Thailand
Tears For The Thai Girl

J. F. Gump

© 2008 by J. F. Gump & Sabai Books
North American Edition
ISBN: 978-0-9714855-3-2
www.JFGumpNovels.com

First English Version Published by:
Bangkok Book House, Bangkok, Thailand
Published as: One High Season
Distribution Rights in Southeast Asia
ISBN: 974-85129-3-2

Cover Photo by: Dickson Yue, Hong Kong
http://www.flickr.com/photos/dicksonyue/2795971231/
Taken in Pattaya, Thailand – 2008

Published by Sabai Books, P.O. Box 138, Kings Mills, Ohio 45034

Printed in the United States of America.

Preface

Pattaya, Thailand. The quaint resort city on the Gulf of Old Siam conjures up fond memories for millions of tourists who have traveled there for relaxation or exotic adventure. Some remember the exquisite hotels, the beautiful gardens, and the abundance of places to see and things to do. Others remember the nightlife, the crazy nights on the town, and the mornings after. All wonder what it would be like to live there and love there.

"Tears For The Thai Girl" is the last novel in this Thailand Trilogy, the final chapter in the lives of the Mike Johnson and the Bongkot family. It's is a love story, an emotional drama, a journey into a world you never knew existed. You've passed these people on the street, or seen them in stores, bars, and airports. Now you can meet them up close and personal. It's an adventure not easily forgotten.

For readers unfamiliar with Thailand, Baht is the local currency and is worth about 3 cents U.S. A wai is a polite greeting with hands held in a prayer-like fashion, a kilometer is about .62 miles, buses are the most affordable means of travel, and U.S. Eastern Standard Time follows Thailand time by exactly 12 hours. I'm sure there are other things I should tell you, but these are the ones that come first to mind. I have included a basic map of Thailand for your convenience.

This book was originally written for publication by Bangkok Book House for distribution in Southeast Asia. It has been revised for the North American market.

Acknowledgements

Thanks to everyone who has supported my work. A special thank you to my fans who bought my trilogy from Bangkok Book House, and to my family who allowed me uninterrupted time to write.

~~ J. F. Gump

Chapter 1

Pattaya, Thailand

Mike Johnson stood on the balcony of his oceanfront condo. Below lay Beach Road, the one-way street that traces the shoreline of Pattaya City from Dolphin Circle at the north to Walking Street in the south. The Gulf of Thailand spread west beyond the palm trees and sand.

Mike had never in his life imagined that he would be living in Thailand at the age of fifty-four. Truthfully, the way he had treated his body over the years he was surprised to be living anywhere. Yet here he was, living the life that some men would sell their souls for. But for him Pattaya had faded from a city of glitter and good times to a tinsel town without substance. He wasn't sure if the city had actually changed or if he had simply become jaded.

A bank of dark clouds gathered at the far horizon rolled east. He watched as the storm worked its way across the water toward the beach. Thunder announced its coming. Cool winds arrived minutes before the first drop of rain reached the shoreline. A flash of lightning heralded a downpour. He stepped from the balcony into his condo, lit a cigarette, and watched through the sliding glass door as the monsoon storm unleashed its fury.

Torrential sheets of rain soaked everything not properly sealed or covered. The palm trees bowed and swayed under the steady assault. The storm sewers quickly succumbed to the deluge and the city streets flooded. Trash and dust scum floated atop the murky water. He knew the storm wouldn't last long, and that it would leave a breath of coolness in its passing, but he also knew the sun would return within the hour and turn Pattaya from a tourist's paradise into a tropical steam-bath.

Mike had lived in Pattaya on-and-off for more than five years, but as hard as he tried he had never acclimated to Thailand's heat and humidity. He supposed his body had been habituated by too many frigid winters and air conditioned summers to ever become accustomed to the unrelenting mugginess of Southeast Asia.

He glanced around his condo. It consisted of two bedrooms, a living room, and a combination kitchen and dining area. The furnishings were tasteful but austere. He didn't need the second bedroom, but the price had been so cheap that he couldn't say no. Besides, at the time he'd signed the lease he thought he had a full-time roommate. That hadn't worked out but he didn't care. During the last couple of months he had discovered that he preferred living alone.

His phone rang for the first time since he had moved in. He answered on the third ring. "Hello?"

"Sawasdee ka," a female voice said. "I am Jintana. I have mail for you."

He recognized her name and her voice. Jintana was one of the receptionists at the Amari Orchid, the hotel where he had lived for months. He had left his phone number with the manager in case they ever needed to contact him. "Thank you for calling. I'll stop by later to pick it up."

"Mai pen rai ka, never mind," the girl replied and then disconnected the call.

Mike looked at the clock; it was two-thirty. He glanced out-side; the storm raged. He turned toward his bed; it promised comfort. He set the alarm for seven.

Chapter 2

Khon Kaen, Thailand

Jarapan's workday had been normal to the point of boring routine. After finishing her shift at the bank, she stopped to buy spices for her mother and then drove past the theater to see what was playing. Her fiancé was coming home this weekend and they'd made plans to see a movie. The coming film was a romance and he didn't like those, but she did. She would convince him to go.

By the time she left the city of Khon Kaen, the sun had faded to early evening but its heat lingered like an uninvited guest. The night's coolness was still more than an hour away.

She was about halfway home when her motorcycle died. Not a sputtering death but a sudden one, as if someone had pulled the spark-plug wire. She cranked the engine until her leg ached but it refused to start. She considered leaving the motorcycle at the side of the road but worried that someone might steal it. For the millionth time in her life she wished she had a cell phone. If her father or brother knew she was stranded, they would come to help. She gripped the handlebars and pushed the motorcycle forward.

She was less than a kilometer from her house when a small gray pickup slowed to match her pace. Two men sat in front and two in the open bed. Their clothes and dark skin said they were either construction workers or migrant farmhands. One had nasty scars on his face. The others were nondescript. She didn't recognize any of them.

"You need help?" one man asked.

"No, thank you," she panted. "My home isn't far."

"I'm a mechanic. Let me look." He jumped from the truck-bed and straddled the motorcycle. He turned the key and then kicked the starter. When it didn't start, he did a quick inspection of wires, hoses, and switches.

In a moment the man smiled and cranked the engine again. This time it roared to life. As Jarapan started to thank him, she was grabbed from behind and her arms pinned against her body. Someone stretched a piece of duct tape across her mouth and around her head. Her screams were muted to less than a whimper. Her hands were forced behind her back and bound with thin plastic straps that dug into her skin.

The men dragged her into a thick copse of young bamboo and stripped her bare from the waist down. One man pushed her to the ground and then positioned himself for his assault. Jarapan squirmed and twisted to avoid his clumsy thrusts.

At that moment the man with the scars appeared and kicked her would-be rapist away. Jarapan looked up and saw his face close for the first time. It was grotesque and distorted as if he had been badly burned, or as if someone had tried to erase his face with a grinding wheel.

"Are you okay?" he asked, his tone polite, apologetic.

She nodded yes, praying he would set her free.

The scar-faced man turned to her attackers and told them what low animals they were. After a minute he turned back and stared at her half naked body. His expression changed from apologetic embarrassment to animal lust. He ordered the others to hold her still and he lay down on her thin body.

When scar-face finished, the other men took a turn. Afterwards they taped her feet together and left her in the bushes. She heard the sounds of her mother's motorcycle being loaded into the truck, and then they were gone. She was still tied up and naked when her father and brother found her hours later.

Chapter 3

Josh Johnson reached the north side of Charleston at six-fifteen in the morning. The coming sun tinted the sky a soft red mixed with dark grays. "Red sky in the morning, sailors take warning," his mother's words floated through his head. With luck he would be south of the city before the sun crested the low mountains to the east. With even more luck, the red sky would turn out to mean nothing except that morning had arrived.

He cracked the car window and took a breath of cool air to shake his drowsiness. It didn't help. He turned up the radio. A classic rock station was cranking it up for the early morning commuters. An old ZZ-Top tune pulsed through the speakers. He didn't remember the title but he had heard the song before. He lit another cigarette and concentrated on the road ahead. White lines on blacktop zipped past at seventy miles per hour. The unending procession had a hypnotic effect. His thoughts drifted.

Probably the worst thing anyone had ever said to him was that he was a sociopath. He didn't know what a sociopath was, but it sounded bad, like he was crazy or something. He had been buzzed on coke at the time and felt like superman, so he had kicked the guy's ass for saying it. Later, when they were both straight, his friend explained that he'd called him a sociopath because of the way Josh treated his parents, like he hated them or something.

Josh had never hated his parents. He had simply found ways to manipulate them to get what he wanted. Life was good right up to

5

the day he dropped out of school, and then things went to hell. First his parents stopped his allowance. Then they started making a lot of ridiculous demands like get a job, be home by eleven, and crazy shit like that. To keep peace, he pretended to have an evening job. Actually, he had started a nighttime business that was fun, profitable, and illegal. He had found his niche in life and it was good.

The day his dad lost his job was the beginning of the end. His dad had returned from a project in Thailand only to find out he was being laid off. "No work," his boss had said. To Josh that meant his dad was the lowest ass-kisser on the totem pole. His mom and dad had been having problems, too. They had even stopped sleeping together. In a way he felt sorry for dad. Not only had he been kicked in the face by the company he had slaved for, but he'd also stopped having sex.

He had tried to be friends with his dad during that time but it had never worked. Every conversation deteriorated into his dad bitching about his friends, his hair, his tattoos, and his work habits. Josh had always found that funny because he didn't have any work habits.

His dad had gone ballistic and kicked him out the day he caught him selling pot from the basement. The man had been so angry that veins throbbed on his neck and forehead, and specks of white spittle flew from his mouth when he screamed. Josh had tried to get him to share a J to calm down but he had responded by calling the cops. If his dad had known the other things he'd been selling, he would have called the National Guard. Josh disappeared like anyone with an ounce of street-smarts would do.

He spent a few weeks with a friend in a small college town directly south of Pittsburgh near the West Virginia border. There was a high demand for what he was selling and the students had plenty of cash. The money came rolling in. He made a couple of trips to Pittsburgh to buy more "supplies" but he never called his parents. He figured he would do that later, after his dad had a chance to cool down and set things right with the cops—and with his mom, too. He figured another three or four months would be about right.

He left the college town when one of his customers got busted for possession. There was no sense taking chances and, besides, he'd always wanted to visit Florida.

The car tires growled across the roadside rumble strips. Josh jerked awake and steered back into the fast lane. He lit another cigarette. The drive was smooth down I-77 through Virginia and into North Carolina. He set his cruise control on seventy-five and let it ride.

Chapter 4

Khon Kaen, Thailand

Jarapan had been born and raised in a small village near Khon Kaen in east-central Thailand. Her family was neither rich nor poor. They farmed the few rai (acres) of land they owned and were considered middle-class within their community.

Unlike many men in her village, Jarapan's father was a hardworking man. Although he had never gone past sixth grade in school, he was one of the smartest people she knew. Everyone in their village looked up to him.

Her brother was cut from the same cloth, only not as smart. He had a gift with rice, pineapples and cassava, and even the stubborn water buffalo listened to him; but things like math and science eluded him. By the time he turned thirteen he had dropped out of school to work on the family farm. Jarapan received her education with the money her parents had saved for her brother's private lessons. That gave her incentive to strive and she was always at the top of her class.

Their farm was less than five kilometers from the outskirts of Khon Kaen. Far enough to be isolated yet close enough to feel like they were still in civilization. They had two motorcycles and an old model pickup truck, all of which were used for farm work and basic transportation. Jarapan shared one of the motorcycles with her mother, but it was never a problem because her mother didn't like to drive. Jarapan did the shopping and that made her mother happy. It made Jarapan happy, too, because it gave her the freedom to see her fiancé. His name was Purachai and he was special.

TEARS FOR THE THAI GIRL

She and Purachai had been classmates in grade school and they had fallen in love during their last year of high school. If her parents—or his—had ever objected to their relationship, she had never heard it spoken. Purachai's father was the manager at the local branch of Thai Farmer's Bank and he had helped her get a part-time job at the bank during her final year of technical school. Her computer and accounting skills were above average and the bank had hired her full-time after graduation.

Purachai was an only child and his father was paying for a Bangkok education. He would graduate in less than two years. Not so long ago, Purichai had asked her to marry him as soon as he finished school and she had said yes. But that was before the incident.

The incident! That's what Jarapan called it. She knew it was rape but she couldn't bring herself to use that word. If no one had found out, maybe things would be different now. But everyone had found out, thanks to her father and brother. They had gone looking for her attackers that night and in their drunken anger they had talked to all the wrong people. The rumors spread like wild bamboo. She remembered the following days like they would never end.

Early on the morning following *the incident*, Jarapan dressed for work. She hadn't slept but she didn't feel sleepy. Her thoughts were disorganized and made little sense. She felt a powerful need for routine and normalcy, but she knew her house would be anything but that today. Work seemed her best refuge.

When she started her five kilo walk toward town, it was light enough to see but not yet morning. She was operating on automatic pilot, on instinct. As she passed the place where she had been assaulted, she kept her eyes straight ahead. Horrid images of the scar-faced man and his attack found their way into her thoughts. The memory made her nauseous. At the edge of town, she hired a motorcycle taxi to the bank.

She was sure everyone stared when she entered the lobby, or

maybe they didn't. Maybe it was just her feelings of shame. She pulled herself erect and went to her desk. Her friend Anya said a nervous good morning and then excused herself to the restroom.

A minute later Jarapan was summonsed to her supervisor's office. She had never spoken with her supervisor in private and it made her uncomfortable. She entered the office and smiled as politely as her pounding heart allowed. Ms. Siriwan motioned her to a chair.

"Khun Jarapan," the woman said, her voice hesitant, nervous. "I've been instructed to reduce our overhead." She paused and turned away.

Jarapan's face flushed as she realized her supervisor knew what had happened, and that she was going to be fired because of it. Surely if Ms. Siriwan knew, so did everyone at the bank. Probably everyone in Khon Kaen knew. Without waiting for the woman to finish, she stood and walked away. It wasn't a polite thing to do but she didn't care. She knew what was coming and didn't want to hear the words. She went to her desk, picked up her purse, and headed toward the exit.

She had almost reached the door when the bank manager, Purachai's father, stopped her. Jarapan felt a shred of hope. Maybe she had misunderstood her supervisor's intent. She waited for him to speak.

"Purachai wanted me to tell you he's not coming home this weekend or the next. He doesn't want you to come to Bangkok, either."

A thousand responses came to her head but none escaped the knot in her throat. She burst into tears as she rushed from the bank. Outside, her knees weakened to the point of collapse. At that moment two strong arms pulled her up and held her close. She recognized the scent of her father. She pressed her face against his chest.

"Why are they doing this to me?" Her voice edged on hysteria. "I've done nothing wrong. Everyone looks at me as if I'm some sort of monster."

"They are shallow people," her father soothed and held her tighter. "They're embarrassed by their own stupidity." He steered her away from the bank toward his truck. "This is my fault. Last night your brother talked more than he should and I didn't stop him. We were both drunk and I wasn't thinking. I'm so sorry."

Jarapan didn't respond.

First he took her to the hospital for an examination. Next he stopped by the police station and filed an official complaint about the stolen motorcycle, but nothing else. After that he drove them home. Jarapan retreated into a shell that shut out everyone.

She had spent the following weeks in a mental numbness, going through the motions of living yet feeling disconnected from life. When the nightmares came, she relived the attack over and over.

On her more lucid days she would ride her father's motorcycle to Khon Kaen and surrounding towns to ask people at gas stations, roadside shops, and construction sites about a scar-faced man. She wasn't sure what she would do if she found him, but she knew it wouldn't be polite.

A few people remembered seeing him and a couple of men even said they had worked with him, but none knew where he was from or where he had gone. One construction laborer said the scar-faced man had left the area, heading south. Jarapan knew it could be true, but maybe it wasn't either. She had no way to know.

Her friends seemed uncomfortable when she was around, so she had stopped seeking them out. Purachai's friends wouldn't even acknowledge her existence. Her own family seemed standoffish, too. Like the others, they had changed. Or maybe she was the one who had changed.

Since her family hadn't filed a formal complaint, the police had taken little interest in *the incident*. They knew what had happened, but they wasted no energy on it. Eventually she gave up her search, but the bitterness of all she had lost remained.

She was relieved when her menses came on time. Two weeks later she went to her family doctor for a pregnancy test just to be sure. She also had herself tested for HIV and other diseases. All tests came back negative which was the one bright spot in her world of depression.

Then a friend she hadn't seen for years came to visit. The girl's name was Rattana, and she and Jarapan had been like sisters when they were younger. By the time they had turned sixteen, Rattana had left Khon Kaen for the resort city of Pattaya. Jarapan had stayed behind with her family and continued her education. She didn't know what her friend did for a living, but she suspected the rumors she had heard were true. No one could make as much money as Rattana by working in a hotel, unless they were doing more in the rooms than cleaning them.

Rattana didn't mention *the incident* and neither did Jarapan. Instead they reminisced about old times and the people they remembered. Later, when Rattana talked about her life in Pattaya, she made it sound magical. Jarapan was captivated by the exotic tales of the city by the sea, and by Rattana's stories of her travels to Singapore, Australia, and England. For Jarapan it was a dream she would never experience, but for Rattana it had become a part of life.

Before Rattana left she handed Jarapan a business card, "Call me if things get too miserable in Khon Kaen. I can help you find work. You may never get rich, but at least you'll have fun."

Rattana's offer rang of escape and excitement. Jarapan wasn't sure how long she could live in small-town Thailand where everyone knew what had happened. A new beginning might be what she needed. "I may come sooner than you think," she had replied.

The day after Rattana went back to Pattaya, Jarapan began making plans to escape her life in Khon Kaen.

A few days later later, while her father and brother were working in the fields and her mother was visiting a friend, she put her plans into action. First she wrote a short note to explain what she was doing and where she had gone. Next she packed her suitcase and strapped it to the back of the family's remaining motorcycle. Finally she drove to the Khon Kaen airport and purchased a ticket. She had boarded the plane before anyone realized she was gone. By the time her mother found the note, she had already landed in Bangkok.

By two o'clock in the afternoon she had arrived at the Ekami bus station and bought a one-way ticket to Pattaya. She called Rattana to let her know she was coming. They agreed to meet at the bus depot on North Pattaya Road at six o'clock, or at a bar known as Toy's if her bus was late. At three-thirty she boarded the bus and took her seat. She hadn't slept much the night before and she was exhausted. She fell asleep before the bus pulled from the Bangkok station.

Her dreams were a collage of scenes from her childhood. Warm, loving things like the time her family had made their own flower-laden floats for the Loy Krathong festival, and the water fights she and her brother had waged during the Songkran holidays, and the first time her mother had allowed her to take the motorcycle into town alone. Then there was Purachai; she dreamed of him, too, and even those dreams were pleasant.

Jarapan awoke when the bus bounced hard across a pothole. Outside, dark clouds had covered the afternoon sun and made it seem early evening. She didn't know where she was, but it was clearly somewhere on the outskirts of Bangkok. Here there were no skyscrapers, only urban sprawl. She glanced at her watch: it was four-thirty. The bus was scheduled to arrive in Pattaya by six o'clock but it would probably be late if it rained.

Ten minutes later the skies opened and rain poured down in torrential sheets. The traffic slowed to a sub-crawl speed and then ground to a standstill. She passed the time wondering what her life would be like in Pattaya. She had heard all of the stories but she didn't know which were true and which were lies. Her friend Rattana had made it sound so glamorous and exciting—too good to be anything except romantic imagination.

She turned and stared though the window. There wasn't much to see except the other vehicles creeping forward. From her elevation she could see clearly inside the car beside the bus. The people were so close that she felt as though she were invading their privacy. When the lady in the passenger seat looked up, Jarapan turned away and closed her eyes.

Apprehension of where she was headed niggle at her senses. She prayed for God and Buddha to keep her safe. In a while she fell back asleep.

Chapter 5

Pattaya, Thailand

When the alarm clock blared, Mike Johnson got up, showered, and slipped into fresh clothes. The storm had ended and darkness had arrived. He stepped outside onto the balcony. The sun was long gone but its heat lingered on. The night's steamy dampness was thick enough to slice. He stepped back inside, retrieved his cigarettes and wallet, and left the condo.

It was eight o'clock when Mike entered the open air lobby of the Amari Orchid Hotel. To his left was the lounge where he had spent many pleasant but expensive evenings. Jeena was tending bar. It had been her job for as long as he could remember.

To his right, beyond a cluster of bamboo chairs and coffee tables, was the reception desk. Nok and Jintana were busy registering a group of tourists. He couldn't tell if the tourists were Japanese, Chinese, or Korean; only that there were a lot of them and they were not Thai. It would be a good half hour before the front desk would get a break.

He turned back toward the lounge. A handful of people sat at the lobby-bar. He decided to have a beer or two while he waited. Whatever mail or faxes the Amari was holding for him would be there later and he had plenty of time before anyone expected him to make an appearance at the Suaee Dee Lady.

Jeena smiled when she saw him walking in her direction. By the time he arrived she had a beer waiting. "Sawasdee ka, Khun Mike, good evening," she said in both Thai and English. "How are you?" She had those phrases practiced to perfection.

"Sawasdee krup," he responded, smiling. "Pom sabai dee, khop khun krup. I'm fine, thank you."

"Not see you long time," Jeena's English reverted to its roots. "Why no come have beer? Miss you too much."

By habit he adjusted his own speech to pure basic. "Not stay Amari now. Have condo far away." He waved his hand in the direction of downtown Pattaya.

"Soi 8 no far. What you think?"

"You know where I live?" he asked.

"Everyone know where you stay, Khun Mike," she answered. "Even me." She glanced around the bar, then said, "Excuse, please. I go see other customer." She smiled and walked away.

Everyone know where you stay, her words repeated in his head. A friend, a Thai woman, had once told him that nothing in Pattaya is top secret. Now he knew it was true.

He gazed casually at the other customers lining the bar. One couple, both westerners, sat to his left. Two seats farther were three middle-aged men talking in German. Directly across the bar from him sat a foreigner and a Thai woman. He didn't recognize the man but he knew the woman. Her name was Meaw.

Meaw worked at the Dockside Beer Bar which was less than a block from his condo. He had stopped at the Dockside enough times that they knew each other. She was a nice girl, very attractive but not quite a stunner. When their eyes met, Mike nodded, barely perceptible. She looked away as if embarrassed, then turned her attention to the man beside her.

Mike looked away, too. His face flushed of its own accord. It was the first time he had seen her away from the Dockside with a customer. There was no reason for either to be embarrassed, yet they both felt it. He motioned to Jeena and then picked up his drink and went to one of the nearby wicker sofas. He sat facing the front desk, the opposite direction from Meaw and her customer.

He counted the number of tourists still waiting to register, divided it by how long the process took for each, and decided his first estimate had been wrong. It would be a long wait.

TEARS FOR THE THAI GIRL

In the background a vintage Eric Clapton song played. It triggered old memories that refused to die. He had been in love back then. Her name was Math, and she had affected him like no woman ever had. She was gone now, but his memories of her were as vivid as yesterday. He would never forget her even if he lived to be a million years old.

"You like more beer, sir?" A soft voice interrupted his thoughts.

He glanced up but didn't recognize the waitress. His eyes flicked to her name badge. *Wanna*, it read. A dozen lewd comments entered his mind but he said nothing. He looked toward the reception desk; it was still busy. "Yes, thank you. And my check bin, too."

The girl smiled and hurried away. A moment later she was back with a cold beer and a frosted glass. He handed her four hundred baht without looking at his tab and motioned that she should keep the change. She smiled and wai'ed profusely as she backed away. He glanced at the bar; Meaw and her farang were gone. He took a drink of his beer, then leaned back and relaxed.

Behind him the lounge musicians clicked on their microphones. "Sawasdee ka," a soft female voice said. "We'll start with a song we wrote about Pattaya and falling in love."

It was a tune they played every night and he had heard it a hundred times before. The band, just a duo, wasn't Thai; they were from the Philippines. Traveling troubadours determined to make a living from their love of music. Mostly they sang English songs but sometimes they did German or Thai. Actually they were quite talented and truly nice people.

"Khun Mike, I hab you mail."

Mike looked up. It was Jintana from the front desk. He reached over and took the letter from her outstretched hand. "Thank you. I was waiting until you were less busy."

"Busy long time," Jintana pulled her lips into a pout and pointed toward the parking lot. Two more tour buses had arrived. "Must work now. Please come see us again." She placed her hands

17

together in prayer-like fashion, raised them to eye level, and presented him with a respectful wai.

Mike suppressed his urge to wai in return. Instead, he smiled and said, "Thank you for not making me wait."

"Mia pen rai, never mind," Jintana returned his smile. She turned and hurried away.

He looked at the envelope. It was from his sister; he recognized her handwriting. A hint of guilt nudged at his conscience. He hadn't called, faxed, or anything since he had moved from the hotel to his apartment. He supposed she was worried that something had happened to him. He folded the letter in half and slipped it in his hip pocket. He would read it later. He took one last drink of his beer and left the Amari Orchid Hotel.

Chapter 6

It was almost eight o'clock before Jarapan awoke. At the edge of the road the bus headlights lit a sign proclaiming Pattaya to be 60 kilometers ahead. Definitely her friend wouldn't be waiting this late. She took a deep breath to calm her growing anxiety.

The bus arrived in Pattaya at eight-thirty. Jarapan collected her suitcase and searched the terminal for Rattana but she wasn't there. Jarapan wasn't surprised. What did surprise her was the number of farangs (foreigners) she saw at the bus station. She had never seen so many in her life, at least not in one place.

She followed a Thai family from the terminal to the sidewalk. She watched as the man waved a baht-bus—a truck-taxi—to the curb. He spoke briefly to the driver then ushered his family into the back. Jarapan wasn't sure what she should do.

The baht-bus driver looked at her and shouted. "Where are you going?"

"Soi 2," she answered. That was where Rattana had said to come if they didn't meet at the bus station. The driver nodded and she joined the other passengers.

Jarapan stared at the restaurants, hotels, and shops that lined the street. Here farangs strolled the streets as casually as the Thais did in Khon Kaen. At a busy traffic circle the baht-bus stopped and the family exited. In the distance she saw a glimmer of water. She knew it was the Gulf of Thailand. She had never seen the ocean before and the sight sent a thrill of excitement through her.

As they entered the street on the opposite side of the circle, the driver pulled to the side of the road. A man, a farang, stepped into the back. Jarapan pretended to look anywhere but at him. He glanced at her briefly and then turned away when the baht-bus steered into the traffic.

She wondered where the farang was from and if he was one of the sex tourists she had heard about. She had heard hundreds of rumors about foreign men and their sexual appetites for young Thai women. She wondered what she would do if he said something to her. She gripped her suitcase handle tighter and prayed Soi 2 wasn't far.

In less than a minute the driver stopped. She looked up at the street sign—*Soi 2*. She leaned her head out of the truck-bed, "Do you know where Toy's Bar is?"

"Just up the street. You can walk there in less than a minute."

Carefully she made her way from the back of the vehicle. The farang moved his knees as she edged by. "Khop khun ka, thank you," she said. She paid the driver and started up the dimly lit street. She didn't look back at the baht-bus or the farang.

Chapter 7

Mike stood at the edge of the street outside the Amari Orchid Hotel deciding whether he should walk or ride. Considering he had broken into a sweat in the short distance from the hotel to the sidewalk, walking to South Pattaya tonight was out of the question. A baht-bus steered toward him. It was filled with passengers so he waved it on. Seconds later an apparently empty baht-bus emerged from Dolphin Circle headed toward Beach Road. Mike lifted his hand to barely waist level and waved slightly. The baht-bus pulled to the side of the street and Mike climbed into the back. He didn't speak to the driver because there was no reason to. He wasn't going anyplace in particular, just south.

As he took his seat, he noticed another passenger sitting in the shadows toward the front. In the dim light he couldn't see her well, but good enough to see that she wasn't dressed like the working ladies of Pattaya. She held tight to the handle of a small suitcase and looked away when he glanced at her. The truck jerked forward and pulled into traffic. By reflex he looked back to see if they were about to get rammed by another vehicle. He had seen that happen once and it had been ugly. This time no other vehicles were near.

The breeze created by the moving baht-bus was a welcome relief. His sweating slowed immediately. They didn't go far before the driver pulled to the curb. Mike figured they were stopping to pick up another fare but there was no one on the sidewalk. The girl spoke briefly to the driver, and then stood from her seat and edged past him. He turned his knees sideways to give her room.

"Khop khun ka, thank you," she said.

"Yen dee krup, you're welcome," he replied in Thai. He had

repeated that phrase so many times that he sounded native.

The girl smiled and then turned to pay the driver. Without looking back, she started up Soi 2. The baht-bus sped south with Mike as the sole passenger.

He paid scant attention to the bars, shops, and restaurants that lined the east side of Beach Road, or to the Gulf of Thailand that lay to the west. He glanced up briefly as he passed his condo and noticed he had left his lights on again. Not that anyone cared except himself but he was annoyed at his own forgetfulness. He pressed the buzzer as the baht-bus neared the side-street leading to the Suaee Dee Lady. The driver pulled to the curb. Mike handed him a ten baht coin and walked away.

He was early for work, but that was okay. His part of running the Suaee Dee Lady consisted of showing up each night to swap lies with customers and to make sure there were no problems. Sometimes he was there for an hour or two; sometimes he was there until closing. Most of the tourists looked up to him in awe. He was living every man's dream of having a successful business in Pattaya. What they didn't know was how screwed up things could be in paradise. In a way he envied the tourists. They would stay a week or two, have an unforgettable vacation, and then go home to their families and friends in England, Belgium, Germany, Australia, or wherever. After they were gone, he would still be here.

The girls working the front door smiled and wai'ed when Mike arrived. He smiled back and said a polite good-evening but he didn't wai. If he had learned nothing else during his time in Thailand, he had learned when to wai and when not to wai. Mostly he didn't wai to anyone. He entered the bar.

It was a Saturday night and the Suaee Dee Lady was packed. He forced a smile to his lips and sauntered to the bar. His manner was that of an old-hand who had seen and done it all. It wasn't true, but the truth doesn't matter in a business where appearances mean everything. Itta saw him and motioned him to her side.

"Last night we did very good." She wrote down a number and

turned it toward him. "We made this much." Her excitement was apparent.

Mike did a quick mental calculation to US dollars. "That's our best night ever," he smiled. "Someday we'll be rich."

Itta beamed, "I feel rich already."

Mike really didn't care about being rich; he was mostly concerned about recovering his investment in the bar. He had agreed to finance the Suaee Dee Lady one night in a state of advanced inebriation, and Itta had held him to his word. She had done all of the work, but he had put up all the money. Her incentive was that she would own the business after he had tripled his investment; his incentive was to get back what he had already spent. They were doing good considering how long they had been open, and the fact that they had opened in the middle of the low season. If the high season was half as kind, he would recoup his investment within a year and triple it within two.

"Where's your new assistant?" he asked. Last week Itta had asked to hire an extra person to help with the daily grind of cleaning, restocking, and accounting. The alternative was that he help with the mundane chores. He had agreed that a new employee would be better. According to Itta, her new assistant would start today. He wondered if something had changed. "I thought she was supposed to be here tonight."

"Rattana called and said her friend's bus was late. I think she won't be here until tomorrow."

Mike shrugged and went to talk with customers.

Before he had finished his first beer, Itta was back. "Rattana just called to say she's on her way to Bangkok and cannot meet her friend. She said that because the girl is our employee, we must take care of her."

Mike tilted his head back and stared down his nose. He had drunk enough beers to make him crass but not quite obnoxious. "Is this some Thai custom I don't know about, or is it just some bullshit to cover for Rattana?"

Even in the dim light of the bar he saw Itta blush. He wished he had used different words but it would be a mistake to change them now. He waited for her to respond.

"It's something I want to do," she answered. "I know how I would feel if I came to Pattaya alone and knew no one."

He took a sip of his beer. "So I should buy her a hotel room for the night?"

"That would be polite, and then she would be obligated to us, too."

Mike sighed. He really wasn't in the mood to hang out with a bunch of tourists, but he wasn't ready to go back outside into the muggy night either. "What time does she arrive at the bus station?"

Itta glanced at her watch. "Unless the bus is really late, she arrived a long time ago. Rattana said you should meet her at Toy's Bar, by Big C Shopping Center."

He knew Itta had already promised Rattana that he would find her friend. Knowing Itta as he did, she wouldn't back away from a promise. Arguing with her would be pointless because he would lose anyway. "How do I find her?"

Itta scrunched her face in uncertainty. "I don't know. Maybe she'll be the girl who doesn't look like a bar girl."

Mike laughed despite the situation. "And will she have long black hair and brown eyes?"

"Yes, that will be she." Itta didn't crack a smile. "Rattana also said she had a ring in her eyebrow and water buffalo tattooed on her left shoulder. You can't miss her."

His smile faded. "Are you serious?"

This time Itta laughed. "I think you should look for the girl who looks lost and scared to death. If that doesn't work, ask Lek or one of her girls."

"Lost and scared to death? That describes about half of the girls at Toy's Bar. But I think I'll find her anyway. I guess Rattana will be back tomorrow and then the girl will go to her house?"

A customer at the far end of the bar shouted that he needed a drink and Itta hurried in his direction.

TEARS FOR THE THAI GIRL

Mike had known Itta for nearly eight months, but he had known *of her* for much longer than that. Itta was the sister of a girl he once loved and then lost to an accident in Thailand's insane traffic. He felt a special bond with Itta, but he knew it was because of how he had loved her sister. At one time he had allowed himself to believe she could take her sister's place, but it had been a false dream.

They had lived together for a while, and during that time they had decided open a go-go bar. Actually, she had mentioned it and he had agreed. He had been drunk at the time, but just like Itta he wouldn't break a promise. He had supplied the money and Itta had done the rest. Once the bar had opened, they drifted apart. He had still been working at the refinery at the time, and their waking hours had been opposite. She was gone when he came home from work, and she was still asleep when he left in the morning. When he moved from the Amari Hotel to the condo, she had gone to spend a few days with her brother and never come back. He had never asked why and she had never explained. Her apparent rejection had bothered him for a few days before he realized he was happy she was gone. Since then they had become better friends than they ever had been lovers.

Itta returned to where he sat. "I forgot to tell you, her name is Jarapan. And Rattana won't be back for two weeks."

Mike nearly choked on his beer. "Two weeks? You mean I have to put her up in a hotel for two weeks?"

"No, you only have to buy her a hotel room for tonight. After that, she can stay in your extra bedroom."

"You're as crazy as the rest of the people in Pattaya. Do you think I want some woman I don't know staying in my condo?"

"You've done it before." Her retort was calm and direct, almost aloof. "I think it didn't bother you then."

He searched for a caustic comeback but found none handy. Itta knew him better than anyone in Thailand, and she knew how he thought. She would suspect that he wouldn't want to pay for two weeks in a hotel, even if it was a cheap dump, and she would be right. She would also know he couldn't leave a naive, defenseless, young woman on the streets of Pattaya if there was some way he could prevent it. He had done it for her sister and he had done it for her. They both knew he would do it for their new employee. The smugness of her words said that much.

"But I didn't like it," he lied.

Itta smiled. She pulled a five hundred baht bill from her pocket and slid it toward him. "Tonight is on me. I think that will be enough for a nice room with air-con. I'll talk to her tomorrow about sleeping in your condo until Rattana comes back."

Mike looked down at the money, and then back up at Itta. He knew she was fucking with him. They had lived together long enough that she knew all of his hot buttons. He slid the baht note back. "I have my own money." He finished his beer then turned and walked away.

"Her name is Jarapan," Itta shouted as he exited the Suaee Dee Lady.

If it had cooled outside, he couldn't tell. A sheen of sticky sweat formed on his skin even before he reached Second Road. He would be glad when he had the girl in a hotel and he was home in his air conditioned condo. He flagged down a baht-bus and headed north toward Soi 2.

"Jarapan," he reminded himself. "Her name is Jarapan."

Chapter 8

Rattana had told Jarapan to come to a place called Toy's Bar if they didn't meet at the bus station. She had said it was at the corner of Soi 2 and Second Road. The baht-bus driver dropped Jarapan at the end of Soi 2 nearest the beach. Up the street, more than a hundred meters away, she could see lights and people. She headed in that direction

Halfway to the lights, the sound of foreign music reached her ears. A moment later she passed a hotel and a karaoke bar on the right. A few meters on, a complex of outdoor bars came into clear. Open-air bars, one next to the other, filled an entire quarter block. Dozens, if not hundreds, of foreigners sat on stools drinking one thing or another. Some bars had bands playing inside. All had colored florescent lights glowing and rotating fans hanging from roofs held aloft by metal posts. As impossible as it seemed, there were more Thai women than farangs, the foreigners who came to Thailand. Most of the girls were young and sexy. A few were older and fatter, but even they looked sexy. She moved to the far side of the street where she could watch without being conspicuous.

At the top of the street, she saw a sign proclaiming to be Toy's Fun Bar. She took a deep breath and walked in that direction. She didn't look directly at any of the farangs for fear they might speak to her.

Her pulse quickened when she didn't see Rattana at the bar. Her first instinct was to keep on walking, but she didn't. Instead she just stood and stared at the colored lights, the sexy Thai women, and the loud farangs. Blaring music filled the night. It was like the biggest and weirdest party imaginable.

27

She noticed an empty table at one side of the main bar. She edged her way there and sat down. A farang turned toward her and smiled drunkenly, but he didn't say anything and for that she was thankful. She ordered a cola from one of the waitresses, then sat back and prayed that Rattana would come soon.

She made mental notes of the interaction between the farangs and the girls working the bar. It was obvious that communication was minimal, yet the girls' smiles stayed ever present as they flirted with the men. The men smiled and flirted in return. It wasn't much different from the way young Thai lovers teased each other when the older adults were out of sight. It was the erotic game of seduction.

She wondered who would be the winners and who would be the losers here tonight. If the farangs played the love game as poorly as they played the game of connect-four, she was sure the girls would come out on top. Considering what the girls were selling and what the men were buying, she figured it didn't make any difference—the girls would always come out on top.

The minutes ticked into an hour and still there was no sign of Rattana. She ordered another cola. She knew she shouldn't spend the money but she was afraid the bar would ask her to leave if she didn't have a drink in front of her.

Half an hour later Jarapan concluded that Rattana wasn't going to meet her. She considered her options. She had baht in her pocket but not much; maybe enough for one night at a cheap hotel if she was lucky. The thought nagged at her. Her escape from Khon Kaen was quickly dissolving into disaster. She decided to finish her cola and ask one of the waitresses for directions to the nearest Thai-priced hotel. Beyond that she had no plans. The only thing she knew for certain was that returning to Khon Kaen wasn't an option.

She noticed the foreigner as he entered the bar. He didn't sit with the other farangs. Instead he went to the back and found a seat. He ordered a drink then looked in her direction. It was the same man who had rode in the baht-bus with her earlier. She turned away from his stare and pretended to be interested in the watching the activities at the bar. More than once she glanced in his direction. She wondered if he was here to find a girl for the night. He looked like the type.

~~~

Mike buzzed the baht-bus to stop when he reached the Big C Shopping Center at the intersection of Soi 2 and Second Road. Below him was Toy's Bar. He looked for Lek but didn't see her.

Lek was part owner of Toy's and several other bars in Pattaya. A long time ago he and Lek had been lovers of a sort, but now they were just good friends. Mike had known Lek almost as long as he had been in Thailand. She was a shrewd business woman and an excellent hostess. She never forgot a face and rarely forgot a name. Her slant on life was as much western as Thai which was probably why they had remained friends after everything that had happened between them.

As was typical for a Saturday evening, Toy's Bar was busy. Also as usual, there were a few vacant stools at the back of the bar. That was where he preferred to sit anyway. It was quieter there. He looked for new faces and saw more than a few. He wasn't surprised. The bar girls came and went almost as often as the tourists. He saw one girl sitting alone at a table away from the crowd. She could be the girl he was looking for, or she could be a freelancer, or a friend of Lek's, or just another bar-girl. If she had a suitcase, he didn't see it. From the corner of his eye he noticed her staring at him. She seemed vaguely familiar but he couldn't place her face. When he looked directly at her, she turned away.

He took a seat and ordered a Heineken. When the waitress brought his beer, he leaned forward and said. "Have you seen a lady with a suitcase?"

She stared dumbfounded. "No speak English." She smiled uncertainly and hurried away.

In a moment she came back with another girl in tow. "Sunee speak English."

"Hello Mike," Sunee said. "Not see you long time."

He had known Sunee almost as long as he had known Lek. She was very nice and polite when she was sober, but unpredictable when she wasn't. She seemed sober tonight. "I've been busy. I stopped by a couple of weeks ago but you weren't here."

"I went to Bangkok with my friend."

He smiled. It seemed that no matter where Thais went, they almost always said Bangkok, but in Sunee's case it was probably true. "I hope you had fun."

"I did," she smiled back. "What did you ask the lady?" She nodded toward the girl who had served his beer.

"I asked if she had seen a woman with a suitcase."

"Jing-jing? She thought you wanted to pay her bar fine."

"Only if she has a suitcase and her name is Jarapan," he grinned at his own private joke. "Just tell her that I think she is very beautiful, but I have a lady already."

"Khun Mike, you have lady already? What name she?"

He took a deep breath. "It's a lie, Sunee," he sighed. "I want you to tell her a lie so I don't hurt her feelings."

"Oh, I understand." She turned and spoke to the girl. The girl blushed and smiled. She wai'ed to Mike and then went about her business.

"What about a girl with a suitcase? She would have been looking for Rattana."

"That is she," Sunee waved her hand casually at the girl sitting at a table away from the bar.

It was the same girl Mike had noticed when he first arrived. He allowed himself a longer look. He had seen her somewhere before, but she was no one he knew. He turned back to Sunee. "I promised Rattana that I would meet the girl and buy her a hotel room for tonight. She doesn't know anything about this. If she doesn't speak English, I might have a hard time explaining everything to her. I might scare her or something. Can you talk to her and tell her who I am?"

"Sometimes I worry about you," she frowned. "You must be

careful with Thai ladies you don't know. But I will talk. You stay here and be a good boy. Okay?"

"Khop khun mahk krup," he smiled. "Wave to me when I should come to the table."

"First you buy me drink. Then I go talk."

"Okay, but you can drink it at the lady's table. I'll buy one for the lady, too."

Sunee hurried away. In less than a minute she was sitting across the table from the girl.

Mike sipped at his beer while keeping the two women in the edge of his vision. He waited for Sunee to motion him to the table, but she never did. The two women were in heavy conversation as if they were old friends. From time to time Sunee would glance in his direction and smile. He wondered what she was up to.

After a few minutes had passed with no signal from Sunee, he decided he should find out what was going on. He picked up his beer and walked to the table. "May I join you?" he looked at Sunee.

"Of course." Sunee slid to the far side of the bench seat.

Mike sat down. "I thought you forgot about me."

Sunee pulled her face into a frown. "I not forget you, Khun Mike. You friend for me."

"I mean about the girl." He looked across the table at Jarapan. She was staring toward the bar and didn't notice his gaze. Her head was turned just so and he saw her face in profile. She was actually quite attractive. Her clothes rang of corporate uniform, no doubt from a past job.

"She is from Khon Kaen, same me. I not know her, but I know her uncle. We talked about Rattana, and that someone would come for her. I not talk about you, except to say you friend for me."

"Does she speak English?"

"I not know."

"I can speak some English," the girl interrupted their conversation. She looked at Sunee and then at Mike. "My name is Jarapan. I'm pleased to meet you."

Mike and Sunee both stared, disbelief on their faces. Neither spoke.

"I'm sorry if my English is wrong," Jarapan interrupted the short silence. "Did I say something not polite?"

Mike spoke first, "No, your English is almost perfect. Have you lived in America or England before?"

Jarapan smiled. "I have never lived outside of Khon Kaen. I learned English in school, and from movies and television. I have practiced too much. Thank you for saying I speak good English."

"Did you understand what Sunee and I said before?"

"Yes, I understand. My friend Rattana cannot meet me, but someone will come. You are Sunee's friend?"

Sunee interrupted, "I forgot to tell you; this is the person who will meet you."

Jarapan's smile remained in place but the rest of her face etched with alarm. She looked at Sunee and spoke rapidly in Thai, "Why didn't you tell me right away that a farang was meeting me?"

"Khun Mike was afraid you would run away. He told me to talk to you."

"I don't understand any of this. Why didn't Rattana send one of her friends? She shouldn't have sent a farang."

"I don't know. Why don't you ask him?"

"No. You ask him. He's your friend."

Sunee sighed and turned to Mike, "Why did Rattana send you?"

Her direct question set Mike back but at least he now knew what they had been saying. He looked at Jarapan as he answered Sunee's question, "My business partner hired her to work at the Suaee Dee Lady. It was Rattana's suggestion. This girl is my new employee."

Their silence overpowered the noise of the bar. Sunee seemed unable to understand his non-pidgin English. Jarapan seemed unable to believe what she had just heard. "You are my boss?" she finally asked.

Mike blushed. Not because of what she had said, but because

of what he was thinking. She was more attractive than he first thought. In fact, she was beautiful. Even without make-up and in her drab corporate clothes she was stunning. "Unless you change your mind," he said, pretending it didn't matter but praying she wouldn't.

Jarapan squirmed in her seat. "No, I cannot change my mind. I need a job. But for tonight I need someplace to sleep. I was going to stay with Rattana, but now I don't know what to do."

"Hey, I have an idea, you can sleep with me." He thought nothing of his comment figuring she would respond with an *I'm-good-Thai-girl* smile and a polite no-thank-you. But from the look on her face it was clear that she had missed the nuance of his dry humor.

Jarapan's face reddened and her smile disappeared. Her eyes avoided his. She turned to Sunee and spoke in rapid Thai.

"What did she say?" Mike asked, feeling uneasy.

Sunee's face twisted, as if trying to remember the correct English words. Finally she turned to him and said, "She no sleep with you. Not her job."

Mike blinked. The girl had taken him literally; that much was obvious. It was also quite clear that Itta's earlier suggestion about the girl staying in his condo was out of the question. He would tell Itta tomorrow, but for the moment a little damage control was in order. "It was a joke," he kept his voice intentionally soft. "I'm not here to sleep with you, either. Khun kow chai na? Do you understand?"

"I think I understand. Your words were not real? Same-same talok?"

"Yes," he sighed. "Talok, a joke. I guess it wasn't very funny. Since Rattana isn't here, my business partner and I have decided to buy you a hotel room for the night. You don't have to sleep with me."

She was silent for a moment, apparently digesting his words and weighing her options. Finally she said, "If you are buying me a room, can we leave soon? I'm very tired."

33

Mike nodded. "As soon as I finish my beer."

"Okay," she responded.

He hadn't considered which hotel he would take her to. When Itta had mentioned it, he had imagined something Thai and something cheap. Now after meeting her, and after insulting her, an upscale room seemed more appropriate. The Sabai Inn was just down the street. It was clean and moderately inexpensive. He decided to take her there.

He chugged the last of his Carlsberg, handed Sunee enough money to cover his bill and a tip, and then stood. "I'm ready."

He picked up her suitcase and walked away.

Jarapan followed behind the farang, studying him as they walked. He was thinner than most of the foreigners she had seen at Toy's Bar. Not Thai thin, but thinner. Looking at his back he could have been any age, but she had seen his face and knew he wasn't young. She guessed him to be fifty but had no way to tell. Old enough to be her father for sure.

They hadn't walked far when he stopped at the hotel she had passed earlier. He explained to the receptionist that he would pay for the room and handed over more money than Jarapan thought appropriate. The transaction done, he handed Jarapan the key.

"I will come for you tomorrow at noon. I'll buy you lunch and take you to the Suaee Dee Lady. Itta will start training you then. Goodnight."

She watched as he walked away. When he was gone, she took the elevator to her floor and found her room. The curtains had been left open and streetlights dimly lit the inside. She rested her suitcase against the wall, pulled the curtains closed, and lay down on the bed. Within a minute she was asleep.

Chapter 9

Josh Johnson
Ft. Meyer, Florida, USA

Josh hit every tourist town on Florida's east coast and most of the west before ending up in Ft. Meyer. Finding girls to party with had been easy. His stash of drugs disappeared before he reached the Keys. His supply of cash disappeared even faster when he started buying coke, meth, and pot at street prices. He tried to get back into the business, but the spics made it clear that wasn't going to happen. They didn't threaten him physically; they simply said that he would probably get busted if he got into the business. He took the hint.

He wasn't quite broke when he decided it was time to go home, but at the same time he wasn't sure where his next meal was coming from. It took him less than a day to devise a lie that he thought his mom and dad would believe. When he finally built the nerve to call them, there was no answer.

Instead of *hello*, he got a recording saying the line was being checked for problems. He wasn't sure what that meant. His parents were always home and the phone was never out of order. He suspected his parents had changed the number so his drug buddies couldn't call any more; and probably so he couldn't call either. The very thought pissed him off. He didn't have enough money to buy gasoline back to Pittsburgh so he stayed where he was.

Desperation is an ugly thing and Josh was desperate—he took a job at a local convenient store. For the first time in his life he traded his freedom for a paycheck. Maybe no one else would think that anything special, but Josh was proud of himself.

He wouldn't get paid for a week so he rented space at a cheap campground and slept in the backseat of his car. A motel would have been better but even the shitty ones were overpriced. He diet consisted of Mountain Dew, Snicker Bars, and an occasional cheap cheeseburger. Within two months he had saved over twelve hundred dollars.

One Friday night he decided to reward himself for his efforts. He went out to buy some weed and nothing else, but it didn't turn out that way. Instead he met a couple of really cool girls and they talked him into buying some coke. Or maybe he had volunteered to buy it and they only volunteered to take it. He didn't remember which.

Josh didn't go back to work that night, or the night after that either. In fact, he never went back to work at all. The next few days were a nonstop orgy of drugs and sex. The good times lasted until the money and dope were gone. After that the girls didn't seem so hot or so friendly so he moved on.

Four days later he called his parents again. Now the recording was saying the number had been disconnected. Obviously his parents wanted to make sure he never called them again. What load of crap. Here he was, a thousand miles from home, hadn't eaten in two days, and was broke. Something had to give. He phoned his Aunt Carol collect.

Aunt Carol is his Dad's younger sister, but sometimes she seemed more like a second mom than an aunt. She accepted his call. As they talked, Josh sensed something was wrong. His aunt's voice was tense through the *where-are-you* and *are-you-okay* routines. When he asked about his parents, there was a long silence.

"Your mother is dead," Aunt Carol finally whispered. "She was killed in an automobile accident. A deer jumped... I'm sorry."

Her soft words tore through him like hot bullets. If there had been food in his stomach, he would have thrown it up. It wasn't possible for his mother to be dead. She wasn't allowed to die. It was all he could do to keep his composure.

"Is Dad okay?" he managed.

"Your dad went back to Thailand," she answered.

That completed his downward slide. Mom's body had barely had time to cool and Dad had already gone back to Thailand. The fucking bastard had run away just when they needed each other most. He wasn't sure what he felt but he knew it wasn't love.

When Aunt Carol offered a place to stay, he accepted. She refused to send him money but she did buy him a plane ticket to Pittsburgh. He sold his car for less than it was worth, had one last night on the town, and then flew north.

Chapter 10

Jarapan was awakened by a soft tapping noise. It took her a moment to realize where she was. She hurried to the hotel room door. "I just woke up," she said to whoever was knocking. "Please come back later."

She turned back to the dimly lit room. Daylight seeped past the edges of the curtains; she'd overslept. She walked to the window and pulled the drapes open. Sunlight streamed inside. The room was a palace compared to her home in Khon Kaen. And it was cool. She had never slept in air conditioning before, but it must have been good because she couldn't remember ever sleeping so soundly.

The hotel room was huge, nearly half the size of her parent's house. The bed was large enough to slept her entire family. The floors were marble instead of wood, and the curtains were real cloth instead of split bamboo. There was a small table with two chairs, a dresser, and a television set. Paintings of places unknown hung from the walls. The bathroom had a western-style toilet like the ones at the bank. She had long ago learned it was proper to sit on a toilet seat instead of standing on it and squatting. She didn't like it much, but it wasn't a problem. She glanced at her watch. It was almost eleven. Her new boss would be coming soon. Her new farang boss. She tensed at the thought.

Jarapan hurried through her shower and combed her long black hair. It took several minutes to decide what to wear. She didn't want to dress too formal, but she didn't want to look like the ladies she had seen last night either. She finally decided on black slacks and a light green blouse. She applied her make-up like she was going to work at the bank; not too much, just enough to be noticed. She had just finished primping when the phone rang.

"Hello," she answered.

"This is Mike. I met you last night. I promised to buy you lunch. Do you remember?"

"I didn't forget. I'll be down in a minute."

"Leave your suitcase in the room. I don't want to carry it all over Pattaya. I've paid for a late checkout. We can get it later."

"Okay," she said, relieved. She didn't want to carry her suitcase all over town either.

When she saw him in the lobby, she smiled and wai'ed politely. "I am sorry if I'm an inconvenience."

"No, you're no trouble at all."

If he was lying, Jarapan couldn't tell. His expression seemed sincere. "Are you sure?"

"Well, to be honest, you are an inconvenience." His lips formed an impish grin. "But a beautiful inconvenience, so I don't mind. Do you like pizza? Sometimes I get a craving for pizza."

Jarapan didn't know what to make of his comment about her being a beautiful inconvenience, so she ignored it. She was even less sure about the pizza. She had seen it advertised, but she had never eaten it. She didn't want him to think she was some backwater girl who had never eaten anything besides Thai food so she said, "Yes, pizza would be fine."

They left the hotel together with him in the lead. She walked far enough behind him that no one would think they were together.

Mike noticed that she kept her distance as they walked down Soi 2. It was obvious she didn't want anyone to think she was with him. He didn't say anything, but it annoyed him nonetheless. He wasn't sure if she had a farang phobia or if it was just him.

At Beach Road he flagged down a baht-bus. It was crowded and she had no choice except to sit close beside him. He intentionally let his leg press against hers. He knew she noticed, but it was too crowded for her to do anything about it. After a moment he began feeling like a dirty old man and pulled his leg away. He didn't expect her leg to follow, but it did. He wondered if it meant something or if she was merely making use of the extra space. It didn't matter anyway so he shrugged it off.

The day was hot and humid. The palm tree fronds stood nearly motionless in the stagnant air. Jet skis and speed boats skittered noisily across the water of Pattaya Bay. The beach was busy with sunbathers, strollers, and other tourists on holiday. On the far horizon of the Gulf a monsoon storm was forming.

At the Royal Garden Plaza Mike buzzed the driver to stop. He stepped from the back of the baht-bus and paid their fare. As he waited for Jarapan to join him, he realized where he had seen her before. She had been the passenger in the baht-bus he had taken from the Amari the night before. He was surprised it had taken so long to remember.

"Have you ever been to the Pizza Company?" he pointed at the sign.

"Yes, there's one in Khon Kaen," she lied.

Mike glanced at the distant skyline. "Com'on. If we hurry maybe we can beat the rain."

The temperature inside the restaurant was as cool as the outside was hot. The place was busy with a mix of Thai and farang customers. A waitress showed them to their table. Jarapan eyed the salad bar as they passed.

"What do you like on your pizza," Mike asked, making idle conversation.

Quickly Jarapan scanned the menu. "Seafood," she answered.

Mike made a look of disgust, "Maybe we'll each get our own pizza."

"You don't like seafood?"

"Yes, but not on pizza."

"Oh," was all she could think of to say.

She glanced at the people around her. Most of the Thais were students and young professionals. Most of the farangs were with

Thai ladies of the night. She wondered how many people were thinking she was a bar-girl. A farang at the next table smiled and nodded. Her face flushed in silent embarrassment.

"I think we should order," she said, pointing outside. "The rain is coming soon."

Mike looked over his shoulder. The distant clouds had grown larger and darker. "You're right. We should hurry. The salad bar looked pretty good and it's a lot faster than the pizza. Wanna try that?"

She stared at him. He had talked so fast that she hadn't understood a word he said except salad bar, and that was what she wanted anyway. "Okay," she answered.

Twenty minutes later they left the restaurant. Now the palm trees bowed and swayed in the wind before the storm. Mike led the way down Beach Road toward the Suaee Dee Lady. They almost made it before the rain arrived. They took shelter inside a street-side shop, but they weren't the only ones. The shop was filled with people, mostly farangs, who pretended interest in the Thai handicrafts and trinkets lining the shelves as they waited for the storm to pass. The reek of sour sweat wafted heavy through the humid air.

Jarapan had been around plenty of sweating Thais but they had never smelled like this. She wondered if it was something the farangs ate that made them smell so bad. She also wondered if she smelled bad to them. Nonchalantly she leaned toward Mike and sniffed. He smelled clean enough. Or maybe he only smelled Thai. She discreetly sniffed at her own clothes. If she stank, she couldn't tell.

In a while the worst of the storm had passed. Mike bought an umbrella from the shopkeeper and stepped outside. Jarapan followed.

"Sorry," he said, "but I couldn't stand it in there anymore. More than one of those people needs a bath and a change of clothes." He tilted the umbrella to cover them both. "If you don't stand closer, you'll get soaked."

Jarapan walked close beside him but they got soaked from their knees down anyway. Water dribbled from their pant cuffs by the time they reached the Suaee Dee Lady.

Itta was already there. She gave them a wry inspection and shook her head, "Even my ex-husband is smart enough to stay out of the rain."

Mike knew she was talking about her ex from Scotland; she had talked about him often enough. Sometimes he thought she still loved the Scotsman though she had always denied it whenever the subject came up. "Hey, at least I'm smart enough to have you as a partner, which is more than I can say for him."

Itta smiled at his left-handed compliment and then turned toward Jarapan. "Rattana recommended you very highly. She said you have a college degree in accounting."

Jarapan blushed in the dim light. "I've been trained in both accounting and computers. I've been told my English is very good. What job will I be doing?"

Itta glanced once at Mike, and then spoke to Jarapan in rapid Thai. "I'll tell you the truth. Mike is my friend and a good man, but he's lazy. He doesn't help with anything except talking with the farang tourists. I told Rattana I needed help and she recommended you. She said you're smart and that you can be trusted. You will be my accountant, my cashier, and anything else I need help with. I expect you to live up to Rattana's recommendation. I can pay you eighteen thousand baht per month and no more. It's enough for you to live in Pattaya."

"You're very generous," Jarapan replied. The pay was almost double what she had earned at the bank. "Can I start today?"

"You can start tonight." Itta glanced down at the girl's wet slacks. "Preferably in dry clothes. Where did you stay last night?"

Jarapan nodded toward Mike. "He bought me a room at a hotel called the Sabai Inn."

That answered her question of whether Jarapan had spent the

night in Mike's condo or not. She wondered how the girl would respond to her next bit of information. "Rattana won't be back for two weeks."

Jarapan wasn't ready for that piece of news. She had never considered that Rattana wouldn't be here to meet her and give her a place to stay. Certainly she had never thought Rattana wouldn't be here for two weeks. She didn't have enough money to stay in a hotel or anywhere for two weeks—not even someplace cheap. "I didn't know that. I need to ask a favor. Can you advance me money on my salary?"

"Mike may be lazy, but he's not stupid. He won't allow it."

Her escape from home wasn't turning out anything like she had planned. "Could I stay at your house?"

"I live with my brother and his house is very small."

Her hopes sank. She didn't have enough money to stay in Pattaya but she had enough to leave. "Maybe I should just go home."

"Mike has an extra room in his condo. If you want, I'll ask him if you can stay there."

Jarapan remembered last night's conversation and Mike's joke about her sleeping with him. Buddha only knew what might happen if she stayed in the same house with a farang, even if it was in a separate room. Besides, what would people think? It wasn't an option. "I could not," she finally said. "I would be embarrassed."

Itta studied the girl briefly. She was reminded of herself not so many years ago. Young and stupid and desperate. "Who would notice?"

"I would notice," Jarapan answered. "Last night Khun Mike said he wanted to sleep with me."

Itta darted her eyes at Mike, and then back. "Are you sure?"

"He said it was a joke, but it's what he said."

"I heard my name," Mike interrupted. "Would you two mind talking in English? I'm getting paranoid."

Itta turned to him, her face serious, "Do you want to sleep with her?" She tilted her head back and stared.

Mike flushed as he pulled Itta aside. "What man wouldn't want to sleep with her? I mean look at her, she's a knockout. Last night I made a joke about sleeping with her, but I would never force myself on her or any other woman. You know me better than that." He glanced briefly at Jarapan and added. "If she's such a prude and can't take a joke, she doesn't belong in Pattaya anyway. She would probably run off screaming the first time Bookman came in and wanted to pay her bar-fine. She would be better off in Korat or Khon Kaen or wherever it is she came from."

"She asked for an advance on her salary for a hotel room," Itta responded, her voice as quiet as his.

Mike's eyes widened. "Now you're the one joking, right?"

"You know I never joke about money. We've talked about that before."

His sigh oozed annoyance. He pulled his wallet from his pocket and extracted two thousand baht. "Here. This should be enough for a couple of meals and room rent for a night or two. If she needs more, she'll have to earn it like every other woman in Pattaya does. I suggest she spend it on a bus ticket home."

Itta held the money for a moment while deciding what to tell Jarapan. What Mike said made sense. The girl didn't belong here. On the other hand she still needed help running the bar. If the girl went home, she would be exactly where she had started, and her friend Rattana would probably be pissed as well. She walked back to where Jarapan waited and said the first lie that came to mind.

"Khun Mike apologizes for offending you. He said you can stay at his place if you want and he promised not to bother you." She handed over the two thousand baht. "This is an advance on your pay in case you need to buy clothes or anything. Or you can use it to buy a ticket back to your home." It wasn't exactly what Mike had said, but it was what he should have said. She didn't know what choice the girl would make, but she expected her to just go home. It was the logical thing to do.

Jarapan stared at the money, clearly studying her options. "I need to call Rattana," she finally said.

TEARS FOR THE THAI GIRL

Itta handed over her cell phone, and Jarapan placed her call. In a moment she handed the phone back. "Rattana didn't answer." Her face twisted with a mix of anxiety and indecision.

"You can decide later," Itta said. "Right now I think you need some dry clothes." She glanced around the room. "You did bring clothes with you, didn't you?"

"Khun Mike told me to leave my suitcase at the hotel, so we didn't have to carry it all over Pattaya."

Itta looked over at Mike, then back at Jarapan. "Since we have paid you, I expect you to work tonight. I'll tell Mike you want to use his condo to clean up and dress for work. You can get a hotel room later if that's what you decide."

Jarapan barely hesitated before answering, "He won't bother me?"

Again, Itta glanced at Mike. "If he does, he'll answer to me."

Jarapan smiled tentatively. "Okay."

"She wants to go to your condo," Itta said in English for all to understand. "And no monkey business while she gets ready for work. Do you understand me Mr. Mike Johnson?"

Itta's tone was threatening, but her eyes and the way she touched Mike's arm said otherwise. She was negotiating a narrow course between his attitude, the girl's fright, and her own need for a helper.

"If she doesn't bother me, I won't bother her," he answered.

Itta turned to Jarapan. The girl nodded her agreement.

Chapter 11

Pittsburgh, PA
Aunt Carol

After arriving back in Pittsburgh, Josh spent a lot of time talking with his Aunt Carol. She was five years younger than Dad, but still an older lady. Their parents, Josh's grandparents, had died before Josh turned ten. There are no other brothers or sisters.

Aunt Carol told him personal things about herself that he'd never expected to hear. Among other things, he learned she had once been married but it hadn't worked out. Her husband had wanted kids but she couldn't conceive and that had ended their marriage. After the divorce, she had taken back her maiden name and continued her life as if the marriage had never happened. She had buried herself in her work and forgot about ever having a family of her own. Dad's letters and faxes from exotic-sounding places satisfied her small need for adventure.

She had shown him a few of Dad's letters and he'd read them, but only in a cursory manner. He was having a love/hate issue with his dad at that time, and couldn't have given a shit less what his father was doing. According to his friends, his old-man was probably screwing every Thai woman who would spread her legs for him. Josh had never said anything, but he hoped his dad would catch some disease that would rot his dick off. With Mom's death and all it didn't seem right for his father to be sexing it up with some Asian chicks.

TEARS FOR THE THAI GIRL

Aunt Carol told him that his dad had opened a business in a tourist resort in Thailand. She thought it was a pub, but with a name like the Suaee Dee Lady Josh figured it was more likely to be a whorehouse.

Eventually Josh made contact with his old suppliers and a few of his old customers. Within a month he was back in business. He'd told his aunt he was working evenings delivering pizzas, and she seemed to believe that all right. He supposed that was why he'd been so surprised the night he came home to find a police officer in the kitchen. Carol said the man was a friend from her church, but that hadn't made him feel more comfortable.

Really, the officer was very nice, but he had been totally blunt. He'd said he would be watching and if he ever caught Josh taking, selling, or even thinking about drugs he would arrest him.

Josh had listened politely, but decided it was time to move on. It was nothing personal with his Aunt Carol; it was simply time to go.

Chapter 12

Mike escorted Jarapan back to the Sabai Inn. Neither spoke during the ride. He had the baht-bus wait while they went inside to collect her suitcase and check out of the room. A few minutes later they were at his condo.

He turned on the lights and pointed toward a door." That's my extra bedroom. You can put your things in there." He pointed to another door, "That's the bath." He looked down at his wet trousers, "I'll change in my room."

For the moment Jarapan had the condo to herself. It was enormous. It had its own kitchen, a separate living area with sofas and chairs, a computer, a stereo system she would never be able to afford, and the biggest television she had ever seen in her life. And it was all for one person. She figured he must be a millionaire or something.

She carried her suitcase to *her* room. It was smaller than the hotel room, but only a little, and it was neat and tidy. There were pictures on the walls, a dresser with a full-length mirror, one cane chair, a bed big enough for two, and a night stand with a touch-control lamp. Compared to her home in Khon Kaen it was luxurious.

She opened her suitcase, hung her slacks and blouses in the closet, and put her personal items in the dresser. The she stripped off her wet clothes and draped them across the chair to dry. Her choice of outfits to wear consisted of the business suit she had worn yesterday, two pairs of dress slacks, a couple of blouses, and a pair of jeans that was tighter than she thought polite. She decided on the jeans. From what she had noticed they would be more appropriate for the bar.

Her good shoes were soaked, maybe ruined. She slipped on a pair of rubber flip-flops, the only option she had left. She checked her make-up, combed her hair, and then walked toward the open living area of the condo. The bathroom door was closed and a hiss of spraying water seeped from inside. Foreign music floated down the short hallway. She had never heard the song before, but she understood the words. She followed the sound; it came from the television.

She sat on the sofa and watched the music video. When the song ended, she picked up the remote and thumbed through the channels. She stopped when she came to a Thai soap opera with a female ghost as the main character. Before leaving Khon Kaen she had been watching the series at her home and was anxious to see what was happening. Within seconds she was caught up in the fantasy.

She didn't notice when the shower stopped or when Mike stepped into the living room. She only realized he was near when he cleared his throat to get her attention. Quickly she switched back to the original station and looked up. "I'm sorry," she blushed. "I thought you were in the shower."

He was dressed in dry clothes but his uncombed hair shined of wetness. In the subdued light of the condo, he looked younger than she had thought earlier. She watched as he sat in one of the side chairs and lit a cigarette.

"I don't care," he finally said. "I only use the television for background noise."

It took her a moment to understand his words. "I only turn on the TV when I want to watch something."

He took a short drag on his cigarette and looked down at her flip-flops. "Are you wearing those to work?"

Jarapan's blush deepened. "My good shoes are very wet. These are all I have to wear. Is it a problem?"

Mike stared at her feet. "You do look good in flip-flops, but I like my business employees to dress better than my dancers and hostesses." He glanced at his watch. "We have time. Come on, I'll take you to the Big C Shopping Center. You can get a new pair of shoes."

Jarapan thought about the 2000 baht in her pocket. If she started wasting it on things like new shoes, it would disappear in quickly time. "I think I'll wait for my shoes to dry."

Mike smiled, "That could take a while and Itta expects you to work tonight. Don't worry about the cost, I'll pay."

"An advance on my salary?"

"Consider it a welcome gift for my new employee."

Her mind raced with a thousand questions as to why he was being so generous, but then decided she was being silly. Maybe he really did like his business staff to dress well. She pushed her suspicions aside. "Okay, if that's what you want."

"Let's go then. Itta is expecting you at work in a couple of hours."

As they left the lobby, an eerie screech drifted through the air. Jarapan stopped and turned.

"What was that?"

"What was what?" he asked back.

The screech came again. "That!"

"Oh, that. It's the monkey. It belonged to the previous condo manager. When he went home to Germany, he left the monkey behind. The current manager hates the animal and is trying to find someone to take her. If he can't, he will have her disposed of."

"I don't know that word, *disposed of*. What does it mean?" She had an idea what it meant, but hoped she was wrong.

When Mike finally answered, his tone had changed. "The manager will have her put to sleep."

"You mean he will kill the monkey? "

Mike sighed. "Yes, but I wouldn't feel too sorry. The monkey hates women and doesn't like men much either. If I were you, I would stay away."

She wondered if the monkey really did hate women, or if he

had said it just to make her feel better about it being killed. "I think they should let it go, or put it in a zoo."

"Maybe they will." He walked away ending the discussion.

One last plaintive screech reached her ears as she followed Mike to the street.

They walked to the Second Road and caught a baht-bus to the Big C. The rain had stopped but the sky remained overcast. The storm had cooled the afternoon air to tolerable temperatures. The breeze from the moving vehicle felt almost cold.

Inside the Big C, Jarapan took her time trying on shoes, comparing prices, and asking Mike's opinion. He figured his opinion wasn't worth much, but he enjoyed the opportunity to look at her from the waist down without seeming to ogle. She had one of those slender-tight bodies that stirred his hormones—no small feat for a man his age. He'd have been happy if she had taken hours to make up her mind, but within a few minutes she had selected a pair of shoes that looked expensive but cost just a little.

As they passed through the ladies clothing department on the way to the checkout counter, Mike stopped. "As long as we're here, we might as well go all the way."

"What do you mean, *go all the way*?" Jarapan asked.

He wondered if she knew the sexual connotation of that American double entendre. As good as her English was, she probably did. But that wasn't his intent, so he made it clear. "If you are going to have new shoes, you should have new clothes too. I want to buy you a dress. Get a nice one, one with a jacket. It will be cold tonight."

Jarapan stared at him, unsure of what to say. Certainly she liked new clothes, but she felt uncomfortable letting a man she hardly knew buy them for her. "Don't you like the clothes I'm wearing?"

"I like your clothes just fine," Mike stammered. His expression said he had no idea why he wanted to buy her clothes. He paused for a moment then said. "There's this guy who owns a bar in South Pattaya and he's always bragging about how beautiful his cashier is. The old bastard decks her out like a movie star. You're more beautiful than her, and if you have a few sexy outfits you'll make his cashier seem like a worn out hooker." He smiled as if he was making sense.

Jarapan didn't understand much of Mike's rapid English, but she had heard him say beautiful and cashier. "Is this a welcome gift, too?"

"Yes, welcome to Pattaya, and to the Suaee Dee Lady."

Back at the condo, Jarapan slipped into her new clothes, touched up her lipstick and mascara, combed her hair, and then stepped into the living room. "How do I look?"

Mike stood from his seat and turned toward her. "Wow," he said. "Khun suay dee mak. You are very beautiful. Khun suay khun."

Jarapan blushed at his compliment. "Thank you," she said softly, lowering her head slightly, smiling shyly.

He glanced at his watch, "It's getting late. I should get you to work now. I can't wait to show you off." He reached out and took her by the hand.

She didn't move. Instead, she stood stiff and pulled her hand away.

Mike cocked his head, "Are you okay?"

"It's not polite for a man and a woman to do that in public."

"Do what?"

She looked down. "Hold my hand. People will think I'm a bar girl."

Mike was acutely aware of the traditional Thai slant on showing affection in public, but this was the first time he had ever experienced it. He had spent all of his time in Thailand hanging around with the more liberal Thais, the ones who had succumbed to influence of western world. "I'm sorry. It's just that you remind me of someone I once knew. We held hands sometimes."

"Never mind. I'm not offended, but I would be embarrassed." She glanced at her own watch. "We should go. I don't want to be late my first day at work."

"Okay," he laughed softly. "But don't worry too much. If you're late, you can blame it on me."

Outside, evening had come early beneath the cloud-covered sky. Already the sidewalks were filled with the tourists who had left their hotel rooms for another night of booze, music, and women. Mike set off down the street toward Beach Road. Jarapan followed a discrete three steps behind.

At the corner they passed a small beer bar. "Hello Mike," came a female voice.

He looked over and waved at the girl.

"Hey, sweetheart," came a man's laughing voice. "Come sit with this fat old bastard."

Jarapan turned her eyes away and picked up her pace. She took hold of Mike's hand. "Maybe it would be okay if we walked like this for a minute." She held his hand as they rode the baht-bus south and as they walked toward the Suaee Dee Lady. She let go when the bar came into view.

Business was slow for a Saturday night, but Mike didn't care. It gave Jarapan time to learn her new job without being pressured. Within the hour, she was tracking inventory, making change, and recording lady drinks like she had been doing it for years.

Mike stayed until closing instead of leaving at eleven as he usually did. He passed the time talking with their few customers, appraising the two new dancers Itta had hired, and filling his eyes with images of Jarapan. By the time the bar closed, he had consumed enough beer to be pleasantly inebriated. Also, he had decided that he would have to thank Rattana for his new employee.

He escorted Jarapan home to the condo where she announced she was exhausted and immediately retired to her room. With nothing else to do, he followed suit. When he slept, he dreamed of Jarapan.

Chapter 13

Jarapan awoke when the morning sun lit her bedroom window. She slipped into a terrycloth robe she found hanging in the closet and then stepped into the hallway listening for any noise that would say Mike was up and about. All she heard was snoring.

She went to the bath, adjusted the taps, and took a long shower. Hot running water was something she didn't have at her home in Khon Kaen. It was a luxury she could easily come to love. As the water sprayed down, her mind wandered.

She had arrived in Pattaya two days ago expecting to meet her friend Rattana who had promised to give her a place to stay until she could find an apartment of her own. Those plans had ended at the bar on Soi 2. Instead of Rattana, she had been met by a farang, her new boss, the man who owned this condo. That hadn't been planned, but it wasn't a bad thing, either. He had been nicer than she would have expected considering what she had heard about farangs. He had even bought her new clothes. It dawned on her that Purichai had never once taken her shopping for clothes. Probably because he never had the money, or maybe because he never wanted to. She shook the thoughts from her head, stopped the water, and grabbed a thick towel from the rack.

In a minute she was dressed in the blouse and tight jeans she had worn yesterday when they went shopping. Mike was still snoring. She used the solitude to inspect her temporary home. The small kitchen had a stove, a microwave, a refrigerator, a table, and a sink with hot and cold running water. The walls were hard plaster. The refrigerator contained an assortment of food and drink, some that she recognized and some that she didn't. There were a few things with green and white mold growing in wild profusion.

On the kitchen table sat a laptop computer and printer surrounded by internet "how-to" books, a thesaurus, a writer's guide to getting published, and a disorganized mess of printed pages. There were old copies of the Bangkok Post and Pattaya Mail scattered about the living room. All were in English and she could read them easily enough, but she wasn't interested in foreigner's news so she didn't bother.

The same screech she had heard yesterday came from outside the sliding glass door. She slid it open and stepped out onto the balcony. Below and to her left she saw the monkey. Its cage was built of bamboo framing and heavy wire screening, really quite large for such a small creature. As she watched, the daytime security guard appeared carrying food and a small carton of milk. If the monkey was dangerous, the man didn't seem concerned. He fed it fruit from his hand and held the milk carton while it drank through a straw. She shook her head. Either Mike had lied or the monkey was having a calm day.

"You're up early," Mike said from behind her.

She spun around. He was dressed in jeans and nothing else. It was the first time she had seen him without a shirt. He was hairier than any Thai man she had ever known. He wasn't as fat as she had imagined, but his skin sagged a little just like her father's. "I'm sorry if I woke you," she said.

He lit a cigarette and glanced up at the morning sun. "It's time to get up anyway." With that he turned and walked away.

She stared after him as he went directly to the bathroom and closed the door. She lost interest in the monkey and followed Mike inside.

Through the bathroom door she could hear him coughing. It was a hard, lung-searing cough that hurt just to hear it. She wondered if he was still smoking his cigarette. One of her neighbors in Khon Kaen had once coughed like that and had died from a heart attack. She hoped Mike didn't die while she was staying at his condo.

In a minute his coughing stopped and the shower started. Jarapan breathed a sigh of relief and turned her attention to the television. She flipped through the channels but found nothing of interest. She finally left it on the Asian version of MTV. Her ears heard the music clearly but her mind tuned it out. It became little more than background noise. She stood and continued her inspection of the condo.

Along one wall was a narrow shelving unit that reached almost to the ceiling. Foreign novels lined the top two shelves. The bottom two held towels and washcloths. On the center shelf stood three pictures. One was a farang woman, one was a boy who looked a little like Mike, and the other was a Thai lady. She guessed the farang woman and the boy to be his family, but the Thai lady was a puzzle. Perhaps he had a Thai wife or girlfriend, or maybe it was just a friend. That didn't seem likely but it was possible.

It dawned on her that she knew nothing about Mike. Why was he in Thailand? Did he have a wife at home? Was he married? Was he divorced? Was he a criminal escaped from America? Those and a million other questions flitted through her head. She would ask him later. Or maybe she would ask Itta; that seemed like an easier thing to do.

When the shower stopped, she hurried to sit in front of the television. The last thing she wanted was for him to catch her snooping around. In a while she heard the bathroom door open but he didn't come into the living room. Instead, he went directly to his bedroom. A minute later he emerged, fully dressed.

"Are you hungry?" he asked. "I can cook something for breakfast."

She thought about the moldy food in the refrigerator. Anything she ate from there would have to be boiled. "Can you cook rice soup with pork? It's my favorite."

He considered her request. "I could, but it might not be very good, and it may take a while. On the other hand, the restaurant downstairs makes excellent breakfast porridge."

"Is that the same as rice soup with pork?"

His lips lifted to a small smile. "Yes, they're identical." He glanced at his watch. "If we don't hurry, there'll be no breakfast at all." He reached out to take her hand, then quickly pulled away. "Sorry. It's an old habit."

"Never mind," she answered, then took him by the hand and led him into the hallway. She kept her hand in his until the elevator opened into the lobby.

The restaurant was very small with only eight tables. It was empty except for one waitress and a cashier. Jarapan thought the waitress stared a little more than necessary while taking their order. She wondered if the girl thought Mike was her lover for the night, or if they'd made love before coming to breakfast. Her face flushed at the thought.

As the waitress moved away from their table, she had another thought. How many other women had Mike brought to this restaurant, and this same table? The picture of the Thai lady appeared in her mind. Where was that lady now? She considered several ideas but not one possibility made more sense than another.

"Are you okay?" Mike asked. "You look like you're in another world."

"I was just thinking this is a nice restaurant," she lied, then asked the question foremost in her mind. "Do you eat here often?"

"I have eaten here a few times. This is only the second time I've come for breakfast." He pulled a cigarette from his pack and lit it. "I had the rice soup the first time, too. It's good, but you might want to add some spices."

That answered part of her question. At least he wasn't in the habit of bringing women here for breakfast. That left only lunches and dinners to wonder about—and the Thai lady in the picture. She started to ask about that, but then changed her mind. "You're not supposed to smoke here," she pointed toward a sign.

"Yeah," Mike grumbled. "Then they shouldn't put ashtrays on the tables."

The waitress arrived with their meals. Jarapan watched as

Mike flavored his soup with a touch of sugar, a dash of fish sauce, and a heavy dose of red peppers. When he finished, she did the same, only not so much hot pepper.

"You like Thai food?" she asked between bites.

"Some of it. The rest I have to disguise with seasoning."

"You mean spices?"

"Yeah, spices."

"Not everyone likes hot food."

"You mean farangs?"

"And Thai people, too."

"I never thought about it."

"How long have you lived in Thailand?" she asked in Thai.

"What? I didn't understand what you said."

"I said, how long have you lived in Thailand?" she repeated in English. The fact that he didn't understand her the first time told her his understanding of Thai was small.

"Five years, on and off," he replied. "What about you?"

She noticed the jest in his answer and smiled in return. "About four times longer than you," she answered.

"Is that an insult?"

"It's a compliment."

His eyes looked as if he wanted to ask why, but he didn't. "Thank you," he said instead and continued his breakfast.

When they finished eating, Jarapan asked, "What will we do this afternoon?"

"I don't know about you, but I'm going to work on my computer. I'm building a web site for the Suaee Dee Lady."

Jarapan had designed a single web page once while she attended school in Khon Kaen. It had turned out okay and she had even learned some HTML coding, but she couldn't imagine building an entire web site with interlinked pages and everything. "That sounds very complicated. Can I see it?"

Mike was quiet for a second. He had been working on it sporadically since moving into the condo. Not only was it not finished, he wasn't even sure what he wanted to do with it. He had done the index page thirty or forty times, but they always turned out looking like cheap imitations of other web sites. Sometimes he thought it would never be finished. "It's not finished yet. I'll show you later, after I put it on the internet. "

He paid for their food, left an adequate tip, and then left the restaurant. Jarapan followed behind.

~~~

Back in the room, Jarapan snuggled on the small sofa and watched television while Mike made himself busy with the computer. The clickity-clack of his keyboard lulled her into a semi-sleep. Conscious thoughts and slumbering dreams mixed together in mass confusion...

Purachai was there, smiling and as handsome as ever. He reached out to touch her, and then pulled away. His smile turned into a frown as his image faded. Clickity-clack, clickity- clack. Suddenly she was at her home in Khon Kaen. The house was full of dust and spider webs. She knew she should clean it before her mother came home, and start the rice too. There was no rice to eat. A voice called to her but she could barely hear the words. It wasn't Thai, it was farang. What was he saying? She had to go see. She felt herself falling.

"Hey, are you okay?" she heard Mike asking.

"I must have fallen asleep. I'm sorry if I disturbed you."

"You were making some pretty strange noises over there. Nightmares?"

She didn't know the English word nightmare, but she supposed that was what she was having. "Big nightmares," she answered as she stood from the sofa. "I think I shouldn't sleep after eating soup."

Mike smiled and turned back to his computer.

Jarapan went to the bathroom and washed the sleep from her

eyes. When she returned Mike was still tapping at the keyboard and ignored her presence.

"Can I see your web site now?" she asked.

"It's not done yet," he answered without looking up.

"Maybe I can help," she offered.

"Yeah, right," he responded.

She was insulted at his curt reply, but said nothing. As she returned to the sofa, the pictures on the shelf caught her attention. Her curiosity overcame politeness and she said, "The farang woman in the picture is very beautiful. Is she your wife?"

This time he looked up. "She was my wife. She died in an accident a long time ago. The young boy was my son. He's into drugs and I've disowned him."

"I'm sorry. That's very sad for you."

"It's been a while and doesn't hurt so much anymore. I keep the pictures to remind myself of how lucky I was when they loved me." He turned back to the computer.

Jarapan thought of Purachai. He had loved her once, too, but now he didn't. She didn't feel lucky about anything. She wondered if she would ever be able to look at a picture of Purachai and feel anything besides his rejection. "Who is the Thai lady? She looks very young."

Mike's fingers stopped in mid keystroke. He looked up. "Her name is Tippawan. She died two years ago."

Jarapan wasn't sure how to respond. His voice rang with sadness, but his eyes sparked with emotions far from dead. "Did you love her, too?" she finally asked.

"I still love her."

"Did you walk with her hand-in-hand?"

"The answer is yes." His tone was suddenly curt. "And you ask too many questions. Can't you see that I'm busy? I can't work while you're bothering me."

She stepped back from his abrupt change of mood. "I'm sorry. I was just wondering who they were. I'll leave you alone now." She headed toward her room.

"Wait, I know you didn't mean anything. You were just being curious, and I was being an asshole."

She wanted to ask what an asshole was, but she didn't want to continue their uncomfortable conversation. "Never mind, I understand."

"I'll be in a better mood later," he said as she stepped into her room.

She closed the door without responding.

She lay on her bed wondering if she should find another place to live. Clearly she was an intruder on his life and his privacy. He had been nice to her, except for just now. But who could blame him? She had nosed into something that was none of her business. She would have reacted the same way if he had asked her about Purachai.

She fell asleep with the image of the Thai girl in the picture walking hand-in-hand with Mike; and doing other things too impolite to think about.

Jarapan was awakened by a soft knock at her door. She glanced at her watch. It was almost five o'clock. She couldn't believe she had slept so long. She jumped from the bed and opened the door. It was Mike, showered and dressed for the evening.

"I'm going out for a while. I have some business to take care of. I'll be back in a half hour or so. You should get ready for work. We'll leave as soon as I get back."

He pulled the door shut and a second later she heard him leave. She couldn't believe he had left her alone in his house. He knew absolutely nothing about her except that she was his new employee and that she was from Khon Kaen. She was an honest person, but he had no way to know that. She decided he was too trusting of strangers.

Thirty minutes later she had showered and dressed in the slacks and a blouse she had brought from home. Purachai had always told her she looked sexy in this particular outfit. She inspected herself in the mirror. They weren't new clothes, but they did accent her female figure in all of the right places.

The first thing she noticed when she entered the living room was that the pictures on the shelf had disappeared. Before she had time to consider what it meant, the condo door opened and Mike stepped inside. He was carrying a plastic bag and he was smiling.

"I bought..." he started then stopped just as quickly. His eyes flicked up and down her body. "Never mind. You look great! Here, I bought these for tomorrow." He handed her the bag.

Jarapan blushed at Mike's flattery. Really, she shouldn't care what a farang thought about her, but she felt good at his compliment. She peeked inside the bag; there was another blouse and a pair of slacks. Somehow, she was sure they would fit. "You shouldn't spend your money on me. You don't even know me."

"It was on sale," he smiled. "Besides, I already told you I want to have the sexiest cashier in Pattaya. I'm doing it for me if that makes you feel better."

She wasn't sure if it did or not. "Thank you. Someday I'll repay your generosity."

"I think you already have."

She didn't understand his comment, but she didn't pursue the subject. She glanced over at the empty picture shelf. If he noticed, he didn't say anything. "Do we have time to eat?" she asked. "I'm starving."

"There's a good restaurant near the Suaee Dee Lady. They have Thai food that even I like. I'm a little hungry, too."

She took his hand in hers. "Then we should go now. I don't want to be late."

He looked down at their hands and smiled. "And I don't want you to starve to death. It would look bad for me."

She didn't let go of him until they were within eye-shot of the Suaee Dee Lady.

The next two weeks passed not much different than that, day, except Mike didn't buy her new clothes every day. They did go to the store for fresh food, and sometimes they would eat in, but as often as not they ate out. Every afternoon from twelve until three Mike would work on his computer while she slept or watched television.

When Mike was busy on the computer, it was like he was in another world. His concentration was so intense that he noticed nothing around him. Sometimes his face became so emotional that Jarapan thought he would cry. She couldn't imagine what sort of website would have that effect. She could hardly wait to see the finished pages.

Promptly at three o'clock he would turn off the computer, grab some clean clothes, and go into the bathroom. Half an hour later he would emerge ready for the evening. Sometimes he would go out while Jarapan showered and dressed, but mostly he just sat and read newspapers. He always had the television on, but he rarely watched it.

Each evening before work they would stop for dinner. Usually they went to Pizza Hut or Burger King or KFC, but sometimes they ate at the Thai restaurant near the Suaee Dee Lady. Of them all, Jarapan liked KFC the best. It was during dinner when they would talk. Mike talked the most but it was always about work or Thailand or some radical group terrorizing the world. He never talked about his past or the people in the pictures. Jarapan often wanted to ask, but she was afraid he would want to know about her own past so she kept her questions to herself.

She enjoyed talking about Thailand and the royal family and the Buddhist religion. On the days that the conversation turned to those subjects she talked more than Mike. He seemed intrigued by the little things she found ordinary. Most nights he would stay at the Suaee Dee Lady until it closed and they would ride home together. Other times he would leave before midnight but never said where he was going. He was always in bed by the time Jarapan arrived at the condo.

Rattana called one evening and said she would be returning a week later than planned. Jarapan thought that should bother her, but it didn't. She had become comfortable living with Mike and didn't care if Rattana ever came back. What did bother her was the idea that everyone would expect her to move in with Rattana when she came home. Jarapan figured she probably would do that just to keep the rumors to a minimum. She knew if she didn't move in with Rattana, there was a chance the gossip could spread all the way to her family in Khon Kaen. How embarrassed would her mother and father be if they found out she was living in Pattaya with a farang? Never mind that they slept in separate rooms and that their most intimate conversations were about Thai superstitions and the daily lives of Buddhist monks. No rumor worth repeating would ever allow itself to be tempered by facts.

At the Suaee Dee Lady on the Wednesday night before Rattana was scheduled to arrive, Mike announced that he was going to Singapore to renew his visa. He was leaving the following morning and would be home Saturday evening.

Itta didn't seem surprised but Jarapan certainly was. Mike hadn't said anything to her about leaving. He'd told her that he had to leave Thailand sometimes for visa reasons, but he had never said when. The biggest surprise was when he told Itta that Jarapan was meeting him at the airport when he returned, and that they were spending a night or two in Bangkok while he attended to some business. Itta took that piece of news as if expected. Jarapan took it with total shock. Mike left the Suaee Dee Lady before she recovered enough to confront him.

Jarapan spent the rest of the evening teetering between excitement and anger. She felt flattered that he wanted her to be the one to meet him at the airport, but incensed because he assumed she would. He was taking her and their living arrangement for granted. She could hardly wait to get home and *discuss* his surprise plans for her. As soon as the bar closed, she hired a motorcycle taxi directly to the condo.

Mike was gone but he had left a note on the table. *Thank you for meeting me at the airport* was all it said. Below he had printed his flight number and arrival time plus the name, address, and check-in time for the hotel room he had reserved. Pinned beneath the his ashtray was ten thousand baht. A yellow post-it note said it was for expenses. Her anger faded and she began making plans for her holiday in Bangkok. Later, she lay down in Mike's bed. She didn't know why she did that, but somehow it felt right.

~~~

The next morning Jarapan wandered aimlessly through the condo. She had become so used to Mike's company that she felt uncomfortable in his absence. She considered going to the condo restaurant for breakfast but didn't. Instead she made a slice of toast and nibbled at some leftover fruit. She never thought she would miss Mike's morning moodiness but she did. She tried to sleep but couldn't. Finally she turned on the computer to see what he was doing with his web pages.

She did a search for all files created or updated within the past week. Only two appeared. One was a web page and the other was a word processing document. The time/date stamp on the web page was six days old. It was titled *Suaee Dee Lady*. The word document was dated yesterday at three o'clock p.m. It was titled *The Joy of Math*.

She opened the web page. It wasn't horrible but it was pretty basic. She had expected more from all the time he spent on his computer. She studied it for a few minutes, picturing in her mind how it could be better. Maybe she would work on it later, after she had time to think. She closed the file.

The word processing document stared out at her from the search results. The title made no sense. Perhaps it was where he wrote things before putting them on the web page. She opened the file and was overwhelmed by what she saw. It was page after page written in English. She wondered what could inspire anyone to write so many words. She went to the top of the document and read. Within minutes she was engrossed in a tale like none she had ever experienced.

Jarapan had never thought that a Thai woman and a farang man could have more than superficial feelings for each other. Thais and farangs were so different that love didn't seem possible. They didn't even speak the same language. Even her friend Rattana had told her it was all a game to see how much money she could get from her English boyfriend. Love had nothing to do with it.

But as Jarapan read, she knew that Rattana was wrong. If Mike's story wasn't about love, then love didn't exist in Thailand or anyplace else in the world. She wasn't one to cry at woeful Thai soap operas or sad movies, but she cried like a baby as she read the tale of Tippawan. She didn't need anyone to tell her that Tippawan was the girl in the picture. By the time she finished the story it was almost six o'clock and she had come to know more about Mike than she ever intended.

As she hurried though her shower, memories of how he had treated her flooded her mind. He had been more than kind. He was always giving and never asked for anything in return. He passed his generosity off with vague comments that she had already repaid him for everything, or that she someday could. She didn't understand any of it. She wondered if all farangs were as cryptic as Mike. More than that, she wondered if he was looking for a replacement for the girl in the story.

Work went as usual that night. Itta served the drinks, Jarapan took care of the cash, and the hostesses and dancers took care of the customers. A few people asked about Mike and nodded their understanding when they learned of his visa run.

When she got home, she again lay in Mike's bed. In the short time before falling asleep she thought about Mike and wondered what he was he was doing at that moment in Singapore. She figured he was asleep in some hotel room. The image of a woman lying beside him found its way into her head. She forced her own likeness onto the imaginary woman's face. Satisfied that he was dreaming only of her, she fell asleep with a smile on her lips.

Chapter 14

During the years that Mike had been in Thailand, he had never made a visa run to Singapore. While working at the refinery, all of his visa runs had been to the US. Since that project had ended and there was no company to pay his way, his only visa run had been to Cambodia. But he'd heard stories of Singapore and wanted to see it for himself. He had heard it was spotless and orderly to the point of being more western than most western cities.

What he hadn't heard was how expensive it was. Or if he had heard, he had ignored it. The travel agent on Second Road near the Big C Shopping Center had found him a room for $80 per night; a twenty percent discount, she had said. He thought it a little expensive, but some of the nicer hotels in Bangkok cost that much, too. He figured it would be comparable to one of those.

At the airport in Singapore he hired a taxi to the hotel. He stared through the windows as cabbie made his way through the traffic. It was exactly as he had imagined from the stories he'd heard. The streets were clean and orderly. Some people waited in queues to catch buses and taxis. Others moved along the sidewalks carrying shopping bags and briefcases as they went about their daily lives. They were oblivious to Mike in the taxi.

His first surprise came when he arrived at the hotel. He supposed it did bear some resemblance to the picture in the travel brochure, but not much. It wasn't a dump or anything, but it was less than he had expected for the money. He sighed and followed the bellboy to his room. He tipped the less-than-enthusiastic young man more than he deserved and sent him away. A quick inspection of his room told him the hotel was far from new. Clearly it had been remodeled at some time in the past, but just as clearly it needed another updating.

He took a quick shower and put on clean clothes while debating what he would do in Singapore. He walked to the window, pulled the curtain open, and looked at the street below. At that second he realized he didn't know where he would go. He knew exactly nothing about Singapore other than what he had already seen through the taxi window. Uncertainty crept through him. It was the same feeling he'd had when he first arrived in Thailand. It was the fear of making a fool out of himself by breaking some law or insulting someone because he didn't understand their customs. He decided to start at a bar, just to settle the butterflies in his stomach. In the lobby he asked the girl on duty where he could buy a beer. She directed him through the front door and across a narrow-side street to the right.

The bar was small to the point of claustrophobic, and it was empty except for a waitress and a barmaid. That didn't matter; he was only here to have a beer or two before going out anyway. The barmaid took his order and brought his beer. He tried to start a conversation but she was more interested in talking to the waitress so he gave it up.

He flipped over the tab the girl had brought with his drink and got his second shock of the day. His bill was in Singapore dollars, but when converted it came to more than $8 US. He almost choked on the beer. He did a quick calculation and decided he couldn't afford a night on the town at those prices.

The girls continued to ignore him while he finished his drink. He put enough Singapore dollars on the counter to pay his bill plus a small tip and then left the bar. Neither girl acknowledged his leaving. He walked to the main road and joined the nearest taxi queue. There were a dozen or so people in line ahead of him. He passed the time deciding where he would go. Just last week he had talked to a couple of guys who'd been to Singapore. One of them had mentioned a Hooter's restaurant. He couldn't remember the last time he had eaten real Buffalo wings, so he decided to go there for dinner. The wings would be a treat and the beer would surely be cheaper than at the bar he'd just left.

Two women edged past him as he stood in the taxi queue. They passed him as if he didn't exist and squeezed into the small space between him and a young Singaporean couple. Their rudeness pissed him off. He had met plenty of line-busters in Thailand, but there he had never hesitated to stand his ground. Here, he wasn't so sure. He had heard the Singapore cops were tough and he didn't want to prove it at personal level. His blood pressure spiked from the effort of keeping his irritation in check.

As it turned out, the line-jumpers caused him to wait less than one extra minute. He told the driver *Hooter's*, then relaxed in the air conditioned taxi. He felt silly for the way he had let the two women line-jumpers upset him. On the other hand he was annoyed with himself for not saying anything to them.

The Singapore Hooter's girls were about what one would expect in Asia. The uplifting bras helped some, but not much. But they were cuter and more attentive than the girls at the bar beside the hotel, a lot friendlier too. It was the perfect place for an order of wings and a couple of beers. When he closed his eyes, he could almost imagine he was sitting in America.

When he received his bill, all imagery ended. Hooter's Singapore was even more expensive than the rip-off bar by the hotel. He nursed his last beer and stripped the wings to the bone. It was as close as he would come to getting his money's worth. Again he did a quick cash count and decided that tomorrow he would have to skip two meals just to keep his budget in line. He didn't want to be broke when he returned to Bangkok.

He was in bed by eleven o'clock but he couldn't sleep. Thoughts of his son Josh filled his head and kept him awake. He knew Josh was back in Pittsburgh, and from what Carol had said he was dealing drugs again.

Carol! He had read his sister's letter but he'd never answered. He would send a note when he got back to Pattaya. He fell asleep composing a letter to his sister. Later he dreamed of Jarapan.

Chapter 15

Pittsburgh, PA USA

Weeks passed before Josh had contact with anyone in his family. It wouldn't have happened then, except that he and his Aunt Carol happened to be in the same store at the same time, and she saw him before he saw her.

"Have you heard from your father?" she asked quick and to the point. There were no polite greetings or pleasantries or anything; just a very terse *have you heard from your father*.

To Josh it was a stupid question. "I have no reason to hear from him. I don't even think about him. I couldn't care less where he's at or what he's doing."

Carol's lower lip trembled and tears formed in her eyes. He hadn't meant to hurt her or anything; he'd only wanted her to know how he felt. But now he felt like shit for making her cry. He loved his aunt, even if she had invited her police friend for a "man-to-man" talk. "I'm sorry Aunt Carol." He put his arms around her and pulled her close. "I'm still hurting about everything."

"Me too," she said. In a minute her crying stopped. "Will you go for a ride with me? I was on my way to do something and would feel better if you were with me."

He glanced at his watch; it was almost three. The Steelers were playing Cincinnati at four. He'd only come to the store for cigarettes, not to wander all over Pittsburgh. "How long?"

"Half an hour; forty-five minutes at most."

"Okay, let's go. But I have to be back by before four, I have something important to do."

"I'll have you back by then. Come on, I'll drive."

They ended up at the cemetery where his mom was buried. It was the first time Josh had been to his own mother's grave. Seeing her name etched in cold marble had a strange effect on him. Aunt Carol put a wreath of plastic flowers near the headstone and then busied herself pulling the weeds that had invaded the grass on his mother's grave.

Josh knew he was expected to cry, and he wanted to, but for some reason he couldn't. He just stood and stared. After a few uncomfortable minutes, he pretended to say a prayer and then said he was ready to leave.

As they drove back to his car, Aunt Carol tried to pry into his life but he didn't respond. He wasn't in a mood to talk. They were less than a mile from his car when she said, "I haven't heard from your daddy in a few weeks and I'm worried something has happened."

He figured she was making something of nothing. It wasn't like months had passed or anything. If his friends were right, his dad had found some gold-digging whore and was busy screwing his nuts off, but he couldn't say that to his Aunt Carol. "I'm sure he's fine. You worry too much."

She was quiet for the rest of the ride.

"Would you consider going to Thailand to look for my brother?" she asked as she steered into the store parking lot.

He thought about that until she stopped beside his car. He had no desire to travel to some third-world country filled with slanty-eyed rice-burners who rode around on elephants and water buffaloes. He wasn't scared or anything like that; a trip to Thailand simply didn't fit into his agenda. He was moving up in the distribution business and making more money than ever. He no longer sold pot by the ounce or coke by the eight-ball. Others below him took that risk. He had a dependable supplier and he was a steady source for his dealers. Instead of peddling every night, he would buy in quantity once a week. It would be gone within hours. That was good for everyone. Certainly it was safer for him.

"I'm too busy right now. Call me if you haven't heard from him in a couple of months."

As he drove from the parking lot, he realized that Aunt Carol hadn't asked for his phone number or his address. He knew it shouldn't bother him, but it did. It bothered him all the way home. Inside his apartment, he grabbed a beer from the fridge and flipped through the channels on his new plasma TV. He had missed the kickoff and the first series of downs. The Steelers had forced a turnover and were in Cincinnati territory. It was going to be a great game. He smoked a joint, laid back on the sofa, and forgot about Aunt Carol, Dad, and Thailand.

Chapter 16

Jarapan spent Friday morning working on the Suaee Dee Lady website. She had just finished her ideas for the front page when the phone rang. She was sure it was Mike. As she reached for the handset, she hesitated. What if it wasn't Mike? What if it was someone she didn't know, like a farang woman, or even a Thai girl? What if his explanations of the pictures were lies? On the fifth ring she answered the phone. "Hello."

"This is Itta. I'm sorry to ask you this, but I need you to come to work this afternoon. I'm switching Ohm to nights until you and Mike come back from Bangkok. I need your help stocking the bar and cleaning up."

Jarapan breathed a sigh of relief that it was only Itta. "Okay, never mind. I'll come right away." She glanced at her watch; it was well after one o'clock. She hurried through her shower, put on clean clothes, and went to work.

As the baht-bus made its way down Beach Road, images of meeting Mike in Bangkok played through her head. Excited anticipation throbbed in her chest. She wasn't sure if it was from the thought of going to Bangkok or from the thought of being with Mike. Whichever it was, it made her feel giddy.

Itta was waiting when she arrived at the Suaee Dee Lady. "I need you to make sure everything is clean," she instructed, "and keep an eye open for the beer man. He'll be here soon. I'll be in the office taking care of some paperwork."

Jarapan watched as Itta disappeared through the doorway and then turned her attention to the bar. As far as she could tell, it was clean already. It should be, because cleaning was the last thing they did every night before leaving. She shrugged to herself and set about making the place spotless. She had almost run out of tables to wipe and bar-tops to shine when she heard the door open. She turned, expecting to see the beer delivery men. Instead she saw a farang, his dress was smartly casual. She figured him to be newbie who didn't know their operating hours.

"We don't open until six," she said.

"I know," the man responded. "I'm not a customer. I'm looking for a woman named Thichakorn Bongkot. Her nickname is Itta. She is part owner of this bar. Is she here?"

Jarapan tensed at his cold announcement of facts. If he were Thai, she would have guessed him to be an undercover policeman or a lawyer. But he wasn't Thai. "Can I tell her who you are?"

"She wouldn't recognize my name, but she'll want to talk to me."

Unsure of what to do, she hurried down the short hallway leading to the office.

Itta was just finishing her daily accounting chores when office door creaked open.

"There's a farang in the bar," Jarapan said. "He wants to see you."

"Do you know him?"

"I've never seen him before. He asked for you by name."

"You mean he asked for Itta?"

Jarapan fidgeted. "Yes. I mean no. First he asked for Thichakorn Bongkot, and then he asked for you."

Itta's pulse quickened, "Are you sure he said Thichakorn? Mike's the only farang in Pattaya who knows me by that name." The idea that it could be her ex-husband entered her thoughts. "What does he look like?" Her chest pounded.

Itta listened as Jarapan described the man. She could have been describing half the foreigners who come to Thailand on holiday, but at least it wasn't Ian. Ian's red-blond hair was a stark contrast to the dark-haired farang Jarapan described. Itta relaxed a little. "I suppose I should find out what he wants. Maybe I've inherited money or something." The idea that Ian had died crossed Itta's mind; it was a comforting thought. She followed Jarapan into the bar area.

The stranger stared as they entered the room. If she had ever seen him before, she couldn't recall when or where. She forced her best smile and walked toward the man. She raised her hands to chin level, put her palms together in prayer-like fashion, and presented him a very proper wai. "Sawasdee ka," she said as calmly as her tension allowed.

"Sawasdee krup," he answered but didn't return her wai. "Please excuse my interruption. I'm sure you're very busy." His calm demeanor and easy smile were disarming.

"You want to talk with me about something? Have you had some problem with one of our girls?"

He shook his head. "Nothing like that." He pulled a paper from his hip pocket, unfolded it, and then held it in her direction. "Do you know this woman?"

Itta took the paper from his hand. Even in the dim light, the face was unmistakable. "It's me," she said, her smile fading. "Who are you, and why do you have my picture?"

"A client asked me to verify who the lady is. Now I will leave."

"Wait. Who is your client? I need to know."

"That's confidential Ms. Itta. I would never betray a client's trust." He turned to go.

"Wait," Itta stopped him again. "Is my husband dead?"

"I don't know anything about that," he replied. "Even if I did, I wouldn't be at liberty to discuss it." Without further hesitation he left the bar.

The incident left Itta unnerved. She had no doubt about the identity of the man's client. It was Ian and he wasn't dead. If he was, the man would have said so. Ian had hired the man to track her down. Nothing else made sense.

She wasn't sure what Ian might do now that he had found her, but she was sure it wouldn't be good. He had a temper and did little to control it. He would be furious that she had disappeared from Scotland without telling anyone she was leaving. He would be outraged that she was part owner of a go-go bar in Pattaya. By reflex, she put her hand to her cheek. She had been the brunt of Ian's rage more than once. For the first time since they had opened the Suaee Dee Lady she didn't want to be in Pattaya. She wasn't even sure she wanted to be in Thailand.

"Are you okay?" Jarapan interrupted her thoughts.

"Yes, I'm okay," her voice quavered a not-so-okay reply. Her hand shook as she reached out to steady herself against the bar.

"Who was that man? Do you know him?"

"He was sent by a monster from my past." She looked over at Jarapan, deciding what she should tell and what she should keep secret. If Ian had hired the man to find her, he would eventually show up here in Pattaya. She knew that as surely as tomorrow would follow today. It was only a matter of time before everyone knew about Ian and her past. Nothing would remain secret for long. She decided to tell Jarapan everything.

"When I was younger," she said, "I met a man from Scotland. His name was Ian and he was working in Thailand. He had money and he was very handsome. He paid more attention to me than any man ever had. He treated me like a queen and I fell in love. When his job in Thailand was finished, he asked me to marry him and go to his home in Scotland. My mother and father do not like farangs and they were against it, but I didn't care. I thought it was my chance to escape my life in Pattaya and live happy forever.

"For a while everything was okay. His relatives treated me like a servant, but he was kind so I didn't mind. Then Ian lost his job and everything changed. He started drinking a lot and when he was drunk he was mean. Sometimes he would hit me. After a while he found a job in England and went away, leaving me alone in our small house. It wasn't a nice house, but it was better than my home in Phitsanulok, except colder. He sent money sometimes, but it was never enough to pay for everything. While Ian was gone, his family ignored me and I had no friends. I found a job at a restaurant and worked there every day. Mostly I worked because I needed money, but partly because I was lonely.

"Ian came home when his job in England ended. He couldn't find new work and he was angry all the time. I started working later and later at the restaurant because I didn't want to be with him at home. Always he would find reasons to hit me. Never with his fists and never on my face, but with his open-hands on my back and stomach where it hurt but where no one could see.

"One night I came home from work and found Ian and two of his friends at my house. They were drunk and talking loudly. Ian was telling them stories about Thailand and calling me a little brown fucking machine. I was embarrassed that he would say things like that to anyone. Before his friends left, one gave Ian money and Ian made me have sex with the man while he watched. Ian even helped hold me down. I cried through the whole thing. After the men were gone, Ian beat me with his fists on my face and my arms and everywhere.

"The next day I covered my bruises with make-up and went to work. Everyone noticed, but I told them nothing. One customer waited until the restaurant closed and talked to me before he went home. He had heard rumors and offered to help me go back to Thailand if I wanted. I didn't have to think very long because I didn't love Ian or Scotland anymore. The man gave me his phone number and told me to call him when I was ready.

"That night when I got home, Ian was passed out on the sofa. I packed my clothes and left. The next morning I was on my way to Thailand. That was almost a year ago. I've been praying to Buddha that Ian would forget me. Now I know that he hasn't. I'm afraid of what he might do if he comes here. He might even kill me."

At that moment the door to the opened again. This time it was the beer delivery crew. Itta told them what she needed and set to work putting bottles into the coolers. Jarapan worked alongside her and the job went quickly.

When they were finished, Itta said, "I'm not feeling well. Can you stay until I return? The girls will arrive soon and will leave if the door is locked."

She nodded and Itta left the bar.

Jarapan was completely stressed after the episode with the farang and Itta's story about her Scottish husband. What if Itta's husband came while she was here alone? What if he came with a gun or a knife or something? If he was as mean as Itta had said, maybe she wasn't safe here alone. She spent the next hour peeking outside, inspecting every farang who passed down the street.

She was relieved when Paw, one of their dancers, arrived with her boyfriend of the week. Jarapan turned on the music and took her place behind the bar. She gave Paw's boyfriend a beer on the house, but paid for it out of her own money. She was happy that she was no longer alone.

Within half an hour, the other dancers and hostesses and DJ had arrived and they were in business. Jarapan did double duty as bartender and cashier until Ohm arrived to help. Itta returned at eight o'clock and acted as if nothing had happened earlier, but Jarapan could sense tenseness in the way she moved and talked.

At ten o'clock Itta said, "You should go home now. You'll have a busy day tomorrow with your trip to Bangkok. Ohm and I can take care of everything until closing."

"Will you be okay?" Jarapan whispered just loud enough to be heard over the noise of he bar.

Itta glanced about the bar. "I'm not afraid of Ian. He won't bother me with so many people around. You go home and get rested for your trip. Knowing Mike, he'll keep you up late tomorrow night. I'll see you Monday evening." She walked away without waiting for a response.

Outside the Suaee Dee Lady, Jarapan hired a motorcycle taxi to take her home. After working until two o'clock or later every night, it felt strange to be home by ten-thirty. By eleven o'clock she had packed her suitcase except for the few things she needed in the morning. By midnight she was in bed waiting for sleep to come.

She wondered at the story Itta had told. Until today she would never have guessed that Itta had once been married to a farang or that she had ever lived in Scotland. Suddenly Mike's book became clearer. Peoples' names were different but the story was the same. One character in the book had married a man from Scotland. There was no mention of her ever returning, but Jarapan was convinced that Itta and the book character were the same. That meant Itta was the sister of the girl Mike wrote about. She wondered how they had met and what their relationship was. Obviously they were business partners, but now she wondered how that had come about. She would ask Mike tomorrow.

Itta's words jumped to her thoughts, "Knowing Mike, he'll keep you up late tomorrow night."

For some reason Itta's nonchalant statement bothered her. She wondered what Itta had meant. Maybe only that Mike would want to go out on the town in Bangkok. Or maybe Itta had been conveying some warning, like Mike might expect her to have sex with him or something. She quelled the thrill that swept though her. Despite what her body was saying, the last thing she needed was to have sex with a farang. She fell into a fitful sleep remembering Itta's tale from Scotland.

Drunk farangs chased her with guns demanding that she have sex with them or they would kill her. Then Purachai was there, naked, sexually aroused, and climaxing as he joined the chase. She stumbled into a copse of bamboo and fell down. The scar-faced man began his oversized penetration.

Jarapan jerked awake. Her heart raced, and her breath came in short gasps. She flicked on the light and glanced at the clock. It wasn't yet five in the morning. She wanted to go back to sleep but was afraid the dreams would come back. She got up and spent the rest of the night rereading Mike's story about the Thai lady named Tippawan.

Chapter 17

It rained in Singapore on Friday; not that it mattered much to Mike. With the price of everything so high, there wasn't much he could afford to do anyway.

He spent the day smoking cigarettes, watching old movies on the TV, and reading Dean Barrett's latest Thailand book. From time to time his thoughts drifted to Pattaya and the Suaee Dee Lady. He knew everything was fine there, but he couldn't shake the uneasiness of not being able to see it with his own eyes. The day dragged on forever. By the time he went to bed he had decided he hated Singapore.

He awoke on Saturday morning at four o'clock. Jarapan was the first thought in his sleep-clogged brain. He reached for the phone to call her but quickly changed his mind. It was early and she was probably still asleep. He had no good reason to call her anyway, except to find out if she had decided meet him or not. Calling wouldn't change anything; it would only make him look unsure of himself

He sat up and lit a cigarette. His flight wasn't scheduled until well after lunch but he was ready to leave now. Yesterday had been a total bust. He hadn't even left his hotel room except for the free breakfast. He definitely hated Singapore. There was nothing for him here except another day in an expensive city that was too antiseptic for his tastes.

He went to the bath, washed the sleep from his eyes, and considered his options. He could sit in the hotel for a few more hours, or he could change his flight to an earlier one and be in

Bangkok by mid afternoon. Bangkok wasn't his favorite place in the world, but it beat the hell out of Singapore. Thirty minutes later he was on his way to the airport.

The earlier flight to Bangkok wasn't a problem and the cost to change his schedule was less than the cost of the wings and beer at Hooters. His new schedule would put him in Thailand at three in the afternoon, five hours earlier than planned. There wouldn't be a problem with his hotel in Bangkok since his check-in time was any time after noon. He had written the same thing in his note to Jarapan.

Jarapan! He hadn't thought of her since morning. He wondered if she would really meet him in Bangkok or if she had blown off his suggestion as beer-talk and bullshit. He wouldn't blame her if she had. He had announced in public that Jarapan would meet him at the airport when he returned from his visa run, but he had never asked her directly. Looking back he thought his tactic crude if not downright tacky, but his dislike of rejection wouldn't allow a different approach. He had asked her to meet him as his employee and nothing else. If she didn't, it wouldn't be a personal rejection, only a business thing. He knew his reasoning was crap, but it was the best he could do.

As his flight cruised north toward Bangkok, he wondered what Jarapan would do. If she was meeting him, and if she had followed his instructions, she would have arrived at the hotel already. If she wasn't meeting him, then she wouldn't be at the hotel. That was pretty simple to figure out. Finally he decided he had no control over what she did so he leaned his seat back and got as comfortable as possible in his coach class seat.

~~~

That same morning, Jarapan hired a mini-van leaving Pattaya at ten o'clock. It was scheduled to arrive at the hotel in Bangkok between noon and one. They were barely past Sri Racha when Itta's comment about Mike keeping her up all night entered her thoughts. The image that flashed through her head made her blush.

In the short time she had known Mike he had always been the perfect gentleman. Except for her father, Mike had treated her better than any man ever had. Sometimes he even sounded like her father when he talked. Not his words or tone, but the way he thought about the world. Sometimes he seemed much younger than he looked, but sometimes he seemed older than her father. Above all, he had always treated her as if she were a grown woman. If she were ever to want another man, she would want one like Mike, only younger.

Jarapan arrived at the hotel at twelve-fifteen. The hotel bellboys rushed to the mini-van when it pulled into the covered entranceway. Their enthusiasm cooled noticeably when she stepped out. No doubt they had been expecting a farang with pockets deeper than hers would ever be. They were polite but reserved as they ushered her inside.

She stared in awe when she entered the hotel lobby. It was grand beyond anything she had ever seen. The dark marble floors were spotless and the heavy woodwork was carved with such minute detail that it must have been done by the finest craftsmen in Thailand. A fountain with multicolored fish and lotus flowers filled the center of the lobby. Farang's, acting rich and confident, ambled casually to and from the lounge located at the far side of the lobby. The hotel employees wore uniforms reminiscent of ancient Thailand. The scene intimidated her. When she said her name at the front desk, everyone's demeanor changed.

"We are pleased to have you as our guest, Mrs. Johnson," the receptionist smiled. At once the bellboys became more attentive.

Mrs. Johnson? She figured they had made some mistake. Probably they had her mixed up with someone else. She glanced down at the paper laying on the counter-top. The room was reserved for a Mr. and Mrs. Michael Johnson. Her Thai name was bracketed beside that in parentheses. Suddenly she understood what Itta had meant about Mike keeping her up late. Images of him making love to her flashed through her thoughts. She blushed despite her best effort to maintain an air of aloofness. She showed her ID and signed where the girl pointed. In a moment, one of the bellboys disappeared with her suitcase and a svelte young hostess escorted Jarapan to her room.

Directly inside was a sitting area with a sofa, a couple of overstuffed chairs, a television, a stereo, and a desk with a computer and printer. Through a doorway, beyond the sitting area, was the bedroom. The bed was the biggest she had ever seen. It could have easily slept four people, six if they snuggled close. The hostess swung open the doors of the dresser revealing yet another television set. A fruit plate sat on a small reading table. Sliding glass doors opened to a balcony complete with a table and chairs. Beyond was the Bangkok skyline.

The bath was a combination jacuzzi, shower, and mirrors with dual wash basins below. Shampoos, lotions, and fancy folded towels lined the counter-top. Even the bath had a television. She couldn't imagine how much this hotel cost for one night, but she was sure it was more than what she earned in an entire week.

The hostess went through her spiel on the controls for every device in the room. Next she handed Jarapan a piece of paper with codes and passwords for computer and gave brief instructions on what they all meant. As she finished, the bellboy entered the sitting area with luggage in hand. The hostess ended with a practiced *we-hope-you-enjoy-your-stay* speech and then wa'ied expectantly.

Jarapan knew she should give the girl and the bellboy a tip, but she wasn't sure how much was appropriate. Ten baht, she knew, would suffice in a normal hotel, but this hotel wasn't even close to being normal. She handed the hostess and the bellboy a hundred baht each, hoping it was neither too much nor too little. They seemed overjoyed at her generosity. Clearly she had given more than they expected. She didn't return their wai of thanks, but she did smile as they left the room.

Once alone, Jarapan inspected every nook and cranny. Using the remote control she turned on the stereo, the televisions, and every other electronic device in each room. She stepped outside onto the balcony with a confusing bedlam of sound pouring through the sliding-glass door. She had never been to Bangkok except for passing through. She had seen the towering city skyscrapers, but from inside a bus they seemed unreal. Now here she was, twenty-eight stories up, gazing out at Bangkok from the balcony of a hotel room fit for a princess, or even a queen.

She wondered what it would be like to live like this all of the time. Not just this hotel, but also the condo in Pattaya, and the entire lifestyle she was sharing with Mike. Surely her family wouldn't approve of her living with a farang, but only because they didn't understand farangs. They thought foreigners were smelly, obnoxious creatures who weren't quite human. Overbearing animals with bad tempers who loved money more than family, country, and customs. She knew her parents were both right and wrong at the same time. Most of the farangs she had met in Pattaya were obnoxious, smelly, and overbearing, and their love of money was almost Thai-like, but Mike was different. He liked to live well but he wasn't obnoxious or overbearing, and he didn't smell different than any Thai she had ever known. Mike was farang, but he acted Thai. If he wasn't so old, she might even think of him as a man she could love.

She turned and went back inside the room. Using the remote she turned off all of the noise she had turned on only minutes before. She had almost seven hours before she was to meet Mike at the airport. She debated what to do in the meantime. Mike had left her a lot of money for incidentals when he left for Singapore. Without effort she convinced herself that if he were here, he would want her to buy a new blouse or slacks or something with the money. She inspected her hair and makeup in the bathroom mirror and then left the hotel.

Chapter 18

Jarapan stood at the front of the hotel and watched the nonstop throng of Thais and farangs walking to places unknown. Each yielded little space to the others, yet they never touched except for an occasional brush of shoulders. Heat beat down from the afternoon sun and radiated up from the concrete below. The humid air waft thick with the smell of food from the street vendors, an occasional scent of jasmine, and the grating odor of exhaust fumes.

She had no idea of where she was going, but she knew she didn't want to walk. She asked a woman at one of the food carts for the fastest way to get to Robinson's Department Store. All of the bargirls at the Suaee Dee Lady talked about Robinson's.

The woman pointed in the air. "Sky-train," she smiled. "Very fast, and cheap. Get off at the Asoke station."

Jarapan had heard about the sky-train system in Bangkok, but she had no idea of where it went or how to buy a ticket or anything. She followed others up an escalator and watched as they bought coins from a change booth, purchased tickets from an automatic dispensing machine, and passed through the turnstiles to the boarding area. One the wall she noticed a map of the sky-train routes in Bangkok. The street names and sky-train stations meant nothing to her, except the one the food vendor had mentioned. It was only two stops away and in the cheapest zone.

She fished coins from her purse, fed them into the indicated slot, and a credit-card-looking ticket appeared. She studied it briefly, noting the magnetic strip on the back. She guessed it somehow kept track where she got on and where she got off. A minute later she was waiting for the next train to arrive.

Robinson's was the most luxurious store she had ever seen, and the most expensive as well. The clothes were nice but way overpriced. The displays were done to perfection and the salesgirls were all smiles and politeness. At the cosmetic counter a beautician was applying her employer's brand of make-up and it was free for volunteers. Jarapan volunteered. The girl expertly applied lipstick and mascara and powder and rouge and other things. Jarapan couldn't stop looking at her self in the mirror. She had always considered herself plain, but suddenly she was beautiful. She wondered what Mike would think of her tonight. She bought the bare basics of the cosmetics just in case Mike liked how she looked.

She felt like a seasoned sky-train rider as she made her way back to her station. It seemed she got more than her share of smiling stares from the other passengers. She was sure it was because of how the make-up had transformed her from plain to beautiful. She pretended not to notice, but inside she was bursting with pride.

She stopped at a sidewalk shop on her way to the hotel and bought a pullover shirt with DNKY embroidered on the front. The shop owner bargained fair and she got the shirt at a good price. It would match the slacks she planned to wear later.

Less than a block from the hotel she passed a small Thai restaurant. Her stomach rumbled at the thought of food. She hadn't eaten since morning and she was starving. She glanced at her watch: not yet five. Mike wouldn't arrive for another three hours. It was more than enough time to eat and still meet Mike.

~~~

Mike hated airplane landings. He knew he should feel exhilarated at the thought of being on good old mother-earth again, but he couldn't. At least not until the plane was physically on the tarmac. The pilot did such a good job there was barely a bump when they touched down. It was almost five o'clock by the time he cleared immigration and customs. Outside he hired a taxi to his hotel.

The driver sped down the freeway passing cars, cutting off other vehicles, and hogging as much of the road as he could. It was frightening, but thrilling. Suddenly he realized how much he loved the chaos of Thailand. It was pandemonium compared to the orderliness of Singapore where strict rules were rigidly enforced. It made him feel alive.

Despite the afternoon traffic they made good time and arrived at the hotel by five-thirty. The bellboys were all smiles and politeness as they carried his luggage into the lobby. The girl at the front desk welcomed him warmly and then proceeded to tell him that his wife had arrived but had gone outside. He smiled at her announcement.

Mike finished the registration form and followed the greeter to his room. As if on cue, the bellboy arrived just as she finished her guided tour. He gave them each a fifty baht note and sent them away. In the bedroom area he saw Jarapan's suitcase. It was unopened. A hand towel had been used in the bathroom but no one had taken a shower. Wherever she had gone, he was sure she would return before going to the airport to meet him. He glanced at his watch. He figured she would be back within the hour.

Mike took a quick shower, shaved, and dressed in clean clothes. He stepped out onto the balcony for a minute while he considered his options. He could stay in the room and watch television, or he could go to the lobby lounge and have a beer. It was an easy choice; he'd never liked television that much anyway.

There were several customers in the lounge. They were mostly foreigners but a few Thai businessmen were there as well. No one was sitting at the bar so that was where he went. He sat where he had a clear view of the main lobby and a partial view of the front doors. He ordered a Heineken from the barmaid, lit a cigarette, and then leaned back to wait.

A few minutes later he thought he saw Jarapan approaching

the front of the hotel. He stubbed his cigarette in the ashtray and stood to await her entrance. When she didn't appear, he wondered if he had been mistaken. He walked to the glass doors of the lobby. At the far edge of the driveway Jarapan was talking to a Thai man. They seemed to know each other, but their bodies were tense. He wondered who the Thai man was.

~~~

It was almost six o'clock before Jarapan finished eating. It didn't matter; Mike wouldn't arrive until eight so she had plenty of time to change clothes and still get to the airport on time. She paid her tab from the money he had given her and left the restaurant.

She was near the hotel entrance when a Thai man called her name. Her heart stopped in mid-beat. She never expected to see anyone she knew in Bangkok—least of all Purachai. She wanted to run but her feet stayed planted. She wasn't afraid of him; she just didn't want to see him. Not after what had happened, and the way their relationship had ended. He trotted toward her, neither smiling nor frowning.

"Hello, Jarapan," he said. "Where are you going?"

It was a normal Thai greeting, nosy but meaningless. Purachai hadn't changed since she had last seen him. He was as lean and handsome as she remembered. She wondered what he would say to her, or what she would say to him. "I'm going out," she gave a typical Thai response.

He smiled. "Looks to me like you're going in. Are you staying here? Your new job in Pattaya must pay very good if you can afford this hotel."

Jarapan tensed at his question. "I got a special rate for the weekend, and I'm sharing the cost with a friend." It was a lie, but she didn't care. It was none of his business anyway. "How is school?" she changed the subject.

His eyes dropped at her question. "Not so good. I'm failing three of my classes. I can't concentrate. I always worry about you being in a city like Pattaya."

She wasn't sure how to respond but she was sure he didn't worry about her too much, not after everything that had happened. "I'm safe enough. I live with a friend. Rattana is now a successful businesswoman and she helped me get a good job."

"Yes, that's what I've heard." He was silent for a long second. "I've also heard that Rattana has become a whore." His words were as much a question as a statement.

Jarapan blushed, wishing he hadn't seen her. "I don't know anything about that. I only know what I'm doing. I work for the Suaee Dee Entertainment Complex. I'm their accountant. They pay me 30,000 baht per month."

It was a lie, but a good one. If he believed her, he would be impressed and stop his snide insinuations.

"Then I'm happy for you," he responded, looking as uncomfortable as she felt. "Do you come to Bangkok often?"

"No, this is my first time," she answered, relieved he had changed the subject. "Do you live near here?"

"Less than three blocks," his face softened to a smile. "If you have time, you can come and see my apartment. It's really nice; I think you'll like it."

Jarapan wondered at his invitation. Just a few weeks ago he had broken up with her, and now he acted as if it didn't matter. "Today I can't. Maybe next time I come to Bangkok."

Purachai blushed at her polite rejection. "I understand, but I wanted to ask. I still love you, you know."

She was nonplussed but managed to keep her smile in place. She had finally gotten over him dumping her, and now he was professing to love her.

"Hey, Jarapan," a shout came from the hotel entrance.

She looked up and saw Mike hurrying across the short drive, a smile on his face.

"I see you've been shopping. Who's your friend?"

Jarapan hadn't expected to see Mike until eight o'clock at the airport. Certainly she hadn't expected to see him outside the hotel at this time of the day. From the corner of her eye she saw Purachai tense. Disaster tweaked at her senses.

"What are you doing here?" she said, trying to act normal, yet scrambling for words. "I just returned from shopping." She held a plastic bag out as if she needed proof. She nodded toward Purachai. "This is a person I went to school with." That much was true. "He was just leaving," she added a lie.

She turned to Purachai and spoke rapidly in very formal Thai, "I'm going inside now and you should leave." She knew Mike would never understand what she said.

Purachai looked over at Mike and responded in guttural Thai, "I think I understand everything now. This is the *friend* you're sharing a room with, isn't it?" He gave Mike a haughty inspection. "I can't believe you are staying with that thing," his words reeked disdain. "A farang older than your own father. How much does he pay to sleep with you?"

His words hit her like a slap. Her forced smile turned cold. "I once loved you, Purachai. I thought you were a man. But when I needed you most, you deserted me. You made your friends hate me, and turned mine against me. I did nothing wrong, yet you made me feel like a tramp. I have never slept with this man. He is just my friend, no matter what you think. And he respects me, which is more than I can say for you."

Purachai's eyes narrowed. His smile turned brittle. "Father was right; you are nothing but a fucking whore. I can't imagine I ever tricked myself into believing he was wrong. I will come to Pattaya one day and I'll buy you from the bar. You will never be my wife but I'll have sex with you, just like your farang."

Jarapan barely controlled her rage as she hissed, "Fuck you, Purachai. I wouldn't have sex with you and your little, fast-cumming penis for all of the money in Thailand."

Purachai's smile disappeared completely. "I should hit you for that, but you aren't worth the effort. I think your family will want to know what you've become. Maybe I'll call them. What do you think about that?"

TEARS FOR THE THAI GIRL

Mike watched as Jarapan and her friend talked. He didn't understand a word they said, but their facial expressions and body language told him it wasn't a pleasant conversation. He stepped closer to Jarapan and slightly in front of her, but his eyes never left the Thai man. "We should get dressed for dinner now."

The two men stared at each other, the atmosphere electric.

Finally Purachai spoke in very clear English, "Your girlfriend is a whore." He turned and walked away.

Mike looked at Jarapan, "I think we need to talk." He took her by the arm and led her through the hotel lobby. They didn't speak in the elevator.

Inside the room Mike said, "What's going on? Who was that man?"

Jarapan didn't respond. Tears welled and flowed. Her beautiful mascara left black streaks on her cheeks. Her thin body quivered.

Mike spoke softer. "Are you okay?"

Without warning, she turned and buried her face in his shirt. "I want to go home."

Mike put his arms around her and let her cry. Something was going on; something he didn't understand. He moved her to the edge of the bed and they sat together.

"I'm sorry," he said when she had calmed.

She looked up. "You have nothing for you to be sorry for. You've done nothing wrong."

"I embarrassed you in front of your friend."

"He is not my friend. Before I came to Pattaya he was my fiancé."

Her comment took him by surprise. "Do you want to talk?"

Jarapan nodded. She took a deep breath and then talked for a long time. She told him about her life, her family, and the farm where they lived. She painted an ideal life. Then she talked about *the incident*. She kept her eyes downcast through her confession. Finally she looked up. "Am I a bad person?"

Mike tried to speak but nothing came out. He pulled her close to his side, and she didn't resist. After a moment he managed to whisper, "You're not a bad person. You are my friend and I love you."

She slipped her arms around him and cradled her head in the crook of his shoulder. In a while, she fell asleep. He eased them down onto the bed and stretched out beside her.

Mike lay awake for hours, feeling the heat from her body and recalling the story she had told him about her life and the reasons she had come to Pattaya. She seemed so delicate, so fragile, and yet she had held up under pressures that would have left most people an emotional wreck. Looking back he could see how her past had influenced recent behavior. From the day she had arrived at Toy's bar she had been friendly but aloof. Despite his attempts to win her affections, she had kept him at arm's length. He had often wondered if she disliked men in general or if it was only farangs. More than once he had considered that it was only him she disliked. Her confession explained a lot. The fact that she had come to Bangkok to meet him said even more. Either she trusted him more than she should, or she wanted to see Bangkok so much that he was nothing but minor inconvenience. Perhaps it was a little of both. Maybe she even liked him.

He mulled that idea for a while then decided it was more likely that she thought of him only as a father figure instead of a boyfriend or lover. After all, he was twice her age plus a few years. He doubted that she had ever had a single sexual thought about him. She probably figured he wasn't even capable of sex at his age. Lately he had been having the same thoughts. Certainly the urges came less often now than in the past. He shook the depressing thoughts from his head.

It was almost midnight when he rolled to his side and laid his arm across her stomach. She snuggled closer but didn't awaken. In a while he fell asleep.

Chapter 19

When Jarapan awoke the next morning, Mike was lying beside her. His left hand rested atop her stomach, his head against her shoulder, his breathing soft and rhythmic. The air conditioner blew cool air but she didn't feel cold, the heat from Mike's body kept her warm.

She knew she should get up but she didn't want to, not just yet. She lay awake with her eyes shut and thought about yesterday. When she had left Pattaya, she had been excited about spending the weekend in Bangkok. The sky-train ride and her shopping trip to Robinson's may have seemed mundane to anyone else, but to her it had been thrilling. Seeing Purachai had put a damper on her excitement but she would have gotten over it if Mike hadn't made his unexpected appearance. That had put an end to what should have been a wonderful day. She couldn't believe Purachai had said he still loved her, or that he had called her a whore in front of Mike. Nothing could be further from the truth. Except for *the incident*, she was still a virgin.

Mike stirred but didn't waken. His arm shifted and his hand came to rest on her left breast. Her heart skipped a beat at his touch. Her urge to move away from him was stopped by a stronger desire to stay. She put her hand on his, pressed it tighter against her, and then snuggled closer against his warm body. The heat swept all the way to her womanhood and impolite images filled her thoughts. She wondered what Purachai would think about that. Even more, she wondered what her mother and father would think. At that moment she didn't care what anyone thought. She gave her imagination full rein and her physical desires ran wild. She was surprised at her yearning. She had never willingly had sex with anyone, yet she suddenly wanted this man desperately. She didn't understand her own urges. Embarrassed, she forced herself from Mike's embrace and left the bed.

In the bath she showered away the smeared make-up from yesterday's shopping trip. As she washed, she pretended it was Mike's hands fondling her body. Her fingers lingered in sensitive places where they caressed her to a climax so intense it made her knees weaken. She hoped the noise of the shower covered her low gasps of pleasure.

After she had recovered enough to stand properly, she turned off the water and toweled herself dry. When she wiped the steam from the mirror, she saw that her face and chest were flushed red. She wasn't sure if it was from the hot shower or her hot orgasm.

She slipped into the oversized bathrobe hanging from a hook on the door, and stepped into the bedroom to retrieve her make-up and clean clothes from the suitcase. Mike hadn't moved. As she dressed and put on make-up, she wondered what Mike would say about last night. If he didn't say anything about them sleeping together, neither would she. After all, they hadn't done anything, except in her imagination.

Finished with her primping she left the bathroom. Mike was still asleep. She watched him for a long time, deciding what to do. Itta wasn't expecting them back in Pattaya until tomorrow, but she was ready to leave today. Now that Purachai knew where she was and with whom she was staying, most likely he would come around again. She didn't think he would be too bold with Mike nearby, but he might try to embarrass her again by calling her names. And what if he had followed through with his threat to call her parents? For all she knew, her mother and father were already in Bangkok waiting for her and Mike to emerge from the hotel. The thought nagged at her as she debated her options.

If Mike wanted to stay another night, she supposed she would. Clearly he had planned his visa run with intentions of spending a couple of nights in Bangkok, either with or without her. She wondered what he would say if she told him she was leaving. Would he get angry? Would he make her move from his condo when they returned to Pattaya? Or would he even care at all? After yesterday, anything was possible.

In a while she began to feel foolish for letting Purachai ruin her weekend in Bangkok. She would be safe as long as Mike was with her, and surely he had understood everything she had told him about Purachai and the incident. In the end she decided she'd do whatever Mike wanted.

At six o'clock she went to the restaurant on the third floor and bought coffee and hot tea. When she returned, Mike was in the bathroom. She could hear water running. A mental image of him standing naked in the shower flashed through her head. She blushed and quickly brushed it away.

"I bought you coffee and a newspaper," she called soft through the door. If he answered, she didn't hear him. She sat in the living room and sipped at her tea while she waited for Mike to finish his shower.

~~~

Mike was awakened by the sound of a door closing. It took a second to realize where he was. The scent of Jarapan's perfume lingered soft around him. He reached out to touch her but she was gone. He sat up long enough to see that her suitcase was still there. He wasn't sure where she had gone, but at least she hadn't run away. He laid his head back on the pillow.

Outside the sky glowed with early dawn. He felt groggy but good. He wasn't sure if it was because he had gone to bed sober, or because he had slept so soundly. Maybe it was only because Jarapan had decided to meet him in Bangkok. He smiled at the thought. Memories of yesterday caused his smile to fade.

Last night Jarapan had said she wanted to go home. After what had happened he didn't blame her. Really he had no reason to be in Bangkok except that he didn't want to be in Pattaya. His original plans had been to take Jarapan sightseeing and to dinner at an upscale restaurant. He had no desire to go to Nana Plaza, or Soi Cowboy, or any of the other nightspots visited by the tourists. He had seen enough go-go's and beer bars in Thailand to last a lifetime.

He hoped Jarapan had calmed down from yesterday's confrontation with her ex-fiancé. The man had called her a whore because she was with him, and that had pissed him off. Until last night they had never so much as held each other. Absolutely they had never had sex. He wasn't sure what he would do if the little prick came around again, but whatever he might do wouldn't be polite. In his mind he imagined himself giving the asshole a mouthful of American fist. His body jerked at the reality of his thought.

Mike got up from the bed, grabbed a change of clothes, and headed toward the bathroom. If she still wanted to go to Pattaya, then that was what they would do. He wasn't one to run away from unpleasant situations, but he would leave if she asked.

He stepped into the shower and let the hot water wash away the tension that roiled inside. He wondered where Jarapan had gone. He hoped she hadn't gone looking for her ex. His scrotum tightened at the thought. He breathed a sigh of relief when he heard her voice softly announce that she had brought him coffee and a newspaper. Ten minutes later he had showered, shaved, and dressed.

"Where would you like to go today?" he asked as he stepped from the bathroom. A broad smile lit his face. "Do you want to see the Grand Palace and Wat Phra Kaew, or would you rather see the Floating Market?" He raised his eyebrows in question, and waited for her to answer. He hoped she didn't say home.

Jarapan noticed that Mike had conveniently ignored the Pattaya option in his list of places to go. But since she had decided to do whatever he wanted, it didn't seem important. "I'll be happy to go anywhere, as long as you are with me."

Mike was caught off guard. Her answer was almost like a

come-on. He had expected her to insist that they return to Pattaya. He wanted to ask if she was worried about her ex showing up again, but decided it best to leave sleeping dogs lie. Instead he said, "Then I'll give you a tour of Bangkok like you've never seen."

"That should be easy," Jarapan giggled, "Because I have never toured anything in Bangkok."

"Well good then." He glanced at his watch to cover his blush. "If we hurry, we can do everything in one day and still be back in time for dinner."

He held his hand toward her and she took it without hesitation. For the first time since he had met Jarapan, he thought of her as something other than a hot chick and a dedicated employee. She was a person with feelings and emotions. And unless he was reading her signals totally wrong she liked him, and her signals had just spoken volumes.

Outside the hotel they hired a private driver to show them around Bangkok. It was still early and they could have gone with a tour group gathering in the lobby, but Mike preferred the freedom offered by a private driver. He had never been to the Floating Market and wanted to see it, but if they went there they would miss a lot of other things he was sure Jarapan would want to see. Today they would visit the Grand Palace, Wat Phra Kaew with its Emerald Buddha, and the ancient canals built by King Rama I and his Khmer prisoners of war. He had seen those tourist sites before, but that was okay; Jarapan had never been to Bangkok and everything would be new to her.

By 7:15 they were making their way through the morning congestion of Bangkok's traffic. Their driver turned out to be a gem. His English was almost as good as his Thai. He talked non-stop about the city of Bangkok.

Krung Thep, the City of Angels, was what the Thais called Bangkok. It had been built when Burmese warriors forced the Siamese from their original capital of Ayutthaya. The name Bangkok had come from a small village in the area known as Bang

Makok or Place of Olives. In time, foreigners had shortened the name to Bangkok, but to the Thais it was still Krung Thep.

Jarapan gave their guide her undivided attention as he retold the history of Thailand and its capital city. Mike spent his time alternately staring at the insane traffic and gazing at Jarapan who sat to his right. If anything was amiss from last night, she didn't let it show.

Their day of touring started at the Grand Palace, followed by a solemn visit to the Wat Phra Kaew. Jarapan added a special touch by lighting candles and incense and saying prayers before they left the temple.

After a lunch at KFC they took an extended ride on a long tail boat through Bangkok's famous canals which had once inspired the name "Venice of the East". Jarapan's never-ending enthusiasm and the constant chatter made it a great day.

They were on their way back to the hotel when Mike directed the driver to Robinson's. "I want to take you shopping," he said.

"You don't have to do that; I went shopping yesterday."

He tilted his head back and stared down his nose. "And you bought what, one cheap blouse from a street vendor? We're going to dinner tonight and I want you to be the classiest woman in the restaurant."

"But I can't go shopping like this. I've been sweating all day and I'm dirty."

Mike laughed, "The store won't mind as long as we have money to spend."

They spent the next hour shopping. By the time they left the store, Jarapan had the dress, shoes, and cosmetics she had wanted so much the day before but was afraid to buy. The prices were outrageous, but Mike didn't blink an eye when he paid the bill.

As they walked back to the taxi, Jarapan couldn't help but notice the smile on Mike's face. He seemed happy that she was happy. If yesterday's scene with Purachai had affected him, she couldn't tell. Actually he seemed even more attentive now than he had ever been before. And the way he looked at her ... well, she wasn't sure what to think about that, but it made her feel good inside.

When they arrived back at the hotel, Jarapan was as full of energy as when they had left, but Mike was tired from the afternoon heat. He commandeered the bathroom and took a quick shower to wash away the layer of oily sweat and dust that had collected during the day. Afterwards he relaxed on the bed while she took over the bath.

When Jarapan emerged, she was wearing her new clothes. They fit her perfectly. The extra time she had taken with the mascara and make-up from Robinson's had transformed her from a princess into a goddess. If he had ever seen a more beautiful woman, he couldn't remember when or where. Maybe he never had.

"You look absolutely wonderful," he said.

"Thank you," she dropped her eyes from his gaze. "You're too kind."

"Are you ready to go? I know a nice French restaurant near here. I think you'll like it." He reached out and she took his hand without hesitation.

Chapter 20

There was no sign of Purachai when they left the hotel or as they walked the two blocks to the restaurant. The clientele were mostly farangs and their clothes were mostly rich. A few were with Thai women, but mostly they were not. Everyone seemed to know each other. Jarapan figured the restaurant was some sort of meeting place for the farangs living in Bangkok. She couldn't stop comparing herself to the women seated at the nearby tables. From the sly stares she received, she knew they were doing the same to her.

When the waitress came, Mike ordered a beer for himself and a glass of wine for her. She had never tasted wine or beer or anything like that and she wasn't sure today was a good time to start. She started to protest but then decided that one little glass of wine wouldn't hurt. In fact it sounded romantic. She had seen movies where glamorous people had wine with their meals and tonight she felt glamorous.

"I won't get drunk, will I?" she asked.

Mike laughed. "I'll be disappointed if you don't."

"What if I can't walk?"

"Then I'll carry you home."

Jarapan had mental images of him toting her across his shoulders like a sack of rice. It didn't seem very lady-like. "I think that's a bad idea."

"You think I'm too old?"

"Oh no," she answered quickly. "But I'm very heavy and it's very far to the hotel."

Mike leaned to one side and inspected her body. "About 45

100

kilos, I'd guess. Not so heavy."

"I weigh much more than that," she smiled. "I'm 46 kilos."

Mike laughed. "Okay fat lady, if you get drunk I'll hire a taxi."

"Okay old man," she laughed along with him. "I think that would be better for both of us."

The waitress arrived with their drinks. With dramatic flourish the girl poured Mike's beer into a frosted mug. Finished she turned to Jarapan and carefully filled a crystal stem glass from a newly opened bottle of wine. Instead of taking the bottle away, the girl put it into a decorative bucket of ice. Then she wai'ed politely and left them alone.

Jarapan eyed the glass of wine warily. Her stomach filled with soft butterflies as she picked up the glass and brought it to her lips. Until this very moment, alcohol had never crossed her tongue. She took a small sip and then sat the glass back on the table. When she looked up, Mike was watching expectantly.

"Is it okay?" he asked.

Jarapan didn't know what to think about the wine. It didn't taste good, but it didn't taste terrible either. Although it was cool, it left a warmth in the back of her throat. She would rather have a cola, but she wasn't about to say that. She didn't want anyone in the restaurant to think that she was some low-class rice picker. She put on her most charming smile. "It's perfect," she answered.

In a minute the waitress returned and took their order. While they waited for their dinner to be served, Jarapan finished her glass of wine and poured herself another. The second glass went down much smoother than the first. A soft glow enveloped her senses. Without asking, Mike poured her a third glass of wine. Really she didn't want it, but she drank it anyway. It was delicious. She wondered if the waitress had exchanged the first bottle with a special flavor. As she ate her meal, she had yet another glass. The warm glow spread through her entire body. She had one last glass as they relaxed after dinner.

In the subdued lights of the restaurant, Mike looked different, perhaps a little younger, definitely more distinguished. Strands of gray streaked his light brown hair, but on him it looked sexy. His blue-green eyes fascinated her. He was talking to her, but she couldn't keep up with the pace of his words. She wished he would slow down so she could understand. She was lightheaded and her face felt flushed.

"Would you like more wine?" he was saying.

She giggled at his question. "No, thank you. I think I've had enough. We should go soon. It's been a long day and I'm tired. "Her words came out a mixture of Thai and English.

"Of course. I'm tired, too." He caught their server's attention. "Ghep tung krup," he said. "Our check-bin please."

When the waitress went to total their bill, Jarapan excused herself to the ladies room. She felt like she was walking on air as she made her way through the restaurant. Once or twice she had to hold onto the back of a chair to keep her balance. She wondered if this was what it was like to be drunk. She giggled at the thought and continued her teetering trek.

She stared at herself in the bathroom mirror. She looked normal enough, though a little out of focus. A slight hum buzzed in her ears. She wanted to splash water on her face but didn't dare; it would ruin her make-up.

She sat in a toilet stall longer than she needed, hoping her giddiness would calm before she went back to the table. Impolite thoughts of her and Mike naked together kept interrupting and she was powerless to stop the images. After a minute she even encouraged them. The warmth of the wine collected into a coherent heat that quickly focused on her womanhood. Memories of her orgasm in the shower flashed clearer than anything around her and she knew she would make love with Mike before the night was through. The butterflies returned and she giggled in spite of herself.

Mike saw her as soon as she exited the ladies room. She had looked a bit tipsy when she left their table, and she didn't seem any steadier now. He stood and walked to meet her. He held out his arm and she took it immediately, clinging gratefully.

"I've already paid," he said. "I'll hire a taxi back to the hotel."

"I can walk," her smile was lopsided.

"It's a long walk for an old man like me," he responded, hoping he didn't sound too glib. She only smiled her silly grin.

As they left the restaurant, Jarapan's legs felt disconnected from the rest of her body. She was walking but not with her usual poised gait.

"Are you okay," he asked.

"As long as you don't fall down," she answered, and tightened her grip on his arm.

Outside, some of the older Thais stared as they passed. In formal Thai society it's considered impolite for a man and woman to show affection in public. Certainly it isn't polite for a farang and a Thai woman half his age to be holding each other so close.

The night air was thick with humidity, exhaust fumes, and food cooking on charcoal grills. The mixed aroma was unique. It was the smell of Bangkok. He hired a taxi to take them back to the hotel.

Jarapan snuggled close as they made the short ride. There was no doubt whether she was drunk or not. Whatever shyness or aloofness she had ever shown in the past disappeared quickly inside the taxi. She leaned against him, put her arms around him, and let her hands caress his body. In a moment she reached up and placed a sniffing Thai kiss on his neck. A wave of chills washed through him.

As they neared at their hotel, Mike had thoughts of rushing Jarapan to the room and making mad passionate love, but he couldn't—not just like that. As much as he wanted her, he wouldn't take advantage of her drunkenness. Maybe later, after her alcohol high had faded, they would make love if she wanted. In the meantime, he would take a Viagra pill just in case.

Mike was on the lookout for Jarapan's ex-fiancé as they exited the taxi but he didn't see the man. He breathed a sigh of relief.

"Whore!" a voice shouted as they stepped into the lobby.

Mike glanced back and saw the Thai man across the street. Jarapan apparently didn't hear, or if she did she ignored it.

Mike could feel the man's eyes on his back as they crossed the marble floors of the hotel lobby. He was tempted to look back but figured that would be a mistake. He wouldn't give the asshole the satisfaction of thinking he was bothered. He slipped his arm around Jarapan's waist and walked her to the elevator.

"While you shower and get ready for bed, I think I'll go to the lounge for a nightcap. I won't be long."

Jarapan smiled her sexiest lopsided smile. "I'll be waiting for you."

He thought maybe a shower and a few minutes alone would sober her up and cool down her wine induced passion. But considering that she continued pressing erotic parts of her body against him in the elevator, he suspected that a shower might not be enough.

Inside the room he took a Viagra tablet from his suitcase and swallowed it dry. If she was still in an amorous mood later, at least he would be ready. He left the room as soon as he heard the shower start.

His senses were in high gear when he stepped off the elevator. He scanned the lobby but Jarapan's ex- fiancé was nowhere to be seen. He was headed toward the lounge when the girl at the front desk interrupted him.

"I have a message for your wife," she said barely loud enough for him to hear.

Mike's body tensed at her words. He tried to remain calm as he walked to the reception counter and took the envelope. The flap wasn't sealed. Inside was a note, hand-written in Thai script. He couldn't understand a word of it. He considered asking the girl what it said, and then decided that was a bad idea. He slipped the note back into the envelope, walked to the lounge, and ordered a beer.

A Thai band played classic American and British oldies for the odd mix of Thai and foreign customers. The waitresses bustled about serving drinks and snacks. He fingered the envelope. Considering who had written it, he was sure it wasn't a letter congratulating Jarapan on her new job in Pattaya.

He finished his Heineken and ordered another. He stopped the barmaid when she returned with his beer, "Can you tell me what this note says in English."

The girl took the envelope, pulled out the letter, scanned it, and then looked up, "It's not polite."

Mike ran his fingers across his forehead. "I don't care about polite or not. I only want to know what it says."

The girl shuffled from one foot to the other for a moment before she translated the Thai into English. "You are a whore," she read, just loud enough for only him to hear. "I have called your family and they're coming to take you home. You have embarrassed them by having sex with farangs. They cannot understand why you have so little respect for yourself or your family. You have embarrassed me so much that I could never love you again. You are nothing but a whore."

She tilted her head downwards and put the letter back on the bar. "I'm sorry."

Mike's anger raged. He glanced at the hotel entrance but there was no sign of Jarapan's ex. He wasn't sure what he would do if he saw the man at this moment. Mental images of him beating the man to a bloody pulp flicked through his head.

"Thank you." he said as calmly as he could. "Please bring my check-bin."

The girl started to say more, but didn't. She hurried away and returned in a minute with his tab.

Mike paid, chugged his beer, and then went to his room.

Jarapan had finished her shower and was in bed, blankets pulled to her chin. "I've been waiting for you," she whispered.

"We have to leave Bangkok tonight."

"We can go later," she whispered. "Right now I want you."

She sat up, exposing her small breasts. "I know you want me, too."

Mike did want her, and clearly she was ready to give herself to him. The temptation to take her was powerful. He shoved it aside and told the first lie that came to his head. "There's an emergency. We must go to Pattaya now, tonight."

She looked like she had been slapped. "You think I'm ugly, don't you? Or a whore?"

"No," he said, shoving his scattered clothes into his suitcase. "There is an emergency. We have to go now."

"What emergency?" she glared as she pulled the sheet over her breasts. "I don't believe you."

"It's a fire or something, I don't know. Please, Jarapan, just trust me." He noticed her nakedness. "Put on some clothes and pack your things. "

"You are nothing but a stupid lying farang and I hate you," she wrapped the bedcover around her body and got up from the bed. She mumbled Thai curses as she staggered her way into the bathroom

"I don't care. Just hurry up." Mike rubbed his face with both hands, trying to shake off the several beers he had drunk. The Viagra had kicked in and it would be so easy to screw her brains out now and worry later about her family and her ex later. But now wasn't the time.

A minute later Jarapan emerged from the bathroom fully dressed and furious. Quickly but awkwardly she packed her things. "I want to get out of here. I hate you."

Mike ignored her comment. At that moment he hated himself, too. He was turning down the piece of ass he had wanted for weeks. After this she would be the piece of ass he would never have. But that wasn't important. If the note from her ex wasn't an empty threat, and if they were still here in the morning, she would suffer a lot more than his polite rejection. It was time to go.

In the lobby he asked the bellboy to get them a taxi to Pattaya and to hurry. He didn't even ask about the cost. At the moment any price would be cheap. Five minutes later he had paid his hotel bill and they were on their way to Pattaya. Jarapan sat in the back seat with Mike, but stayed on her side of the taxi as far from him as she could get. She fell asleep before they were outside of Bangkok's city limits.

He wondered if he should tell her about the note. If he didn't tell her, and it was true about her parents and everything, she would eventually find out and hate him for hiding things from her. On the other hand, if he showed her the note, she might panic and disappear whether it was true or not. The thought plucked at his emotions. The last thing he wanted was for her to disappear. He pulled the note from his pocket, wadded it into a ball, and threw it out the window.

In a while he pulled Jarapan from her side of the taxi to rest against him. She didn't protest, or even awaken. Instead, she laid her head on his shoulder, put her arms around his waist, and snuggled closer. She slept like that all the way to Pattaya.

Chapter 21

Jarapan awoke when the taxi turned right off the Sukhumvit highway onto North Pattaya Road and headed west toward Dolphin Circle and the Gulf of Thailand. She cracked her eyes open long enough to realize where she was and who she was with and then shut them again.

She felt better now. Her giddiness was gone but the effects of the wine still lingered. In bits and pieces she remembered the events of the evening. The wine, her euphoria, her desire for Mike. She blushed at her memories yet longed for the feelings to return. And she was thirsty, really thirsty.

"Mike," she said, "I need something to drink. Can we stop at a Seven-Eleven or something?" In recent years, Seven-Eleven stores had popped up all over Thailand like mushrooms on steroids. They were everywhere and they were open twenty-four hours a day. American convenience had taken old Siam by storm.

"Okay," he answered. "You tell the driver. Your Thai is better than mine." He smiled at his own dry wit.

Inside the store Mike bought three large bottles of Beer Chang while Jarapan stared at the coolers. "Is there a problem?" he finally asked.

"They don't have wine like the restaurant."

"Do you think you need it?"

She glanced at the beers sitting on the counter. "Yes."

Mike raised his brows. He hadn't expected her to want more to drink after getting sloshed earlier. "They have wine coolers which are pretty good. If you really want wine, that's as close as you'll find here."

Jarapan took four Spy-brand wine coolers from the shelf and sat them on the counter next to Mike's beer. "Why should you be the only one who has fun?"

Mike smiled at her and then retrieved four more bottles from the cooler. "There," he said setting them on the counter. "Now you can have twice as much fun. Besides, why should I be the only one with a hangover in the morning?"

"What do you mean?" she asked, eyeing the eight wine coolers cautiously.

"Never mind. I just mean that I don't want to have more fun than you. That wouldn't be fair, would it?"

She thought about that for a second before answering. "No, it wouldn't. I deserve to have as much fun as you."

Mike paid for their drinks and carried them to the waiting taxi. "Have you ever seen Pattaya at night from Buddha Hill?"

"What is Buddha Hill?"

"You know, up there." He pointed to the short mountain that separated Pattaya City from Jomtien Beach. "I know a place on this side that has a terrific view. It's really neat at night. Would you like to see it?"

"Will it be fun?"

"Yes, and romantic too." He opened one of the wine coolers and handed it to her. "Tell the driver I'll pay him double if he drives us there."

Jarapan took a drink of the wine; it was even better than what she'd had at the restaurant. It didn't warm her throat like before, but it did quench her thirst. She spoke to the driver and he pulled back into the flow of traffic.

Mike gave directions, Jarapan interpreted, and the driver drove. She finished her first wine cooler before they reached the road at the bottom of Buddha Hill. Mike opened another and she took it without hesitation. Minutes later they were high on the hillside overlooking Pattaya City. Mike was right, the view was spectacular.

They sat in silence watching the vehicles move along Beach

Road and the fishing boats bobbing across Pattaya Bay. As Jarapan finished her second wine cooler, her earlier sense of euphoria crept back and she welcomed it. She leaned against Mike and felt the heat of his body. She remembered waiting for him in the hotel room in Bangkok, and she remembered him telling her to get dressed because there was an emergency. Now, sitting on Buddha Hill, nothing seemed very urgent. She wondered what had been so important before.

"Why did we come back to Pattaya?" she broke the silence.

Mike slipped his arm around her and pulled her close. "You said you wanted to leave Bangkok," he lied. "I felt guilty making you stay. I was being selfish."

Jarapan pondered his statement as she finished the wine cooler. She remembered saying she wanted to leave Bangkok, but that had been more than a day ago. And then tonight, just when she wanted him to take her, he had insisted they leave at once. The alcohol emboldened her. "I wanted to make love with you." She blushed in the darkness and buried her face in his shirt.

Mike's face reddened at the lie he had told before and from the urges rushing through him now. The viagra was still having more effect than he thought possible. He opened another wine cooler and handed it to her. "We'll have one more drink and then we'll go back to our condo."

She noticed that he said *our condo* instead of my condo. She wondered if it meant anything or if it meant nothing. "Will we have sex?" she asked, her face still buried in his shirt.

He took her hand and guided it to his lap. There could be no mistaking the hardness of his manhood. "Up to you."

She allowed herself to touch him for a moment then pulled away and stood. She turned the nearly full bottle upside-down and finished it without stopping. "We must hurry," she said the same words he had told her in the hotel room. "There's an emergency."

He stood beside her. "What emergency?"

"I think it's a fire or something," she smiled her lopsided, sexy grin and headed toward the taxi.

Mike tried to be as nonchalant as he could with his jeans bulging. If the driver noticed, he didn't say anything.

It was a slow ride back to their condo on the far side of Pattaya. Jarapan ignored the driver and the traffic around them and did everything except make love to Mike in the taxi. By the time they reached the condo, he was ready to explode.

"I need a shower," he whispered. Really he needed to cool off a little or it would be a very short session of lovemaking, but he couldn't say that. "I want to be clean for you."

"Please hurry; I need a shower, too."

By the time Mike had finished bathing, his passion had eased a little but his erection had not. When he opened the shower curtain, Jarapan was there and completely naked. She stared at his aroused manhood as if she had never seen one before. His desire to take her then and there, on the bathroom floor, was as powerful as anything he had ever felt. He stepped aside to let her into the shower. "It's your turn to hurry."

Jarapan caressed her body as the shower sprayed down against her skin. She couldn't believe how excited she was. And terrified. She had never had sex with a man. Not voluntary sex anyway, so *the incident* didn't really count. Certainly she had never made love with a farang. Mike wasn't good looking according to Thai tastes, but he was exotic. Her mind raced with erotic images of his erection. Her nipples hardened and a needful warmth filled her womanhood. She rubbed herself to the point of climax before stopping. Finally she turned off the shower, toweled herself dry, and hurried to the bed. Her head whirled with an intoxicating potion of hormones and alcohol.

Mike was waiting for her. He took her in his arms and pulled her close. She expected him to kiss her on the lips like farangs always do in the movies, but he didn't. She was relieved when he kissed like a Thai.

After a moment she relaxed and enjoyed the attention he paid to her body. The sensation of his lips on her breasts drove her desire higher. When his fingers found her womanhood, she opened her legs to give him access; her hips pushed upward of their own accord. When his tongue joined the action, she gasped aloud from pure physical pleasure. She reached out with her hand and found his manhood. She twisted her body until she could take it into her mouth. She heard him moan, but he didn't stop his gentle assault until he had teased her to the point of orgasm.

Suddenly he stopped and pulled away. In the next moment she was on her back, his body positioned atop hers. "I love you," she heard him whisper. She didn't believe his words but she spread her legs wide in surrender. "I love you, too." She guided his pulsing manhood forward. She climaxed before he was completely inside.

Mike felt Jarapan tense as he entered her, but had no idea that she was having an orgasm. He thrust slowly, rhythmically, gently, until his manhood was completely enmeshed by Jarapan's body. The Viagra kept him strong, while the beer kept him from ending before he had even started. Suddenly he pulled her close and rolled to his back with her ending up on top. Her silky black hair hung down and brushed his cheek. He raised his head and took her right breast in his mouth as he increased the tempo of his in and out stroking. In a moment she caught his rhythm. For Mike, the world beyond their union ceased to exist.

Jarapan had been startled when Mike rolled to his back. She ended up on top with him still firmly planted in her womanhood. He continued his lovemaking without missing a stroke. In a moment he took her small breast in his mouth and ran quick laps around the nipple with his tongue. She matched his thrusting with her hips and her passion built faster than a monsoon storm. Within seconds her undulations overwhelmed any rhythm he tried to maintain. She was in control of her destiny and it was coming fast. Just as she thought more pleasure wasn't possible, Mike's manhood became stiffer, thicker, and longer than it had been a second before. She convulsed in orgasmic ecstasy as he reached his own explosive climax.

Afterwards they lay together touching gently, breathing heavy, and putting soft Thai kisses on each other's face and neck. It took fifteen minutes for Mike's heart to slow to a normal pace. It took Jarapan only minutes longer to decide she wanted to do it again.

She started by letting her hand slide to his waist and snuggling her head against his chest. She crossed his leg with hers and pulled herself close, moving her hips seductively. "I need you again," she purred in his ear. "Please take me now." Her hand slid toward his manhood.

Mike panicked. Quickly he reached down, pulled her hand to his lips and kissed it gently. "I love you," he said

When she tried to move her hand downward again, he gripped tighter.

"Are you okay, teeluk?" she whispered.

Mike turned on his side and rose up on his elbow. "When I was eighteen, I could have made love to you three times without stopping. But I'm not eighteen anymore. At my age, I'm lucky if I can do it three times in one week. That's the problem with old perverts like me." Embarrassment crept through him. "I want you Jarapan, but I can't. Not now."

Her face flushed; she hoped it wasn't glowing in the dark. "I'm sorry. I'm very stupid about men. What is a pervert?"

"Never mind," Mike whispered.

Jarapan put his hand on her stomach and eased it toward her womanhood. "Can you touch me here Mike? For just a minute? It would make me happy."

Mike let his hand be led astray. "Yes, that I can do. I want to make you happy."

That night, she dreamed of Mike.

Chapter 22

The next morning Jarapan awoke early. She tried to fall back asleep but couldn't. Her head was fuzzy and her stomach queasy. Sick, but not enough to vomit. She wondered if she had a hangover or if she just hadn't gotten enough sleep. She finally slipped from Mike's bed and went to the bath.

A seed of anxiety sprouted as the shower poured across her body. She and Mike had made love, and they hadn't used protection. Since coming to Pattaya she had lost track of her menses and wasn't sure if she was fertile now or not. But that was a small concern compared to how little she knew about Mike's past. He had been living in Pattaya for a long time and Buddha only knew how many bar girls he had slept with. Maybe he hadn't used protection with them either. At the same time she knew he didn't use drugs and he seemed healthy enough. Surely, if he had any concerns, he would have been more careful.

On the other hand, she hadn't been so drunk that she didn't know what she was doing. She had been planning to seduce Mike since the morning she'd left for Bangkok, but she had been thinking about it for a lot longer than that. What they had done was her fault as much as his. That realization didn't make her feel any better, but by the time she finished her shower she had convinced herself that she was worrying over nothing. Besides, it was too late to change anything.

Minutes later she had dressed, applied a thin coat of her new make-up, and was back in the bedroom. Mike hadn't moved. The lines on his face seemed more pronounced than yesterday but maybe it was only a trick of the morning light seeping through the curtains. His eyes were still shut, but she didn't think he was sleeping.

"Khun Mike," she said softly, "I'm hungry."

He grunted in response.

From the waist down he was covered by a blanket. He was naked from the waist up. Last night flickered through her head and she remembered the pleasure he had given her. She smiled at the memory.

"Khun Mike," she said again, "I need to eat soon. Can you get up now?"

He stirred for a minute and sat on the edge of the bed. He kept the blanket strategically in place. He coughed to clear a rattle from his lungs.

"I hate mornings," he mumbled, reaching for his Marlboro's. "Especially when I've had too much to drink." He lit a cigarette, took a couple of silent drags, and then added, "I won't be very good company for a while. If you're hungry, maybe you should go downstairs to the restaurant by yourself. I'll feel better later."

Jarapan had the distinct impression he was trying to get rid of her but didn't say anything. She was hungry, and if he didn't want her around, she would eat alone. "Can I bring you anything?"

"If they'll let you, bring me some cantaloupe and pineapple. A cup of hot tea would be nice, too."

Jarapan nodded and started toward the door.

"Hey," he stopped her. "Bring me a newspaper, too. Steal one from the restaurant if you have to."

She was sure she wouldn't steal anything from the restaurant, but didn't say it. She left the condo and went downstairs. She didn't know what to think of Mike's mood. She had never seen him so gruff. She wondered if he was hung-over or if he was feeling guilty because of what they had done last night. Or perhaps, she thought, he was like that just because she was there. She had heard that some men only chased a woman until they had sex with them and then they lost interest. She wondered if Mike was like that. The notion nagged at her through breakfast.

When she finished eating, she asked the waitress for a small pot of tea to go and then loaded a plate with pineapple and cantaloupe. Thoughtfully, the girl gave her a serving tray. That made it easier to carry the food, but it made her feel like a maid. She hoped Mike appreciated what she was doing for him.

After Jarapan had left, Mike finished his cigarette and stood from the bed. He felt like shit but it had nothing to do with the beers he had consumed the night before. He felt like shit every morning, even when he didn't drink a drop. Sometimes he could hide his morning moods but sometimes he couldn't. This was one of those mornings when he couldn't. He glanced at the clock. Jarapan wouldn't be gone long.

He headed for the bathroom, his joints ached with every step. He had showered the night before but he took another anyway. He didn't even wait for hot water. He needed something to jolt him back to life.

Twenty minutes later he had finished his morning bathroom routine. He felt better, but still not good. After dressing he went to the living room and read an old Bangkok Post. He was on his second cigarette when Jarapan returned with the tray of fruit and hot tea. "Thank you," he said, carefully polite.

"Are you awake yet?" she asked.

"Almost," he smiled. "Give me another ten minutes. Where's the newspaper?"

"I didn't see one. Someone must have stolen it already."

Mike sighed. "Never mind; it wasn't important anyway."

Jarapan nodded and excused herself from his presence.

He could hear the sounds of her unpacking her suitcase, putting the clean clothes into the dresser, the dirty ones into the laundry basket, and her toiletries in the bathroom cabinets. Images of last night crept into his thoughts. They'd had sex. He couldn't decide if that was a good thing or not. He felt the satisfaction that always came when a woman gave herself to him for the first time, but his usual sense of *by-gawd-I-showed-her* was missing. Spotty memories of their lovemaking flashed through his head. Jarapan had been drunk when she gave herself to him. Actually, she had been drunk since before they left the restaurant in Bangkok. She had sobered a little by the time they arrived in Pattaya, but the wine coolers on Buddha Hill had reversed that quick enough. He felt like he had taken advantage of her in a moment of intoxicated weakness. Yet she had been aggressive, as if she wanted it as much as he.

He tried to pretend it was all her fault, even as he remembered he was the one who had taken the Viagra just in case. He hadn't planned to seduce her although the idea had crossed his mind more than once. But that had been before the note from her ex-fiancé.

A pang of guilt nudged at him as he remembered the lie he had told her about the note. It pressed harder when he remembered the story she had told him of why she had come to Pattaya: The man she had planned to marry, the assault that had ended their engagement, the alienation she had experienced from her friends and family, and the desperation she had felt when she arrived in Pattaya. The last few months had turned her life upside-down.

Fifteen minutes later she was back. "Are you feeling better now?"

Mike nodded but otherwise ignored her question. "Is it raining?"

Jarapan shook her head. "The sun is shining. I think it's a good day."

What was left of his morning mood evaporated. "I think you're right." He reached out and took her hand in his. "It is a good day."

"Yes, Khun Mike, it's beautiful outside."

"By the way, I wish you wouldn't call me Khun Mike." He had never gotten used to being called khun. It was probably something left over from his younger days.

"What should I call you?" she asked.

"Mike would be nice. The "khun" thing sounds so formal. You don't call your brother khun when you talk to him, do you?"

"No, I call him Pee."

"Well, I don't want you to call me Pee, either."

"What if I call you teeluk?" she smiled coyly.

He paused at her question. He knew she meant it as a compliment, but it bothered him. No one had called him teeluk since Math had died. In fact, no one but Math had ever called him teeluk except in jest. Somehow it didn't seem right that anyone except Math should ever call him teeluk. "I think for now you should just call me Mike." His words came out colder than he intended. He forced a feeble smile to his lips. "Maybe you can call me teeluk next week."

Jarapan had been expecting him to react with happiness, and was surprised when he didn't. Then she remembered the story of the Thai woman and wondered if she had accidentally overstepped her bounds. She blushed slightly and lowered her gaze. "Okay, next week."

Neither spoke for a long minute. Finally, Jarapan said, "Last night in Bangkok, why did we leave so suddenly? You said there was an emergency but I've seen no emergencies since we've been home."

"You know already; I had a fire to put out."

"You could have done that in Bangkok." She gripped his hand hard. "Maybe there you could have put the fire out more than once."

This time Mike blushed. "Like I said last night, at my age I'm lucky if I can even find the fire."

"I don't believe you."

"You don't believe I'm too old?"

"No. I don't believe your reason for coming to Pattaya in the middle of the night."

Mike squirmed. "Okay, you're right. I really wanted to show you the city from Buddha Hill."

Jarapan only stared.

Mike squirmed even more and his smile faded. Finally he sighed and said, "Your friend came to the hotel again last night."

Jarapan tensed. She suspected their sudden departure had something to do with Purachai. After their confrontation she had been expecting him to show up again.

"What did he say? Did he threaten you? He knows many people and his father has money. He could be dangerous to you."

"I've been through too much shit in my life to let some street punk scare me."

His words raked at her. "Purachai isn't some street punk, and he could cause you trouble. What did he say?"

"He didn't say anything." Mike sighed again, deeper this time, resigning himself to telling her the truth. "He left you a note at the front desk."

Jarapan's heart skipped a beat. If Purachai had left a note, it wouldn't be a love letter. It was all she could do to keep panic from her face. "Can I see it?"

Mike blushed. "I threw it away."

"Do you know what it said?"

"It said that he had told your family about us, and they were angry because you had embarrassed them. It said they were on their way to Bangkok to take you home."

"What do you mean, *he told them about us*?" her voice pitched higher now. "There is nothing to tell. In Bangkok we did nothing. We only slept. Purachai is a liar. My mother and father would never believe I'm living with a farang. I must call and tell them the truth."

"That you're not living with me?"

Jarapan blinked at Mike's words. "I'll tell them I'm okay, and not to believe Purichai because he's a liar."

"Maybe you should just ask if they're okay, and tell them you love them. Do they have a phone?"

"My family has a handy, a cell phone."

Mike pointed at the phone on the desk. "You can use that one to call them. Or if it would be better, you can use my handy."

She hesitated for only a moment before taking his cell phone and disappearing into the bathroom.

Mike finished his breakfast while Jarapan called home. His headache had gained momentum and his sinuses were pounding. He wasn't sure if it was from the last night's beers or from the tension that coursed through his body. He searched the kitchen cabinets for aspirin or sinus medicine or Tylenol or anything, but came up as empty as Old Mother Hubbard's cupboard.

Against his better judgment he lit another cigarette. The smoke felt harsher than it should and he coughed slightly in response. His second drag wasn't any better so he crushed it out. The package said Marlboro Lights, but only God and Buddha knew what sort of garbage the Thais put into their version of American cigarettes.

Jarapan came out of the bathroom looking relieved. "Purachai is a liar. My family is still in Khon Kaen and he never called them. I told them I was living with Rattana." She paused then added, "They want me to come home."

Suddenly the room felt cold, "What did you tell them?"

"I cannot go back to Khon Kaen," she answered as she reached for his hand. "I don't want to go home. I think you understand."

"Yes," was all he could think to say.

"Mike," she whispered after a moment. "Would you be angry if I lie down for a while? Suddenly I feel very tired. I think maybe I didn't sleep enough last night, or I had too much wine."

He figured she was suffering from more than a hangover or lack of sleep. The way her mood had changed so quickly he was sure she was experiencing a major touch of homesickness. "No, I won't be angry. I could never be angry with you. I'm not feeling that great myself. I think I'll lie down, too."

Jarapan smiled and squeezed his hand in hers. "Thank you teeluk... I mean Mike. I'll feel better later." She turned and went to her bedroom and closed the door.

Chapter 23

During the next hour Mike's headache intensified from a throbbing pain to pure misery. He felt awful, even his eyeballs hurt. He decided to walk to the Big C Shopping Center for aspirin or sinus medicine or whatever he could find to stop the pain. He wrote Jarapan a note explaining where he had gone. By the time he reached the pharmacy he decided he would never drink Beer Chang again. Maybe he would even quit smoking.

He bought a package of the sinus pills, took four, and then sat on a bench inside the mall waiting for the medicine to take effect. Twenty minutes later the throbbing had eased and he headed home.

He had gone less than a block when he saw a familiar figure headed in his direction. The man's eyes were focused on the broken sidewalk more than the oncoming pedestrians. It was a man he had met months ago, a fellow American. He didn't remember his name, but he remembered his nickname.

"Hey, Greene County," Mike shouted when he was within earshot. The nickname was a reference to the man's home turf in America. Mike had dubbed him that the night they met.

The man looked up. A smile of recognition lit his face. "You can call me Jon."

"Okay, Jon it is, but I like Greene County better." Mike smiled even though he didn't feel like smiling. "What are you still doing in Thailand? I thought your job here was finished a long time ago."

"They needed someone to work evenings and I volunteered. I'll probably be here for another few months but I don't care, I don't have many reasons to go home. What about you? If I remember right, you were here on a short project. Still with the same company?"

"Nope, I just never went home. I'm now the proud owner of a new go-go bar; part-owner that is. I have a Thai partner but it's all my money. I made that ridiculous decision one night in a state of extreme intoxication. If it works, it works. If it doesn't, I guess I'll go home with my tail between my legs and a whole lot poorer."

Jon nodded his understanding. "You wouldn't be the first or the last. I'll keep my fingers crossed for you. What's the name of your bar?"

Mike pulled a business card from his wallet, wrote on the back, and handed it to Jon. "Your first beer is on me. After that you're on your own."

Jon took the card and read the front. "Suaee Dee Lady! I've heard the name somewhere."

"It's the talk of the town. We have the hottest dancers in Pattaya."

"I'm sure you do," Jon grinned at Mike's sales pitch. "But like I said, I work evenings so I don't get home until late."

"We're open until one. A couple of beers will help you sleep better. Stop by sometime."

Jon smiled. "How can I say no?" He held up the business card. "After all, my first beer is free. Maybe I'll stop by tonight."

"Mondays are always slow, but maybe that's better. You'll get more attention from the girls. I'm usually there until closing, but if business is slow I go home early."

"That's good to know. I'll take your presence into consideration. Shit, if I try hard, I'll miss you altogether." Jon laughed at his own joke.

"Fuck you, Greene County," Mike grunted.

"You can call me Jon."

"Yeah, I know," Mike smiled. "By the way, what ever happened to the girl you wanted me to meet."

Jon's face reddened, "I think she went home."

Mike sensed this was a conversation he didn't want to pursue. "They usually do," he responded. "Hey, I have to go, but I'll see you later at my bar." He extended his hand. "Good to see you again Jon."

The two men shook hands and then continued their separate ways.

Despite the midday heat, Mike felt a deep chill creeping through him. By the time he got back to the condo his nausea had returned and his lungs burned with each breath. He was getting sick, really sick. No doubt he had picked up SARS or the chicken flu or some other fucked-up disease in Singapore. He took two more sinus tablets, wishing he had bought aspirin and antibiotics instead. The note he had left for Jarapan was still on the table. Apparently she was still asleep. He folded the paper and slipped it into his pocket.

The room felt like an icebox. He turned off the air conditioner, wrapped himself in the bed covers and shook violently. In a while he fell into a sleep filled with grotesque dreams and fever induced hallucinations.

Chapter 24

When Jarapan awoke, the condo was hot. She didn't remember turning the air conditioner off, so Mike must have done it for some reason. She glanced at her watch; it was after four. She forced herself out of bed, went to the living room, and turned the air conditioner to high.

She peeked into Mike's room before going to the bath to get ready for work. He was asleep, curled in a ball under the bed-covers. She wondered how he could sleep covered like that in the sweltering heat of the condo. Since the day she had moved in, he had always kept the temperature set on cold and then would complain about how hot it was. She decided he must be exhausted from his trip to Singapore and the late night in Pattaya. She would let him sleep until she finished her shower.

By five o'clock she had dressed for work. The air conditioner had done its job and the condo was tolerable again. Mike was still asleep and she decided not to disturb him. She wrote a note and left it on the kitchen table next to a package of sinus medicine. She told him she had gone to work and would see him later. She checked on Mike one last time and left the condo.

Jarapan arrived at the Suaee Dee Lady shortly before six. Itta hadn't yet arrived, so she let herself in with the key Mike had given her. The bar had been stocked and cleaned and was ready for business.

She turned on the music and the stage lights, and then checked her cashier's desk. It was neat and tidy. The girl who had filled in for her had done a good job. Suddenly she felt guilty for taking off work to meet Mike in Bangkok. She knew the time off had been okayed by Itta, but she felt guilty nonetheless. The door opened jarring her from her thoughts. It was Itta.

"Did you have a pleasant holiday?" Itta asked as she stowed her purse behind the bar.

Jarapan wasn't sure how to answer. Except for Purachai's unsettling appearance and Mike's decision to leave early, it had been good. But it had gotten much better when they returned to Pattaya. "It was fine," she finally said.

"Did you do any shopping?"

"I went to Robinson's. How did you know?"

Itta smiled, "I know everything in Thailand. Besides, I know Mike pretty well and would be surprised if he *didn't* take you shopping. "

Jarapan knew that Itta and Mike had known each other for a long time and that they had once been more than friends. That had been confirmed long ago by the gossip that floated through the Suaee Dee Lady. She wondered if Mike had bought the clothes that Itta was wearing today. A pang of jealousy jabbed at her emotions. Her smile stayed warm, but her words came out cold. "Yes, Mike likes to spend money too much. But I guess you know that already."

Neither spoke for a second.

Finally, Itta took a deep breath and said, "Don't believe everything you hear in Pattaya. This city has more rumors than farangs have dollars. Yes, I know Mike very well. I knew him even before I met him. You see, Mike loved my sister Math before she died. Math told me all about him but I never met him until I came home from Scotland. We pretended to be lovers for a while, but that didn't work so we became business partners instead. Mike and I are like brother and sister."

Jarapan blushed. "Why did you tell me that?"

"Because you wanted to know," Itta answered, her voice calm and quiet, almost apologetic. "The truth is that Mike is a good man. And if he likes you, then I'm happy. I would like to see Mike find a woman who can fill the emptiness my sister left in his heart. That is something I could never do. But never mind that; it's time to get ready for opening. We have to make Mike enough money to pay for your new clothes." Itta's smile was warm and genuine. "Okay?"

Jarapan breathed a sigh of relief. "Yes, thank you for understanding everything."

Itta laughed. "You're like a young sister to me. Now let's get to work. Our dancers will be here soon and the customers will be close behind. I have to finish some paperwork in the office. You can sit outside until Noi or Ba or a customer arrives."

Mike didn't come to the Suaee Dee Lady at his usual time that night. In fact, he never showed up at all. Itta seemed unconcerned, but Jarapan worried that something was wrong. No one could possibly sleep that long. She had mental images of Mike at another bar flirting with a common bar girl. As hard as she tried, she couldn't shake the thoughts from her head. By eleven-thirty she was totally distraught. At midnight Itta told her to go check on Mike, even though closing time was still an hour away. Jarapan protested, but Itta insisted. Jarapan left the Suaee Dee Lady and raced home to the condo.

The lights were off when she opened the door. If Mike was there, he clearly wasn't awake. She suspected that he had gone out and hadn't come home yet. Or maybe he had come home and had a woman in his bedroom. Her chest tightened with jealousy.

She flicked on the kitchen light. Everything looked the same as when she had left for work. Her note was still on the table. She went to the bathroom and looked. If Mike had showered, he hadn't used a towel. A sense of disaster crept through her. Something wasn't right. She went to Mike's room and eased the door open. He was there, completely covered by blankets, not moving. She had the eerie feeling that he was dead. It was all she could do to keep from running out of the condo screaming in terror.

"Mike?" she finally managed to whisper.

He didn't respond.

"Mike?" she repeated, louder this time, her voice high-pitched and rising. "Are you asleep?"

The blanket moved slightly but he didn't answer, look up, or anything. She reached to turn on the overhead light but then changed her mind. Instead she walked to the bed and sat beside him. Now she could hear him breathing, shallow, raspy, and labored. She put her hand against his cheek. It was hot, really hot. She switched on the lamp and looked at his face, it was blood red.

"Teeluk," she shook his shoulder gently. "Are you okay?"

When he still didn't respond, her alarm grew. She pulled the blanket from him. He was fully clothed and soaked with sweat. He shivered beneath her hand and his body curled into a tight ball against nonexistent cold. She shook him again, harder.

"Teeluk, you're sick. Please wake up. You need to go to the hospital right now, tonight." She continued shaking him until he finally opened his eyes and looked up at her. The whites of his eyes were as red as his face, and glazed like someone on drugs.

"Math?" he said, a weak smile formed on his dry lips. "What are you doing here? Where have you been? I missed you teeluk. Can you hold me for a minute? I'm so cold."

Jarapan winced at being called another woman's name, even if the other woman was long dead. She knew he hadn't done it on purpose, but it still bothered her. He was probably hallucinating from his fever. She pushed her jealousy aside.

"I have come to help you teeluk," she said. "You're very sick and need to see a doctor right away. We must hurry."

"I'll be better now you 're with me again," his words came out slurred. His eyelids drooped heavily. "I love you Math," he whispered and then fell silent.

Her alarm exploded into panic. She shook his shoulder and pulled on his hands and arms, but he didn't respond. Her heart raced as she decided what to do. She ran to the phone and picked up the handset before realizing she didn't know who to call. She put the phone down and ran to the bathroom. There she soaked a towel with cold water and then hurried back to Mike.

She wiped gently at his face and arms hoping the coolness would awaken him. It only made him shiver harder. Her mind swirled with images of Mike dying because she couldn't get him to the hospital. Suddenly she knew what she must do. If Mike couldn't go to the hospital on his own, she would get an ambulance to take him, or find a doctor to come to him. She stood from the bed feeling calmer now that she had a plan.

"I'll be back in a minute teeluk." she said and hurried downstairs to the lobby.

The young man at the front desk was asleep.

"Sawasdee ka," she said loud enough to awaken him.

The man pushed himself erect. "I was just thinking," he smiled sheepishly. "May I help you?"

"Khun Mike is very ill," she said, her voice high-pitched. " He came back from Singapore two days ago and he seemed fine. Even last night he was okay. He was sleeping when I went to work and he was still sleeping when I came home. I touched his head and he's very hot. He won't stay awake, and he doesn't even know who I am. I want him to go to the hospital, but he can't get out of bed. I need help. Maybe you can tell me how to call an ambulance or a doctor or something."

Instantly the boy was caught up in her panic. "We have a doctor on call for the residents," his voice was almost as shrill as hers. "You go and take care of your friend. I'll call the doctor." He picked up the phone and began dialing.

"Thank you," Jarapan said and hurried away.

When she arrived back in the condo, Mike was awake and sitting on the edge of the bed. Sweat poured from his face despite the fact that the room temperature was too cool to cause anyone to sweat.

"It's hot in here," he said when she entered the bedroom. "Can you turn the air conditioner on? I feel like I'll be sick to my stomach."

"Do you know who I am?" she asked, walking toward him.

"What kind of question is that? Of course I know who you are. And I would be eternally grateful, if you would cool this place down some."

She touched his forehead with the tips of her fingers. The fever that had ravaged him just minutes ago had faded by whole degrees in her short absence. At that moment he began breathing in quick gasps. He hurried past her and ran to the bathroom.

From outside she could hear him vomiting. She felt sorry for him but there was nothing she could do. Now that he was awake and moving, she wondered if she should cancel the doctor. Maybe he had a twenty-four hour flu or something and wasn't dying after all. He might even get angry if he found out she had called for a doctor without telling him. She turned the temperature down a few degrees and waited for him to come out of the bathroom.

His vomiting seemed to last for hours. When it finally stopped, it was replaced by a harsh coughing that hurt Jarapan just to listen. When he came out of the bathroom, his breathing was strained.

"It's cold in here," he wheezed. "I'm freezing." He hurried to the bed and again pulled the covers over himself.

Jarapan turned the air off and then went to sit beside him. She touched his cheek again. That quickly, the fever had returned. "I called for a doctor. You are very sick and I'm very worried."

He coughed long and hard, to the point that Jarapan thought he might pass out from lack of air. When he could finally speak, he said, "I don't need a doctor."

At that moment came a knock on the door. "It's too late. The doctor is here already. He will make you well in quickly time."

Mike didn't protest as the doctor listened, poked, peered, and prodded. After a number of hmm's and uh-huh's, the doctor said to Jarapan, "I think maybe a virus. Antibiotics won't help, but I'll leave some anyway. I don't want to take chances of a secondary infection. He needs to rest for a few days. If he gets worse, or if he's not feeling better by this time next week, make him go to the hospital."

The doctor turned to Jarapan, "Make sure he rests. No solid foods until he stops vomiting and stops having diarrhea. Clear broth and cola will be okay. Lots of water, too. No beer or whiskey."

"I don't think he has diarrhea," Jarapan said.

"I think he will before he's better. He shouldn't smoke either."

Jarapan nodded her understanding. The doctor gave Mike an injection of antibiotics and gave Jarapan the pills for Mike. After repeating his instructions, he left.

Mike's illness ravaged him for two days before easing from horrible to merely miserable. Jarapan went to work just long enough to tell Itta she had to stay home and care for Mike. Itta was understanding and told Jarapan to take as much time as she needed. It was four days before she was willing to leave Mike alone. By then his fever had gone away, but his lung-searing cough remained. He returned to solid food but ate little no matter how much Jarapan nagged.

Mike figured that he had caught some strain of flu in Singapore, and maybe a touch of pneumonia, too. Whatever it was, Jarapan seemed immune and she remained healthy. Both were thankful for that small miracle.

Chapter 25

The downside of Josh's lifestyle change was boredom. Most people assumed he was stoned 24/7, but actually he wasn't. He had tired long ago of living his life in a semi stupor. Just as important, he couldn't take the risk of being caught with possession of any of the hard stuff. He never kept more than a small supply of pot for himself. He had stopped coke and meth altogether.

When Josh bought a computer, he had the crazy notion he could somehow use the internet to expand his business. He also bought it to give him something to do besides watch the afternoon gossip and smut shows. He never got any new customers from the internet, but it kept him occupied for hours on end. It was a harder addiction than any drug he had ever taken. Within a month he had downloaded every song he ever liked and burned them to CD. His music collection was awesome.

One day he typed "Thailand" into a search engine. The number of matches was overwhelming. He narrowed the search to Pattaya, the city where his dad had gone. The volume of matches reduced, but not by much. He picked one at random and entered a world he never knew existed. His waking life became a nonstop inspection of Pattaya web sites interrupted only by his Thursday afternoon buys and his Thursday night sells. He became obsessed.

It didn't take Josh long to figure out what Pattaya was all about. The web boards said it all. Thousands upon thousands of men flocked to the seaside resort each year looking for temporary love. What sorry losers they must be, having to travel halfway around the world for a piece of ass. He hoped someone would blow his brains out if his life ever fell to such a pitiful state.

Chapter 26

On the same night that Mike fell ill, Jonathan "Greene County" Yeager went to the Suaee Dee Lady after finishing his afternoon shift. He scanned the bar for his friend but didn't see him anywhere. He figured Mike had gone home early and didn't give it more thought.

The tables were filled with tourists and working girls. He found an empty stool at the bar and waited to be served. The lady tending bar had her back to him as she served another customer. When she turned, his heart jumped to his throat. In the dim light she looked exactly like a woman he had once lived with. A Thai lady named Nuang. As she approached, he realized it wasn't Nuang, but the resemblance was remarkable.

"What would you like to drink?" the woman's smile sparkled.

"What's your name?" was his response.

She laughed at his question. "My name is Itta. I've never seen you here before. What's your name?"

"I am Jon."

"Would you like something to drink?"

He slipped the business card from his wallet. "The owner said my first drink is on him. I'll have a Heineken."

She took the card, read the writing on the back, and then said, "Mike is my partner. Did you and Mike work together before?"

"No, but Mike and I once lived near each other in America. I really don't know him, but I'll have to thank him for inviting me here. Otherwise I would never have met you."

Itta blushed at his compliment. "I'll get your beer now."

Jon stared at the girls dancing on the raised stage but it was the image of the bartender and her resemblance to Nuang that filled his head. *Nuang*! He hadn't seen her in months. He had once loved her and she had loved him, too, or so he had thought at the time. Then one night she had gone crazy and disappeared. He had waited weeks for her to come back, but she never did. In time he gave up the hope of ever seeing her again. And now here, in his friend's bar, he had found a woman who looked enough like Nuang to be her sister. He knew that was silly but it stuck in his head.

"What time do you get off work?" he asked when Itta delivered his beer. "I would like to see you later."

Her smile turned apprehensive. "I'm sorry. I am the owner and I don't go with customers, even if you are Mike's friend."

Jon blushed, realizing she had interpreted his comment and wishing he hadn't been so forward. "I meant only for something to eat. I just got off work and I'm hungry. I thought maybe you could show me where I can find good food at this time of the night."

"I can have one of the girls go outside and buy something if you're hungry."

"I'd rather have dinner with you later." He stood from his seat, held his arms up, and turned around slowly. "See? No hidden weapons, no drugs, no anything. I'm just tired of eating alone, that's all."

Itta smiled at his antics. "Okay, I do know a small restaurant with good food. It's not far away. My friend Kamra is the cook. But she only cooks Thai food. "

"I love Thai food," he lied. He would eat pig slop if it meant she would have dinner with him. "So you'll go with me?"

She pretended to think for a minute. "Okay, but only this one time." She stood straight and added, "And as long as you pay."

Jon laughed, "I wouldn't have it any other way."

Jon managed to drink three beers before the lights were turned up and the remaining customers left. Itta gave him another on the house while she and a couple of the girls cleaned up the bar from the night's business. The beer was gone by the time Itta was ready to go. She locked the door behind them as they left.

"I have a motorcycle," she said once they were outside. "I'll drive us to my friend's restaurant."

As they walked toward her motorcycle, Itta kept looking over her shoulder as if she were looking for someone or something.

"Expecting the boogey-man?" Jon smiled.

She looked up at him but didn't return his smile, "That's exactly who I'm expecting."

Before he had time to think about what she had said they arrived at her motorcycle. He felt uncomfortable riding behind a woman, but it turned out that she was a very careful driver. Ten minutes later they were ordering food from Kamra.

While they waited for their meals, Jon did his best to make small talk. Soon he ran out of things to say. In the growing lull he said, "I know this may sound factitious, but you are one of the most beautiful women I have ever met."

"What does that word mean? I never heard of factitious."

Jon scrambled for an answer. He wasn't sure what it meant. He wasn't sure he had pronounced it right or if it was even a real word. "It means that I'm not saying I think you're beautiful just to flatter you. I'm saying it because I mean it."

"Oh," she blushed. "Thank you."

The waitress arrived with their food and the conversation gave way to satisfying their hunger.

Itta noticed that Jon couldn't keep his eyes off her. She couldn't remember anyone ever being so attentive. Not Ian, not Mike, nor any of the men she had slept with when she worked as a bar-girl. Despite her attempt to remain nonchalant, she was flattered.

When she finished eating, she glanced at her watch, "Dear Buddha, I didn't know it was so late. I don't mean to be rude, but I have to go home now. I have things I must do in the morning."

In return, Jon looked at his own watch. "You're right; it is late. Can you give me a ride home, so I don't have to bargain with a baht-bus driver?"

Itta leaned back and smiled, "Okay, as long as you don't think I'm being factitious."

Jon laughed at her clear misuse of the word. "You, factitious? That is the farthest thing from my mind."

Ten minutes later Jon was in his condo alone, and Itta was on her way home.

Jon came back to the Suaee Dee Lady the next night, and every night after that as well. He flirted shamelessly with Itta, and she enjoyed his attention just as shamelessly. By the fourth day the girls in the bar and the late night customers at Kamra's had come to know them as a couple. Jon and Itta heard the gossip but they didn't care; the truth was whatever anyone wanted to believe.

One night Itta told Jon about her family. She had two brothers and three sisters. Her mother and father had separated years before. Her oldest brother, with whom she lived, owned an advertising business in Pattaya. Her younger brother was still in school. One of her sisters had died a couple of years earlier in a motorcycle accident. The other two were married and had families of their own. One was named Neet and the other was Nuang. When he heard the name Nuang, he had wanted to pry but didn't. Probably it wasn't the same Nuang he knew. It didn't matter anyway; he had gotten over her a long time ago. He kept silent about his past affair with a Thai woman.

"I would like to meet them someday," he said when she finished talking.

"I would like that, too."

As they waited for the waitress to bring their check-bin, the breeze intensified and became noticeably cooler.

"Rain is coming," Jon said. "You go start the motorcycle while I pay the bill."

Itta nodded and hurried away. She was waiting and ready to go when he stepped from the restaurant.

Two blocks from his condo the sky split and water poured down in torrents. By the time they entered the covered parking area beside the lobby they were sopping wet. If there was a dry spot on either of them, it didn't show. The engine sputtered and died as Itta braked to a stop.

Jon got off the motorcycle, inspected himself from top to bottom, and then looked at Itta. Water dripping from her clothes had formed a puddle beneath the motorcycle. Her hair was soaked and matted tight to her head. Rain smudged mascara left dark circles under her eyes and black streaks on her cheeks. She looked like a raccoon he had once seen in a cartoon movie. "You look like a drowned rat," he said smiling.

Itta looked at herself in the side mirror of the motorcycle. "But I'm a beautiful rat," she retorted.

"Yes," he leaned near and whispered. "A very beautiful rat."

She blushed. "I should go now. My brother will be worried."

She kicked the starter. The engine coughed two dull chugs but remained lifeless.

"You should come inside and get dry. "

"That wouldn't be polite," her voice quavered. She kicked the starter again. It backfired in response.

The security guard looked in their direction.

"Sorry," Itta shouted to him. She put down the kickstand, stood from the motorcycle, and turned to Jon. "I think it's too wet to start. She looked down at her waterlogged clothes. "I think I'm too wet to go anywhere, too."

Her blouse clung to her body like a wet tee-shirt. Clearly she wasn't wearing a bra. Her small breasts protruded erotically through the thin cloth. Her nipples stood out in hard enticing knots.

"Are you cold, or just happy I'm here?"

"What do you mean?"

"Never mind," he reached out and took her hand. "Let's go, I'm freezing."

Inside the elevator Jon kept his distance. His intentions were honorable, yet he felt uncomfortable. "You're safe with me," he said for no reason.

Itta smiled up at him. "I always feel safe with you, Jon. What about you? Do you feel safe with me?"

Her question caught him off guard. "I think you're too little to hurt me."

"I think I'm just the right size," she responded

"The right size for what?"

"For anything."

The elevator door opened.

"Let's hurry," she said. "I'm freezing, too."

Jon's hand shook as he fumbled the key into the lock; not so from the cold as from nervousness. Itta had never been inside his home before. In fact, no woman had been inside his condo since Nuang had disappeared.

Nuang! His head filled with erotic scenes of her teaching him to love again after he'd given up on women altogether. She had rekindled his desires at a time when he believed himself impotent. Nuang had made him feel like a man again for the first time in years. He wondered if Itta could bring that same magic to life.

"There," he said, finally managing to open the door. "I'll be glad to get out of these wet clothes."

"Me too," Itta followed him inside.

Jon switched the lights on and the air conditioner off and then turned to look at her. Even soaking wet she was beautiful. His erotic imagining returned, only this time it was Itta in his thoughts. His face flushed at the vividness of his imagination.

"I, uh ...," he stammered. "I think I have some clothes you can wear."

Itta cocked her head. "You mean you have women's clothes?"

His nodded and his blush deepened.

Her smile faded. "They are yours? And you wear them?"

"Not unless I lose about forty kilos and shrink several inches."

"Then you have another lady?"

"No," he answered, deciding what to tell her. Truth would be easiest, but maybe not the smartest. "The people who lived here before left them behind," he finally lied.

It was Itta's turn to blush. "I was only joking about you

wearing lady clothes."

Jon laughed. "So was I."

Itta's smile returned. "Okay then, show me the lady's clothes you don't wear."

"This way, madam," he bowed slightly and extended his arm toward the closet.

What Itta found was one pair of Levi's, two Thailand tee-shirts, and a dress. The dress would probably fit, but it wasn't practical for tonight. She selected the jeans and tee-shirt instead. "I will change in there," she pointed toward the bathroom.

"Okay, don't hurry. I'll change right here."

She shut the door and inspected herself in the mirror. She really did look like a drowned rat. She wrinkled her nose at her reflection. As she stripped off her wet clothes, she had images of Jon doing the same thing in the room outside. It was easy for her to picture him naked, his body lean and sexually aroused. Her heart skipped a beat as hormones flooded her body with a heady craving for male closeness. Her womanhood wetted intensely as she imagined him taking her, his breathing heavy, eyes filled with animal lust. Her coldness from the rain disappeared in the warmth of her own desires.

"Does everything fit okay?"

Itta jumped at the sound of his voice. Her mental movie ended and she felt foolish. "I don't know yet," she answered. "I'll take a shower before I try them on."

When he didn't say anything else, she adjusted the water to hot and stepped into the shower. Her arousal intensified as she imagined Jon rubbing the washcloth across her breasts and hips and places intimate. As she toweled herself dry, she made plans to seduce him. She wondered how he would react.

The tee-shirt was oversized, its bottom seam dangled to mid thigh. She started to put on the jeans then changed her mind. She didn't want anything to interfere with what she had decided to do. She glanced at herself in the mirror one last time, and then opened the bathroom door. Her heart raced at her daring.

After Itta had gone into the bathroom, Jon slipped out of his wet clothes and put on a comfortable pair of jogging pants and a casual shirt which he consciously left unbuttoned. He was in reasonably good shape for a man his early fifties and was far from embarrassed by his body. Besides, he wanted Itta to see him as relaxed and confident, and showing a little skin might get her to thinking. He shook his head at his adolescent thoughts but left the shirt unbuttoned anyway.

He went to the bathroom door and asked if everything fit okay. She responded that she was going to take a shower. He figured he would do the same when she was finished. When the water started, he had vivid mental images of her naked in the shower. The effect was immediate but the physical results were less than inspiring. He went to his dresser and found the small plastic baggie of Viagra tablets he hadn't touched since Nuang had disappeared. He couldn't remember if he was supposed to take a whole one or half of one, so he swallowed a whole pill. Maybe nothing was going to happen tonight, but he didn't want to take the risk of failing if it did.

A few minutes later the shower stopped and Itta emerged from the bathroom. She had taken jeans and a tee-shirt with her into the bathroom, but now all she had on was the tee-shirt. It stopped inches above her knees. He wondered if she was wearing panties underneath. His body responded to the possibility that she wasn't. Probably just the Viagra, he decided, or maybe not. Whichever, the sensation was intoxicating.

"I should take a shower, too," he said, even though a shower was the last thing on his mind. His words came out husky.

"Up to you," she smiled coyly. She walked to his bed and slipped beneath the covers. "I'll wait for you."

Jon's mind raced a thousand miles an hour. His manhood grew even faster. "I'll hurry," he said as he stepped into the bathroom.

He had taken Viagra before and mostly he remembered it making his face flush and burn like blood pressure run amok. He didn't feel that now, but his entire being throbbed with an anticipation he hadn't felt since his first time with Nuang. He rushed through his shower.

In less than five minutes he slipped beneath the covers beside of Itta. Her soft skin beneath his fingertips triggered a heady release of hormones to powerful to ignore. They touched and teased each other as if old lovers. The hormones and Viagra worked their magic and they made love—twice. If Itta didn't climax both times, she was one hell of an actress.

Jon fell asleep feeling better about himself than he had in months. He held tight to Itta through the night in fear that she might disappear like Nuang had done.

In the morning Jon took her to breakfast. He expected to feel uneasy, but he didn't. He felt more like a teenager than a fifty year old man. The way they talked and laughed any casual observer would have thought they had been together for years.

After breakfast, she excused herself to go home. On impulse he asked her if she would come live with him but she didn't answer. Instead she pulled him close and placed a sniffing Thai kiss on his cheek. When she left, he watched until her motorcycle disappeared in the distance.

~~~

Itta was on cloud nine as she made her way to Anan's house. She was relieved when he wasn't there. She stayed long enough to clean up, put on fresh clothes, and write a note.

"I have found an apartment closer to my work. I will move there tomorrow." She knew her brother would eventually learn where she was living, and she knew his dislike of Thai women living with farangs so she added, "Don't make me lose face."

She packed a few things into an overnight bag and drove back to the condo. She hoped she was making the right decision.

Chapter 27

For Jarapan and Mike the weeks passed like a whirlwind. They spent more time together than they did apart yet never tired of each other's company. The few doubts Jarapan had about falling in love with a farang had long faded. She no longer thought of him as a man old enough to be her father, but a man mature enough to be her husband.

Mike's cough had lasted for nearly three weeks before returning to his usual morning hacking. Jarapan nagged him politely to quit smoking and he promised he would, but he never did.

Her friend Rattana had married her boyfriend and moved with him to England. Jarapan supposed it had more to do with money than with love. She figured Rattana would be back soon enough, and would be a whole lot richer for her time in the U.K.

Ohm had left the Suaee Dee Lady and had gone home to Korat for a few weeks, and Jarapan was now working afternoons and evenings. Mike had been unhappy about the double shifts, but Jarapan was so ecstatic with the extra money that she didn't make an issue of it. Sometimes he even came to the Suaee Dee Lady in the afternoons and helped with the bar stocking, cleaning, and accounting. It all came to an end the day Itta bought a new motorcycle.

Jarapan had been working both shifts for about three weeks when one afternoon Itta said she had something to show her. Outside the Suaee Dee Lady Itta pointed to a shiny new motorcycle.

"What do you think?" she asked.

"It's very nice. Did you buy it today?"

"I bought it last week. They delivered it just today. But that's not what I want to show you."

Jarapan looked at her quizzically.

"I want to show you my old motorcycle. The dealer wouldn't give me much for it so I didn't sell it to him. Why don't you ride it for a few days? If you like it, I'll sell it to you for what he offered me, maybe less. Up to you."

Jarapan couldn't believe what she was hearing. Itta's old motorcycle was less than a year old and almost like new. "Yes, I will drive it for a couple of weeks. How much do you want for it?"

"The dealer offered me 10,000 baht. I'll sell it to you for 8,000. It's a good deal."

Eight thousand baht! Jarapan had never imagined anyone would sell such a nice motorcycle for eight thousand baht. "I'll take it."

Itta smiled. "Drive it for a while before you decide. I'm in no hurry."

"Thank you," Jarapan said, wai'ing profusely. "How can I ever repay you?"

"Take good care of Mike. He deserves happiness."

Jarapan smiled, "That I can promise."

Later that afternoon, after they had finished cleaning and stocking the bar, Jarapan hurried home on her new motorcycle. "I have a surprise," she squealed as she bolted into the condo. "Please come see."

"Are the Germans peeing in the pool again?" Mike smiled.

Jarapan laughed remembering what had happened two days before. "Even better." She grabbed his hand. "Come on, I'll show you."

In the parking lot Jarapan pointed at her new prized possession, "What do you think?"

Mike shifted uncomfortably from one foot to another. His eyes flicked from the motorcycle to Jarapan, and then back to the motorcycle. "I think you should take it back," he finally said. With that he turned and headed toward the elevators.

Jarapan's pride shifted to fury in less than an instant. She had expected him to be happy for her, not tell her to give back the motorcycle. It wasn't right for him to do that. For the first time since they had met, Jarapan felt true anger towards Mike. She caught up with him in the lobby.

"What's wrong with you?" There was no smile on her face and no love in her tone.

"Nothing's wrong. I just don't like motorcycles, that's all."

"It's that girl, isn't it?" The thought popped into her head uninvited.

"What girl?"

"The girl in your book. The girl in the picture."

"What are you talking about?"

"I read the story on your computer. I'm not a stupid lady. You're still in love with her, aren't you? A dead woman, killed in a motorcycle accident. I thought you could love me, but I was wrong." Itta's past words echoed through her head. "You only wanted me to replace her, didn't you?

"Don't say things like that." His face flushed. "You're pissing me off."

"No, I won't stop," she screamed.

"Then get out," he screamed back.

At that moment, their world became silent. Even the usual sounds of the lobby were muted. Their eyes met briefly, but neither held the gaze.

"I'll get my things," Jarapan said as she turned away. "And don't ever shout at me again."

"I didn't mean it," Mike forced his voice quieter.

"Well I did." Jarapan stepped past him, bypassed the elevator, and charged up the stairs. In a minute she had thrown a few clothes and her make-up into a suitcase. She was leaving as Mike reached the condo door.

"I don't want you to go," he whispered.

"I don't want to stay," she responded tartly.

"Then don't let the door hit you in the ass!" he snapped back.

"I wouldn't give it the pleasure." She hefted her suitcase and strutted out.

"You'll be sorry," he shouted down the hallway.

"So will you," she retorted without looking back

Jarapan felt the stares of the condo employees as she walked through the lobby. She had a ridiculous urge to explain everything, but she didn't. She held her head erect as she walked to her new motorcycle. She strapped her suitcase to the back and drove away.

Once she was out of sight, she stopped and cried. Later she went to the Sabai Inn and rented a room. They made her pay cash in advance but she didn't care. At that moment money meant nothing to her. Mike had insulted and embarrassed her, and that was all that mattered.

At five o'clock she showered, dressed for work, and drove *her* motorcycle to the Suaee Dee Lady. She wasn't sure what she would do when Mike came to work. She hoped he didn't try to talk to her.

Mike didn't come to work that night, or the night after that either. When Jarapan told Itta about their argument, Itta called the condo but Mike didn't answer.

"He treated me like a baby," Jarapan complained.

"And what did you do? React like an adult?" Itta paused dramatically then continued, "Maybe he's just concerned about you. He's right you know; motorcycles are dangerous."

"He only hates motorcycles because of that girl."

"You mean my sister?"

Jarapan looked away. "I'm sorry how that sounded. I'm upset, that's all."

"Don't worry," Itta spoke softly. "I understand jealousy."

"I'm not jealous. I hate him."

"Would you like him back?"

"I want him to apologize."

"Do you love him?"

"I never thought about it," Jarapan blushed at her lie. She had thought about it plenty; more than ever since she had moved out. "Maybe I love him a little."

"Well," Itta smiled, "Mike loves you a lot. He told me so himself."

"Alai nah?" Jarapan thought she had misunderstood.

"I said Mike loves you a lot. If you can't see it, you are the only one in Pattaya who can't. I have an idea."

"You can make him apologize?" Jarapan asked.

"No more than I can make you apologize. Sometimes it's better to forgive and forget than it to hear or make an apology. Do you know Saturday is Mike's birthday?"

"Oh dear Buddha. He told me last week but I have been so busy hating him that I forgot. Tomorrow's Saturday; I should buy him a gift or do something special."

"That's exactly what I have in mind. I've been planning a surprise party for him. I never told you because I was afraid you would let it slip. Maybe it's better that you're not living at the condo because now you can help me."

Jarapan lowered her voice to a conspiratorial level. "How?"

"First we must make sure Mike doesn't find out. Then we need to make sure he comes to the Suaee Dee Lady tomorrow night, but not until after eight o'clock. The afternoon shouldn't be a problem because he never comes around when there is real work to do. I'll get Jon to distract him and make sure he doesn't come here until we're ready. Here's my plan."

Chapter 28

When Mike awoke on Saturday morning, his first thought was of Jarapan. She had been gone since Wednesday and hadn't called or come by for the rest of her clothes or anything. He hadn't gone to work since she moved out, so he wasn't even sure if she was still in Pattaya. For all he knew she had gone back to her parents' house in Khon Kaen. After the way he had behaved about the motorcycle, he wouldn't be surprised.

He had replayed it through his head a thousand times, but even now, three days later, he didn't understand his reaction. Jarapan had said it was because Math had died in a motorcycle accident. He supposed that was part of it, but surely not the whole reason. Everyone in Thailand who could afford a motorcycle had one.

Before meeting Jarapan he had lived with Itta and she'd owned a motorcycle, yet it had never bothered him. But for some reason the very thought of Jarapan on a motorcycle set off feelings he didn't understand. Maybe it was because somewhere in his paranoid brain he worried that she would become too independent and leave him. Well now she had left, but it had nothing to do with becoming independent. He glanced at the clock: it was past noon. He forced himself from the bed and stumbled to the bath.

He caught a glimpse of himself in the mirror as he waited for the hot water to arrive. Deep sleep wrinkles etched vertically from hairline to eyebrows on both sides of his face. Horizontal lines crisscrossed from left to right. His eyelids puffed and his cheeks sagged, giving him a skinny bulldog sort of look. A mix of gray and brown hair stuck out from the left side of his head in defiance of gravity. He couldn't see his bald spot from straight ahead, but he knew it was there. It seemed he now had more hair growing from his nose and ears than he had growing on the top of his head. And he looked old. Worse, he felt old. He turned away from the mirror, adjusted the taps, and stepped into the shower. By the time he stepped out, he felt as close to normal as he would for the day. He had shaved and was strategically positioning his thinning hair across his bald-spot when he remembered today was his birthday. That wasn't news; it was just the first time he had thought of it since getting out of bed.

He finished dressing and took a baht-bus to the Pizza Company at the Royal Garden Plaza. It had once been a Pizza Hut, but as things often do in Thailand it had changed. It didn't matter. Neither of them tasted exactly like the Pizza Huts back home anyway.

He was almost back to his condo before his birthday crept back into his head. He wondered if anyone besides himself would remember. It wasn't typical for Thais to forget a birthday unless they wanted to, and so far everyone had wanted to. On the other hand, at his age turning another year older wasn't anything to celebrate. Still, it would have been nice if the Suaee Dee Lady had a party for him, but apparently that was only wishful thinking.

Itta had called a couple of times to make sure he was okay, but she had never mentioned anything about his birthday much less a party. Also, Itta hadn't mentioned Jarapan. He had wanted to ask about her, but somehow he couldn't. He'd just told Itta that he wasn't well, and that he would come to work when he felt better. Jarapan hadn't even called.

When the baht-bus stopped near the condos, Mike got out, paid the driver, and walked toward home. As he stepped inside the lobby he saw Jon "Greene County" Yeager. Maybe someone had remembered his birthday after all.

"Hey, Jon. What's up?"

"Can we talk?" Jon seemed nervous, his smile strained.

Mike nodded. Whatever Jon wanted, it wasn't to wish him a happy birthday. "Sure, why not? Anything to help a fellow West

Virginian."

"I'm from Pennsylvania."

"Yeah, I know. Just busting your balls. What do you want to talk about?"

"I want to talk about Itta."

Mike tensed but feigned indifference. He knew Jon and Itta had been seeing a lot of each other during the past few weeks, and he suspected they were sharing more than late-night meals. But that was none of his business, so he had kept his thoughts to himself. He wondered if there was trouble in paradise. "Okay, shoot," he said nonchalantly and took a seat at the small lobby bar. He waved for the waitress to bring them a beer. He hoped Jon wasn't going to make a scene by dredging up the past.

Jon sat on a stool next to Mike, fidgeted a moment, and then said, "You know I've been spending a lot of time with Itta."

"I've heard the rumors. Does it bother you that I know?"

Jon sat erect. "I was going to ask you the same thing."

Mike relaxed a little. If Jon was worried about his relationship with Itta, it was for nothing. "I love Itta like my sister. I'm happy you're making her happy."

"Would you be so happy if I told you I was taking her to America with me?"

Jon's question caught him off guard. "What do you mean? Do you mean for a holiday?"

Jon wiped at the sweat on his upper lip, "No, I mean forever."

Mike didn't answer. What a great frigging birthday this was turning out to be. He turned his stool to face Jon and leaned forward, "How soon?"

"Not for a while. Maybe two or three months. It'll give you time to find another partner."

"I'm surprised Itta didn't tell me."

"She doesn't know."

Mike laughed in spite of the situation. "You had me going there for a minute Greene County. I thought you were serious."

"I am serious. Itta and I have talked about it, but we haven't made any real plans. Sometimes it seems like a joke between us, but it isn't. I'll ask her formally one day this week. Maybe tonight. I love her Mike, and she loves me. It might take a while before she says yes, but she will. Then we'll get married and I'll take her away. I thought it was only right for you to know my intentions. Even if you don't need another partner, you need to make plans. You have your business to take care of."

Mike was blown away by Jon's announcement. He had never thought that Itta would ever be anything except his business partner. She was making more money than most Thais ever dreamed of, and she was majority owner of one of the most popular bars in Pattaya. She seemed happy with her life and she was his friend. He couldn't imagine her leaving everything to disappear with a farang; not after what had happened with her Scottish husband. But Itta wasn't getting any younger, and the bar business in Pattaya was a high risk venture without guarantees of longevity or ongoing success. The Suaee Dee Lady could never match what Jon was putting on the table. He was offering personal, long-term security. "How well do you know her? There may be reasons why she can't go with you."

"If you mean her life in Scotland, I know about that already. It's not a problem. I've hired a lawyer to put an end to it. The Scotsman will be warned politely if he enters Thailand. Things won't be polite if he comes to Pattaya."

"You can do that?"

"My lawyer is very influential," Jon said matter-of-factly.

"The U.S. visa process won't be easy."

"I've hired the best, and he's a friend of Itta's family. The visa won't be a problem, either."

Mike knew that a good Thai lawyer armed with a lot US dollars could perform miracles in Thailand. "I would never stand in the way of love. I wish you and Itta the best. I won't tell her we've talked unless she asks, or until you tell me it's okay. Thanks for the heads-up."

"No, thank you for understanding. If not for you, I would have never met Itta." Jon paused for a moment then added, "I've heard the rumors about you and Itta. They don't bother me much. At our age, there aren't many virgins."

Mike had talked with hundreds of men about hundreds of women, but this was the first time anyone had admitted that they knew he had made love with their bride-to-be and didn't care. "Itta is a lucky woman, and you are a lucky man."

"Hey, look," Jon stammered, uncomfortable. "I have to go. There is a birthday party tonight for a friend. I promised to help decorate. I'll stop at your bar later to see Itta." He stood and left.

Mike wanted to say it was his birthday, too, but didn't.

Once Jon was gone, Mike took the elevator to his floor. His conversation with Jon had left him melancholic. The fact that he hadn't heard from Jarapan only made him feel worse. The lack of a happy birthday from anyone depressed him. Whatever urges he had to party by himself had disappeared with Jon's announcement.

Inside his room he flipped through the TV channels trying to take his mind off of what Jon had said. He found the usual Thai channels he couldn't understand, a couple of news stations he didn't want to watch, and one B movie with a storyline he couldn't follow. He finally left it on the Asian version of MTV. It wasn't that great either, but it was a distraction. He settled into a chair, sipped at a Chang Beer, and closed his eyes. He fell asleep before the beer was finished. Weird dreams flittered through his head.

In one he was with Math, his long deceased lover. She was talking to him in her broken English, making plans for their future. She seemed so real that he could smell her perfume.

In another dream, he was fishing with his son Josh, ten years old at most. Mike had never taken Josh fishing but he had thought about it often enough. He was always too busy with work for such things. Even in reverie, guilt made itself felt.

His last dream, the one that woke him up, was about Vietnam. He had dreamed the nightmare before, but this time it was different, and totally screwed up. Crazy shit left over from the war, jumbled together like the onions and peppers in a Spanish omelet.

TEARS FOR THE THAI GIRL

The searchlight fanned across the night landscape and focused on a small brick and bamboo hut. It looked frail compared to the heavily-armed soldiers. An order barked in Korean and all hell broke loose. Within a minute enough bullets and shrapnel had entered the house to sink it several millimeters into the dirt. Then, as if on cue, the barrage stopped. Gun-smoke and dust hung heavy in the night air. A slender hand appeared at the doorway.

"Please don't shoot me," a woman begged in Vietnamese. It was Yvonne; he recognized her voice. She stepped through the doorway with her hands pushed high over her head. Her eyes focused on him. He wondered how she could see him behind the glaring searchlight. He couldn't take his eyes away from her. At that instant alarms sounded, a rifle cracked loud, and Yvonne's face disappeared.

Mike jerked awake. The bottle of Chang skittered across the marble floor. The phone was ringing. "Hello," he answered, still lost in his nightmare.

"This is Itta. I'm sorry to call and ask you this when you're not feeling well, but I need you to work for me this evening. I have a personal problem I need to attend."

His earlier conversation with Jon found its way through his grogginess. Apparently Jon hadn't wasted any time informing Itta of his plans to take her away. "I just woke up. I can cover for you but I can't be there for an hour or so." He looked at his watch: it was almost seven. "I can be there by eight. Is Jarapan working?"

"Yes. You two need to talk."

You're right, he thought. "I'll be there as soon as I can."

He retrieved the Chang bottle from the floor, wiped up the spill, and tossed the mess into the trash. Twenty minutes later he had showered, shaved, dressed, and was on his way to the Suaee Dee Lady.

Chapter 29

At seven forty-five Mike was walking toward Beach Road. As he passed the Dockside Bar, someone shouted his name. He knew without looking that it was Meaw. Mike sighed and angled toward the bar.

"I buy for you, Khun Mike," she said, putting an open Heineken in front of him. "Happy birthday to you."

Mike couldn't help but return her smile. At least someone had remembered. His depression lifted a little. "How did you know it was my birthday?"

"You say me before. You forget already?"

He didn't remember, but he might have told her. "Oh, yeah," he blushed. "Thank you for remembering. You're the only person to wish me happy birthday. I think everyone else forgot."

Her smile widened. "I remember for sure. We have happy birthday together, you and me. I think you like too much. Good idea, yes?"

Mike laughed, "Yes, good idea."

He bought Meaw a drink in return but wasted no time downing his own. He finished his beer before hers was half gone. He couldn't remember that ever happening with a bar-girl before. She looked at him expectantly.

"I have to go," he said. "Itta is sick or something. I have to watch the bar."

Meaw pouted out her lower lip. "You sure you come back? I have nice birthday surprise for you."

"How can I turn that down?" he smiled, squeezing her hand. He winked at her and walked away. It was eight o'clock.

TEARS FOR THE THAI GIRL

He caught the first baht-bus that came along. The other passengers squeezed tighter together to make room for him to sit. Toward the front of the baht-bus were four middle-aged men dressed in tee-shirts, shorts, and tennis shoes. They were speaking in German. Across from him sat a young Thai woman and a foreigner. They were holding hands but neither spoke. Sitting next to him was an older Thai lady who was trying hard to ignore everyone around her. Mike followed the old woman's example and stared at the shops, bars, and restaurants that slid past.

They were more than two blocks from the Suaee Dee Lady when the baht-bus braked to a quick stop. Mike leaned over and looked ahead. A long string of taillights stared back. He figured there had been an accident or something. He stepped from the baht-bus, handed the driver ten baht, and continued on foot toward the Suaee Dee Lady.

Half a block from the bar he saw Jarapan. She was standing at the edge of the street near a vendor selling toy rats on a string. She seemed nervous. Her head turned back and forth like an oscillating fan, her eyes alternately looking for the accident down Beach Road and scanning the throngs of tourists moving along the sidewalk. When she finally saw him, she ran toward him at breakneck speed.

"Hey, are you okay?" he asked when she was within earshot. "You look like you're ready to pop a gasket."

"Mike, I'm glad I found you. Something is happening at the go-go. Come quickly, we must hurry." She took him by the hand and tugged him down the street.

Outside the Suaee Dee Lady all seemed normal. He couldn't imagine what the big problem was. When the door-girl saw them coming, she darted inside. Now his heart raced. His head flooded with images of bloody faces, dead bodies, and accusing Thai policemen. He picked up his pace, pulling Jarapan behind him. In a minute they stepped inside the bar. It was pitch black. There was no music.

"Where in the hell are the lights," he shouted into the dark silence.

Suddenly it was light. "Happy Birthday," came a chorus of voices from the customers and employees.

Jarapan stood on her tip-toes and placed a sniffing Thai kiss on his cheek. Someone took a picture and everyone cheered.

"A free drink for everyone," he heard Itta's voice above the noise. This time the cheer was even louder.

Mike's eyes watered, but he didn't cry. Instead he shouted, "Make that two free drinks."

Everyone surged toward the bar. It was going to be a great birthday. His depression was put on hold for the evening.

After the excitement died down, Mike was given presents to open and admire. Mostly they were small things, like the Thailand letter opener with an elephant on the handle. Or silly things, like the naked lady ashtray.

Itta gave him a wallet. Inside she had put a 1,000 baht and a note that read, "Enough to have fun on your birthday, but not too much fun." At the end of the message she had drawn a smiley face with one eye winking.

As the gifts were opened, Mike laughed, blushed, and thanked as the occasion demanded. When the presents ended, the dancers went back to the stage and the night returned to normal. The beers he had given away were nothing compared to the number of drinks the customers bought on their own. During the evening, Jarapan smiled at him more than he had expected. When things reached a lull, she came to him and whispered, "I'm sorry for what happened the other night."

His first impulse was to maintain his previous attitude, but he couldn't. He didn't understand why he'd taken that attitude in the first place. "I'm sorry too. "

Jarapan blushed. "I want to come home."

He reached out and touched her arm. "Are you sure?"

She didn't look up. "Yes. I'm sure."

"Me too."

By the time the party died down, Mike had consumed all of the happy birthday beers he could hold. At eleven-thirty he told Itta that he leaving with Jarapan and she smiled her approval.

"Can we walk home?" Jarapan asked as they left the bar.

"What about your motorcycle?"

"I don't need it when I'm with you. I only need it when I'm coming home alone at night."

A second passed before he said, "I never thought about that."

"Mai pen lai, never mind," she whispered. She took him by the hand and they walked toward their condo. Mike got some strange stares from the girls at the Dockside Bar as he and Jarapan passed by. Meaw in particular seemed unhappy to see Jarapan with him.

When they arrived home, Mike excused himself and went to the bathroom. When he stepped back into the living room, Jarapan was no where to be seen. He wondered if she had left while he was in the bath. He stepped into the bedroom and turned on the light. There she was, the blanket pulled up to her neck.

"I want you to hold me teeluk," she whispered.

Mike didn't need more encouragement. He sat on the edge of the bed, leaned over, and laid his face against her breasts. "I love you Ms. Jarapan," he whispered.

"Me, too, Mr. Johnson." she whispered back.

Their lovemaking was exquisite.

Later, Jarapan lay awake listening to Mike's low snoring. She knew many women who complained about their husbands keeping them awake with their night noises, but she didn't mind at all. Before falling asleep she decided she would do whatever it took to make Mike love her more than he had ever loved any woman. She didn't know why it was so important to her, but at the moment it seemed paramount. She prayed to God and Buddha for guidance and blessings.

~~~

Jarapan awoke early the next morning but pretended she was asleep when Mike slipped from the bed and went to the bath.

When the shower started, she got up from the bed and went to his desk. Mike would be in the shower for at least ten minutes. That was plenty of time. She turned on the computer. As it booted up, she found her purse and took a CD from inside.

During the three days they were apart, Jarapan had spent most of her free time on the computer at the Suaee Dee Lady developing pages for their website. It was done except for inserting a few pictures and uploading the files. She didn't have the codes and software to do that from the Suaee Dee Lady, but Mike had those on his computer. She logged into her email account and prayed that Jon had kept his promise.

She had a one new message and it was from Jon. The pictures were attached. He hadn't forgotten. She started through them one at a time but stopped when she came across the picture of her kissing Mike on the cheek. He looked happy and surprised. It was perfect. She inserted the picture into the index page, put the others on a separate page, and uploaded the entire site to the internet. She keyed www.suaeedeelady.com into the address bar and waited. A moment later it appeared. It looked exactly like she had imagined. She couldn't wait for Mike to see what she had done.

When Mike stepped from the bath, she grabbed him by the arm and pulled him toward the computer. "I have one more birthday surprise for you."

She opened the web-site and stood back, proud of her creation.

Mike stared, "You did this?"

She couldn't tell if he liked it or if he was only surprised that she had done it by herself. "I did it for you. Is it okay?"

"It looks terrific." He turned and looked at her. "This is the best birthday present anyone ever gave me. Thank you." He reached out and pulled her close. "I really do love you."

Jarapan wasn't sure if he meant what he said, but she allowed herself to believe it was true. "I love you, too, Mike. Please don't ever let me leave you again."

Mike put his fingers beneath her chin and lifted her face until their eyes met. "I promise to never let you leave me, as long as you promise to love me. You must also promise to keep the motorcycle."

Jarapan eyes opened wide. "Do you mean that?"

Mike smiled and nodded.

"Then yes, I promise to always love you."

He pulled her close. "Thank you, teeluk."

Jarapan looked up in surprise. "You called me teeluk."

"Is that okay?"

"It's more than okay. It's perfect."

"Can we make love now? Suddenly I want you very much."

Later, after their passions were sated, Jarapan said, "Teeluk, I promised Itta that I would come to work early today. Last night she said she had to talk to Jon and wouldn't be staying to clean the bar. I told her I would help her today. I should be back by three."

"Do you want me to help?"

"I want you to get some rest," she smiled. "I want you full of energy when I come home."

"You're putting a lot of pressure on an old man."

Jarapan only smiled. Ten minutes later she was on her way to work.

Chapter 30

Josh Johnson – Pittsburgh, PA

Josh nearly fell out of his chair the day he clicked on an internet link and his dad's face appeared on the screen. He was smiling and a Thai woman had her lips pressed against his cheek. The girl was beautiful. "Mike's Birthday" read the caption at the top of the page.

Josh had imagined his dad with oriental chicks often enough, but seeing it in real life really pissed him off. It didn't seem right for Dad to be with anyone except Mom. She had been dead for less than a year and Dad had no business being with another woman. He knew their life together hadn't been all that great, but that was no excuse for his dad's insensitivity. He checked the web address. It was SuaeeDeeLady.com. He wrote it down figuring Aunt Carol would be interested.

Later he sent an anonymous email to the webmaster. "The birthday boy looks like an asshole." He really didn't mean it, but he didn't know what else to say. On impulse he added, "The old bastard probably can't even get it up anymore."

Josh spent the rest of the day scrutinizing every picture on the site but his dad wasn't in any of them, except the one on the front page. At six o'clock he called Aunt Carol and she looked, too. He suspected she sent an email after they hung up.

Chapter 31

Jarapan and Itta had finished cleaning and stocking the bar by two o'clock that afternoon. She was on her home way home on her *new* motorcycle when the traffic slowed to a crawl near the intersection of Second Road and Pattaya Klang. The cars, buses, and motorcycles crept forward with irritating slowness. It was mid afternoon and the pavement beneath her was as hot as the sun blazing overhead. If there was a breeze, it wasn't noticeable. Exhaust fumes poured from cars, motorcycles and buses and burned at her eyes and her nose.

Ahead she saw a few of the local motorcycle taxi drivers steering down a narrow alleyway. She figured they knew a way around the traffic jam so she followed. The side street was littered with potholes and her progress was almost as slow as it had been on the main route. In a minute the other motorcycles turned back toward Second and Beach Roads. The traffic was congested there, too, but at least they were moving.

She came to a stop beside a construction site where a new hotel was being built. It was visible from Second Road and she had seen it dozens of times in passing. This was the first time she had seen it from this angle. Through the lobby windows the inside looked finished. At the entrance workers were installing false marble tiles inlaid with the hotel's name and logo. She guessed rooms would cost a fortune for a night.

As she reached the very front of the hotel, one worker turned and looked in her direction. His face was less than five meters from hers. It was him, the man from her nightmares. She turned away, hoping he hadn't seen her. She steered her motorcycle from the hotel as calmly as she could and sped back the way she had come.

Images of the day she was raped whipped through her head and her body shook in response. The man's hideous face dominated her thoughts. She stole a quick glance over her shoulder but he was gone. She wondered if she had really seen him. It was unimaginable that he would be here, at this very moment, on her way home from work.

At Pattaya Klang she turned east, away from the congested area and drove to Sukhumvit Highway. From there she rode north to North Pattaya Road, and then back toward the Gulf of Thailand. By the time she reached Dolphin Circle her encounter with the scar-faced man had faded, leaving her with lingering doubts of whether she had really seen him or not.

Ten minutes later she was at Mike's condo. He had left the key at the front desk along with a note saying he wasn't feeling well and was going to take a nap. She wondered if he was really sick or if he was just worried that he couldn't have sex again so quickly.

As quietly as possible, she showered and dressed for her shift at the Suaee Dee Lady. Before leaving the condo, she wrote Mike a short note to tell him she had come and gone, and that she would see him later when she came home from work. As an afterthought, she added that if he didn't feel better later he shouldn't come to work. She remembered how ill he had been a few weeks earlier when he returned from Singapore, and she didn't want a repeat of that. If he still felt bad tomorrow, she would make him go to the doctor. She signed the note with love and left the condo.

Later that evening, when she arrived home from work, Mike was still asleep. She touched his forehead. It was warmer than normal, but not burning hot like the last time. She slept in their second bedroom so as not to wake him. She said a short prayer for his health before she drifted off to sleep. Her dreams were a continuous stream of nightmares of the scar-faced man.

Chapter 32

Jarapan awoke as the first hint of daylight lit the eastern sky. She went immediately to check on Mike. He stirred awake when she touched his cheek.

"Good morning, teeluk," she whispered. "Are you feeling better today?"

He responded with a short fit of coughing.

"You should see a doctor," she said.

Mike sat up and reached for his cigarettes.

"And you should stop smoking, too."

"Yeah, I know." He lit a cigarette anyway.

"What about the doctor? I wish you would go today. They will give you medicine and you'll feel better in quickly time. I don't want you to be sick like before."

Mike sighed. "Believe it or not, neither do I. I'm sure I'll feel better tomorrow, but if it will make you happy, I'll go to the doctor this afternoon."

Jarapan smiled. "Yes teeluk, that would make me very happy. If you go this morning, I would be even more happy. I can give you a ride on my motorcycle."

Mike frowned. "I'll take a baht-bus after you've left for work."

Jarapan blushed remembering the problem the motorcycle had once caused. "Okay. As long as you go, I'll be happy."

At eleven o'clock, Jarapan told Mike she was going to the Suaee Dee Lady early to make changes to the computer spreadsheet. It was a lie. What she really wanted was to go back to the new hotel and see if that man was really there or not. By now

161

she had convinced herself that it had been some strange illusion from her imagination, but she needed be sure.

She cruised past the construction site eight times but didn't see the scar-faced man or anyone who even resembled him. Finally she stopped at the very place where she had seen him before and looked at each of the workers; he wasn't there. She breathed a sigh of relief and drove away, happy to know it had been a bizarre hallucination. She sped to work.

Jarapan didn't notice the black motorcycle that followed her on the multiple trips past the construction site, nor did she notice it when she finally gave up and headed toward work. She did notice the man who stopped half a block from the Suaee Dee Lady, but his attention was on his motorcycle and not her, so she didn't give him a second thought.

Itta hadn't yet arrived, so Jarapan let herself in and began the daily task of prepping the bar for opening. She had just finished turning on the lights and the air conditioner when she heard the front door opening and closing. She figured it was a customer who didn't know their business hours.

"We're not open yet," she said, turning. A man stood just inside the door. His dress and his posture said he was not farang. "We're not open yet," she repeated in Thai.

The man reached up and lifted the motorcycle helmet from his head. "I wanted to make sure it was you."

Razor-sharp emotions sliced through her. She stepped backward as her thoughts whirled out of control.

"You're safe," he whispered. "I won't hurt you. There's something I must tell you."

Jarapan glanced toward the bar looking for the anything she could use as a weapon. She saw the knife they used for slicing lemons, limes and oranges. She ran to the counter, grabbed it up, and turned back. "If you come close, I will kill you."

"I won't stop you," he said softly. "I followed you here to tell you I'm sorry for what I did. I came to beg your forgiveness."

She wasn't sure what she had expected him to say, but it was anything except what she had just heard. She couldn't believe he had the nerve to ask her forgiveness, not after what he had done. He had taken away her life and her dreams. Images of her stabbing him with the knife flickered through her head. The thoughts made her nauseous. She eased farther away. "You're crazy. If you leave now, I won't call the police."

"Before you call anyone, I want you to read this." He took his wallet from his pocket, removed a folded paper, and tossed it in her direction. It fell short. He backed away and motioned that she should pick it up.

When Jarapan didn't move, he added, "It will only take a minute. I think you should read it."

Jarapan retrieved the paper and unfolded it in the pale light. The print was worn and smudged in places, but it was still readable. Her heart jumped when she saw the medical logo at the top of the page. Her eyes scanned the page. It was filled with medical terminology she didn't understand.

"What does this mean?" Thoughts of Mike exploded inside her head. "Have you given me some disease?" A fist cold as ice gripped her chest.

"It says I have no diseases. I wanted you to know."

Jarapan's mind reeled as her hatred and terror collided with relief. In a moment she found her voice and it was filled with bitterness. "I should forgive you because you have no diseases? What about your friends? Do you expect me to forgive them, too?"

"They're *not* my friends!" his voiced raised for the first time. He closed his eyes, took a deep calming breath and then continued, "I worked with them on a construction project for a few weeks, that's all. Our job had ended and I was giving them a ride as far as my hometown. We started out that morning drinking beer and smoking ganja. By noon we had switched to Mekong and yaba. I don't even remember driving through Khon Kaen. The first thing I remember was when I walked into the bushes and saw what the men were doing. When I saw you lying there, something happened. I knew what I was doing was wrong, but I couldn't stop myself. I was too drunk to care about anything except having you. Afterwards I hated myself. I wanted to keep the others away, but I was afraid. I couldn't tell them no, not after what they had seen me do. I told them to hurry and not hurt you or I would hurt them."

He paused, as if waiting for Jarapan to respond, but she only stared.

"There's something else I want you to see." He held his wallet in her direction. When she didn't move to take it, he tossed it to land near her feet. "Please, look inside."

Jarapan picked up the wallet and spread it open. Inside was a picture of a man and a woman with two young children. They were dressed in traditional Thai garb. The man was handsome and the woman beautiful. The children looked enough alike to be twins. Everyone was smiling. She inspected the rest of the wallet then looked up. "What am I supposed to see?"

"The man in the picture. Have you seen him before?"

She stared, checking the image against her memories. "No, I have never seen him. Should I know him?"

He ignored her question. "By the time I got home that night I had sobered a little, but I was still drunk and high. I sat outside my house for a long time, thinking about what I had done. I never knew it was possible to feel so much guilt. I had to tell someone. I woke my wife and told her everything."

"Your wife?" Jarapan whispered. "You have a wife?"

"I had a wife once. She's the woman in the picture."

"And you're the man?"

"I haven't always looked like this. It was a motorcycle accident and it almost killed me. Sometimes I wish it had. It killed everything else." He paused for a moment as if deciding what to say. "You probably won't believe this, but I'm a college graduate. Nothing special, but a degree nonetheless. Back then I was young and handsome. I had a good job in sales, I was married to the most beautiful woman in Thailand, and I had been blessed with a son and daughter I love so much that it hurts. My wife stayed with me but everything was different. She still loved me, I'm sure of that, but she wouldn't look at me. My scars repulsed her. We haven't slept together since the day this happened." He pointed at his face for emphasis. "I don't blame her; I'm surprised she stayed as long as she did. She left the night I told her what I had done. I'm every evil word she called me. She took my babies and went back to her family."

Jarapan stared at him, strangely moved by his revelations. "I don't know what to say."

"There's nothing you can say. I have brought disgrace to everyone, especially you. Yet I come to ask your forgiveness so I can die in peace."

Jarapan was confused by the emotions coursing through her. Here stood the monster of her nightmares, the focus of her hatred. But now, at this moment, he seemed different from her memories. She felt sorry for him even though she knew it was the last thing she should be feeling. She tried to walk away but her feet stayed riveted. A million thoughts flashed through her head but she said nothing.

"Please, can you can forgive me?"

To her surprise she nodded her head.

A heavy sigh escaped his body. He placed his palms together and brought them to his face in prayer-like fashion and then bowed forward and presented her with a wai of respect and deep gratitude. When he looked up, there were tears. "Thank you," he whispered.

Jarapan's eyes watered in response. The knot in her throat rendered her voiceless.

"Do you own this bar?" he asked, breaking their silence.

"No. I'm only the accountant," she managed to say.

He smiled. "Somehow I knew that."

"You knew I was the accountant?"

"I knew you were not a dancer."

Jarapan blushed. "Why should that matter to you?"

"I don't know."

Neither spoke for a long time. Finally he said, "There's a note in the wallet. Please read it to me." His voice was soft, pleading.

Jarapan fumbled through the wallet for a second and found the note. She read it aloud. "Please don't hate me. I will love you forever."

Another long silence followed. Jarapan studied his face. "Did you write this?"

The man looked down. "I wrote it for my wife, but I never gave it to her."

"You should. Maybe she would forgive you."

He looked back up. "No, she never will. She has made that clear. She's living with her family now. They protect her to make sure I don't get close. They won't even let me see my children."

Jarapan blinked at his words. "How can they do that?"

"I'm the ugly monster who rapes women."

The truth of his statement shook her back to reality. She was having a conversation with the man who had ruined her life. Regardless of everything else, he didn't belong here. "You should leave now."

"I want you to take the note to my wife."

She thought she had misheard him. "What do you mean?"

"I want my wife to meet you. Maybe once she knows you have forgiven me, she can forgive me too. I have no right to ask you to deliver my message, but that is what I'm doing."

"I don't think I can do that. You should deliver it yourself. I'm sure she'll take you back."

He shook his head then turned and walked away.

"Wait. You forgot your wallet."

"I don't need it anymore. There's enough money inside for a trip to Phitsanulok. You keep it in case you change your mind." He disappeared through the doorway.

Jarapan didn't realize how tense she was until after he had gone. Her body shook as the adrenaline subsided. Her knees weakened and she leaned against the bar to steady herself.

The man was as ugly as she remembered, but nothing like she had been imagining since *the event*. At that moment the door opened again, it was Itta. Jarapan broke down and cried as relief rushed through her.

Itta ran to her side. "Are you okay?"

"Yes. I mean no. I mean I don't know what I mean."

Itta took Jarapan by the hand. "I listen well."

Jarapan told her everything, her entire life. Then she told her why she was in Pattaya. Finally she told what had just happened.

"Do you think he'll come back?"

"I don't know. I hope Mike doesn't find out he's in Pattaya."

Itta squeezed Jarapan's hand in hers. "I understand. Maybe you should get away from here for a week or two. The hotel will be finished by then and the workers will have moved on. Why don't you go home and visit your family?"

"I don't want to go home."

"I'm sure they miss you."

Images of her mother and father and her brother flashed through her head. As much as she denied it, she missed them, too. "Mike is sick again. I'll go to visit my family when he's better."

Itta smiled kindly. "Mike is a big boy. He'll be fine. I'll check on him every day to make sure he doesn't need anything. Besides, whatever he has, you don't need to come down with it too."

Jarapan fingered the note she still held in her hand. She could go to Phitsanulok before going on to her hometown. "Will I have a job when I come back?"

Itta laughed as much from Jarapan's question as from the relief of knowing that Jarapan would be taking her advice. "Yes, you will still have a job."

Jarapan retrieved her purse from behind the bar. "Thank you for everything Itta. You're truly a nice person."

"Get out of here before I change my mind."

Jarapan left the Suaee Dee Lady.

Mike wasn't at home when she arrived. She figured he had gone to the doctor as he had promised. Maybe it was just as well; she had already decided to go away for a week or two, and he might try to talk her out of leaving if he was there. She didn't think the scar-faced man would bother her again, but only Buddha knew what would happen if Mike found out the man was in Pattaya. Itta was right, the hotel would be done soon and the workers would go away.

The note for the scar-faced man's wife entered her thoughts. *Please don't hate me. I will love you forever.* The words haunted her. She knew she should forget about the note, but she couldn't. Phitsanulok was only a day out of her way, and the woman needed to know what her husband had written. Perhaps even more, the woman needed to know what her husband had said.

Jarapan pulled the wallet from her jeans pocket and rifled through it. In one compartment she found twenty, one-thousand baht bills: enough for her to go from Pattaya to Phitsanulok and Khon Kaen several times.

She packed a few clothes into her small suitcase and then wrote a short note to Mike. "Teeluk," she said. "There has been an emergency and I must go to my home for a few days. I will call you when I can. I love you very much and will be back with you in quickly time."

She kissed the note and put it on the table where he would see it. She picked up her bag and left the condo. She hoped the doctor made him quit smoking.

Chapter 33

It was after noon before Mike finally went to the hospital. He wouldn't have gone at all except that he didn't want to listen to any nagging about going to see a doctor. He loved Jarapan and everything, but female nagging drove him nuts.

He really didn't feel all that bad. He just didn't feel good. The worst was the coughing and the pain in his back. There had been some blood specks in his spittle, but barely enough to be noticed. He figured he had ruptured a blood vessel with one of his coughing spells. The way he had been hacking lately he was surprised he hadn't burst them all. Thankfully he wasn't as sick as he'd been when he came back from Singapore.

The hospital clinic was neither faster nor slower than those in the U.S. The patients were a blend of Thais and foreigners with a few couples who were a mix of both. An hour passed before it was his turn.

The doctor went through his routine of listening, looking, and probing. He took a throat culture, a urine sample, a vial of blood, and a chest x-ray. Then he left Mike alone while the tests were being analyzed. Later, he returned carrying a clipboard.

Mike coughed to ease a tickle in his chest. "So, what do I have Doc? Some sort of flu?"

The doctor kept his eyes on the report for a long time before he answered. "Your cough is being caused by pneumonia, Mr. Johnson."

Mike breathed a sigh of relief. There were medications for pneumonia. "So," he smiled, "how long will it take for this to go away? A few days, right?"

The doctor didn't return the smile. Instead he looked back at the report. In a moment he looked up, "It's more serious than that," his English pronunciation was stilted but crystal clear.

Mike's smile faded. "What do you mean?"

"I'll give you medication while you make plans to go home for treatment."

"You're not making sense. Why would I go home? You can treat me here. I have money and I have insurance. Payment isn't a problem. Thailand is my home now and I have a business to take care of."

"Your condition is serious. If not treated properly, you will die."

A knot grew inside his chest. "Die? What are you talking about? What the hell kind of pneumonia thing do I have anyway?" He thought of Jarapan and Itta, "Am I contagious?"

The doctor's attempted smile failed. He cleared his voice. "Anyone can get pneumonia, especially if their immune system is weak. Chances of you giving it to anyone healthy are small."

Mike felt like they were talking in circles. He would have to go back to America to be treated for something that wasn't all that contagious. It didn't make sense. Something wasn't being said. "This is bullshit, Doc. You're not telling me everything. I want to know what's going on."

The doctor took a deep breath. "It's obvious you don't know, I'm sorry to be the one to tell you this, Mr. Johnson, but your condition is much more complicated than just pneumonia."

He knew it, his symptoms were clear enough. The cough, the pains in his back, the constant acid burning in his throat and chest. His father had died of lung cancer and he was going to die from it too. No, he thought, he wouldn't die from lung cancer or any other cancer. He would do exactly what his father had done; he would kill himself before cancer had a chance. "I have lung cancer don't I?"

"No, Mr. Johnson, I believe you have AIDS."

Mike felt as if he were floating off his chair. *AIDS*? The doctor and everything around him blurred. He grabbed his legs and jerked himself forward. In a moment the feeling passed and cold terror took its place. "What do you mean, I have AIDS? That isn't possible. I'm not gay, I don't use drugs, and I don't visit brothels. I've never even received blood from anyone. You've made a mistake. I can't have AIDS. It was the short test, wasn't it?"

The doctor pursed his lips and dropped his eyes from Mike's stare. "Yes, it was a short test. It makes mistakes but not too often. The new tests are quite accurate. However, I'll send a sample to the lab in Bangkok for confirmation. You really should consider what you will do, just in case."

Heavy depression overtook every other emotion, "Do you think they'll make me leave Thailand? Will the police come and take me away in handcuffs or something?"

"I don't know? Does it make any difference?"

"No," his tone was resigned. "I guess it doesn't." Not knowing what else say, he stood to leave. "When will my real test results be back?"

"Check with me the day after tomorrow, they should be here by then." The doctor hesitated for a moment then continued. "You can pick up your medication at the hospital pharmacy. By the way, you should stop smoking."

"Does it make any difference?" Mike asked.

The doctor paused at the question. "No," he finally answered, "I guess it doesn't."

Mike walked to the door and then looked back "Doc, does anyone besides you and me have to know? I would rather leave on my own. I don't want to be escorted to the Bangkok airport by any authorities. You can understand that, can't you?"

The doctor sighed. "We'll wait for the lab results and then we'll talk."

Despite the dark emotions assaulting him, Mike felt gratitude. "Thank you. I have one more favor to ask."

The doctor raised his eyebrows.

"I have friends who need to be tested. I'll tell them it is for a deadly fungus or something, but you can test for the uh … for the other thing," he couldn't bring himself to say AIDS. "I will pay."

The doctor's smile was compassionate, "Yes. I'll do that. I'm sorry this is so complicated for you."

A baht-bus was parked outside the hospital but Mike ignored it. He didn't want to be near anyone right now. Even the back of an empty baht-bus would put him too close to another human being. He turned right and headed down a narrow lane. A million emotions rushed through him.

He had AIDS! He was going to die! The thoughts repeated themselves in an endless procession. He didn't feel like he was going to die, he felt like he had an upper respiratory infection, a chest cold. The thought triggered a coughing frenzy that left him lightheaded.

At North Pattaya Road the deserted soi ended and he encountered his first pedestrians. He stayed far from them, as if he might infect them by close proximity. He hurried across the street and continued his way home. The heat and humidity caused him to sweat heavily, but he barely noticed. Other, more horrifying things filled his existence.

As he neared his condo, he wondered if Jarapan had come home from work yet. Even more he wondered what he would say to her. By the time he arrived he had decided not to tell her anything until the real test results were back. He would just tell her he was contagious and that she should stay away from him. She could get a hotel room for a few days until he was better.

His key was at the front desk which told him that Jarapan wasn't there. He breathed a sigh of relief. It would give him time to get himself under control. Inside his room he splashed cold water on his face and arms to quash the emotions rippling through him. It didn't work. He inspected himself in the mirror.

AIDS! He didn't look like he had AIDS. What did a person with AIDS look like anyway? Shit, he didn't even feel that sick. He hadn't lost any weight as he supposed happened when people had

AIDS. His mind spun, trying to make sense of it all. There was no sense to be found. It had to be a mistake.

A coughing attack ended his train of thoughts. By the time the coughing stopped, his stomach muscles hurt and several wads of pink speckled mucus stared up from the basin. He washed them down the drain.

He went to the kitchen and took a beer from the fridge. Maybe three or four of those would help settle his nerves. He tossed a couple of the pills into his mouth and washed them down with a long chug of beer. A minute later the beer was gone, too. He grabbed another and headed toward his bedroom.

As he passed the desk, red lipstick on white paper caught his attention. He picked it up. It was a note from Jarapan. She had come and gone while he was at the hospital. The note was short and to the point. She had gone home but would be back in a few days. There was a family emergency, but nothing specific was mentioned. For the first time since he had met her, he was glad she was gone.

He went to his bed and lay down. Images of Jarapan and Itta flooded his thoughts. If his long test came back positive, he would have to tell them. It was possible they were infected too. And Lek! Dear god, maybe he had given them all AIDS. Or maybe they had given it to him. The reality of his situation overwhelmed him and he cried for himself and everyone he loved.

Chapter 34

Jarapan left her motorcycle in the condo parking lot and took a baht-bus to Pattaya's northern terminal where she bought a ticket to Bangkok with the money from the scar-faced man's wallet.

While she waited for her bus, she thought about what she was doing. She was running away from Pattaya because of the scar-faced man, yet she was going to deliver a message to his wife because he had asked her to. The whole thing didn't make sense. She wondered if she had finally gone insane. She prayed for guidance but no inspirations came.

From Bangkok's Ekami Eastern Bus Station she hired a meter taxi to the airport. There were no flights Phitsanulok until morning. She purchased a coach-class ticket for tomorrow and then asked the girl for the name of the cheapest nearby hotel.

Jarapan didn't sleep that night. She lay awake contemplating how she would approach the scar-faced man's wife. Each new idea seemed as ridiculous as the others. In the end she devised a plan that would keep contact with the woman to a minimum. At five o'clock in the morning she showered and dressed for her trip. She felt nauseous from the tension but not enough to vomit and certainly not enough to cancel her plans.

Before leaving her room she wrote a note on the hotel stationery: *My name is Jarapan. Your husband asked me to deliver the enclosed message. Since you are reading this, I have fulfilled his request. I don't understand everything that has happened in your lives, but I think your husband is not the evil man you believe him to be. He's a tortured soul who loves you and his children. I'm the woman he raped, yet I have forgiven him. Maybe it's time for you to forgive him, too. I think he is considering suicide and needs your love. If you want, I can tell you where to find him.*

She shoved her note into an envelope along with his message and the picture from his wallet and then threw the empty wallet in the trashcan. Five minutes later she was on her way to the airport.

The flight to Phitsanulok was uneventful. Her return ticket was for later in the day and she didn't have time to waste. Outside the airport she hired a tuk-tuk driver and showed him the address. After conferring with another driver on directions, he said he could take her there.

Twenty minutes later they were passing through a more prosperous section of the city. Jarapan was impressed with the houses. Clearly, anyone who lived in this neighborhood had money. Finally the driver stopped in front of a house surrounded by a brick wall with shards of glass cemented along the top. A heavy iron gate secured the entrance.

A young boy, maybe eight years old, was playing near the front door of the house. Jarapan compared his likeness to the picture from the scar-faced man's wallet. It could be his son, but she couldn't tell. The boy was older and looked different than the one in the photo. It was possible she had the wrong house, or maybe the man's wife and her family had moved. He had said his wife never answered his letters. She asked the driver to wait and walked to the iron gate.

"Hello," Jarapan shouted to the boy.

He looked up but continued to play with his toy truck.

"Is your mother home?" she said loud enough for him to hear.

He shook his head yes.

"Can you give her this letter to read?" She held the envelope through the bars of the gate.

The boy came over, took the letter, and raced inside the house.

Jarapan waited, feeling like she would explode at any moment. After a long minute a woman appeared on the front porch. Jarapan recognized her immediately from the picture. The woman stared at Jarapan for a second, reread the two notes she held in her hand,

and then looked up again. Neither of them spoke. Finally Jarapan turned back toward the tuk-tuk.

"Wait," the woman shouted. "I want to talk with you."

Jarapan stopped but didn't return to the gate.

The woman walked until she was within speaking distance. "You are the girl?"

"I am."

"I'm so sorry for everything."

Jarapan collected her thoughts before responding. "I don't want your sympathy. It means nothing to me. I don't even know you. Yesterday I met your husband, the monster from my past. He took everything from me. My family, my fiancé, my job, and my virginity. I hate him more than any person I know. But he asked me to forgive him and I did. I don't know if you still have feelings for him or not, but I know he loves you. I think that if you don't contact him, he'll soon be dead. Maybe that's what you want. Maybe that's what he wants too. I don't know. He's working on a new hotel in Pattaya. Now you can do what you want. I have to go." She climbed aboard the tuk-tuk.

"Where is the hotel in Pattaya?"

"On Second Road, just south of Pattaya Klang. You will talk to him?"

"I'll ask my father's advice."

Jarapan shook her head ever so slightly. "There's nothing more I can say or do, except pray for his spirit." She tapped the driver on the shoulder and they were gone.

Jarapan didn't realize how tense she was until they were away from the house. She felt weak, emotionally drained. She didn't know what the woman would do but one thing was certain, the man would be gone from Pattaya by the time she returned to Mike.

Jarapan spent the night in the same hotel near the Bangkok airport. The next morning she was sick again. This time she threw up. She couldn't remember if Mike had been throwing up before he developed his horrible cough. She hoped she hadn't caught his illness. By the time she left the hotel to catch her flight, the nausea had passed.

It was Wednesday evening when she arrived at her parents' house in Khon Kaen. Everyone was surprised at her unexpected visit. Her mother had a hundred questions. Her father didn't say much, but made certain he didn't miss any of the conversation. Her brother didn't say anything; he only watched. Jarapan told lies as necessary to cover her life in Pattaya. Before long she pled exhaustion and went to bed.

Chapter 35

On Thursday morning Jarapan was sick again. This time was worse than before and it went on for over an hour. He mother stood by helplessly asking if she had eaten bad food and insisting that she go to see a doctor just in case she had food poisoning. The way she felt, and after the way she had nagged Mike about going to a doctor, she couldn't argue with her mother.

When she finally stopped vomiting and felt well enough to travel, she borrowed her mother's new-used motorcycle and drove into Khon Kaen. The doctor's office was busy but eventually it was her turn and the nurse escorted her to the examination room.

The doctor came in almost as soon as the nurse left. He had been her doctor since she was child. He was the same doctor who had treated her in the days following *the incident*. "How are you today, Jarapan?" His smile was warm but strained.

"I feel fine," she answered.

"I see," the doctor said. "Then why are you here?"

Jarapan blushed. "I mean I feel fine now. I got sick yesterday and this morning was even worse. My mother thought maybe I had food poisoning or something."

"Your mother is a smart woman. But since you feel better now, I think it will be nothing serious."

He asked her a series of questions, had her give a urine sample, and then had the nurse take a vial of blood for testing. No doubt he was running the same series of tests he had done months earlier. Those tests had all been negative and she had no reason to think these would be any different.

Twenty minutes later the doctor returned.

"So, will I live or die?" she joked to take the edge off her tension.

"Me? Well, I think you will live," the doctor chuckled. "Now let's see what the tests say."

He took a seat on a short stool with no back and opened her medical folder as if for the first time. He studied it for a minute and then said, "Jarapan, according to this report, you're pregnant."

The word *swoon* barely described the rush that passed through her entire being. A million emotions flickered and faded in a frenzied assault. Her heartbeat shifted from anticipated pulsing to disorganized fluttering. It took her breath away.

"Are you sure?"

"Ninety-nine percent," he answered. "We'll take another test to be positive. I'll need to take more samples, if you don't mind."

"Yes, of course." She wasn't sure if what she felt was happiness or horror. "I need to know 100%."

After Jarapan had left, the doctor reviewed her results once more. He had little doubt about the results of her pregnancy test, but he would have it verified by an independent laboratory anyway. As long as he was sending samples to the lab, he would also have tests run for HIV, hepatitis, and other things. He had known Jarapan and her family since opening his practice. They were good, hard-working people. He hoped there was nothing in the tests that would interfere with her pregnancy. He glanced at his watch; it was barely past noon. It was going to be a long six hours before he could go home.

~~~

Jarapan's heart raced as she left the doctor's office. Pregnant! Ninety-nine percent sure. She had to tell Mike. At that moment she realized she hadn't called him since she'd left Pattaya. She stopped at the first public phone booth she found and dialed his condo number. There was no answer. She wracked her brain to remember his cell number but it wouldn't come. Finally, she called the condo's reception desk number and left a message for Mike to call her parents' house. If she didn't hear from him by evening, she would call Itta.

As she turned toward her motorcycle, she saw Purachai. He stood with his feet spread apart, arms crossed, a smile on his lips. He reached up and removed the dark sunglasses hiding his eyes.

"Trouble in Pattaya? It seems to follow you around."

Jarapan's heart thumped. Purachai was the last person she expected to see. "I thought you were at school."

"I'm taking some time off. I'll be going back next semester. What about you?" He nodded toward the telephone. "Problems with your farang? Did he find a hotter piece of ass and kick you out?"

Jarapan felt her cheeks burn. He had been listening to her phone conversation and now he was taunting her. "I have to go." She moved to step around him.

Purachai cut her off. "What's the hurry?"

"Look. I'm not in the mood for your childish games. I have food poisoning and need to get home. If you don't get out of my way, I swear to Buddha I'll vomit on you."

Purachai didn't move, but he didn't stop her when she stepped around him. "I'll stop by your house later to make sure you're okay."

Jarapan started the motorcycle and glared, "You stay away from my family."

Purachai smiled and waved as Jarapan sped away.

Chapter 36

Mike walked to the hospital on Thursday afternoon. His medication had worked like a miracle drug and he felt almost well. He still coughed more than usual but there hadn't been any blood for two days. He spent most of the walk convincing himself that the quick test had been wrong and that he and the doctor would have a good laugh at the whole thing.

When he signed in, the receptionist made a quick phone call and then told him he wouldn't have to wait in line with the others. The special attention unnerved him. As the nurse led him to an examination room, he felt like a prisoner walking the final mile to his execution. The doctor was already there.

"Good afternoon, Mr. Johnson," the doctor smiled. "You look better than the last time we met. I guess the medicine is doing its job."

"Yeah, I feel great. Look Doc, I don't mean to be rude or anything but I'm not in the mood for small talk. Are my test results back?"

The doctor's gaze dropped from Mike's face. He stood and held a piece of paper out toward Mike. "The important notations are in English."

The temptation to look was powerful. He studied the doctor's expression. Finally he took the paper, folded it up, and slipped it into his back pocket. "I don't need to look, do I?"

"Mr. Johnson, there are medications. And I think you'll get better treatment in America than in Thailand. Have you made plans to go home?"

Mike had a weird urge to giggle. He wondered if he was going into some sort of hysterical shock. He took a deep breath and braced himself against the desk. Disorganized thoughts assaulted him. "I haven't made plans for anything, but I can promise you that I'll be gone from here within the week."

"Your family will be happy to see you."

An image of Josh flashed through his head. "Maybe not all of them."

The doctor nodded. "Same with my family. By the way, none of your friends have come by for testing."

"I haven't told them yet, but I will. Probably tonight. It won't be easy."

The doctor sighed. "I can only imagine. Is there anything you need from me?"

"Can you give me something to make me sleep? I think I might have a problem with that."

The doctor scribbled on a piece of paper. "Take this to the hospital pharmacy. The medicine will make you sleep."

Fear of death cannot be completely understood until it is so close that you can hear its breath and smell its sweat. That thought and more rumbled through Mike's head as he returned to his condo. Between morbid thoughts, he made plans for the rest of his life. It wasn't hard to plan for less than a week.

When he entered the condo lobby, the receptionist waved him to the front desk. "I have a message for you." She handed him the note.

He slipped it into his pocket without reading it. He was sure it was from Jarapan. She had promised to call when she could. He mumbled thanks and walked away. By the time he reached his condo he had steeled himself enough to call her. He wasn't sure what he would say, but he was sure he couldn't tell her the truth. Not just yet. He would need a few beers before he would have the nerve to do that.

Five beers later he sat at his desk and dialed her parents' number. The woman who answered the phone apparently spoke some English because she seemed to understand when he asked for Jarapan. He was relieved when the woman said that Jarapan wasn't there because it meant he didn't have to lie. He hung up without trying to leave a message.

He rummaged through his suitcases and found the small stash of ganja he had hidden there months ago. He unplugged the phone so he wouldn't be disturbed, then spent the next two hours smoking pot, drinking Chang beer, and gathering the nerve to do what he had to do.

~~~

The first thing Jarapan discovered when she got home was that Mike had called. Her mother grilled her about the farang caller. Who was he? Why is a farang calling you? Where is he from? And a lot of other irritating questions. Jarapan endured her mother's inquisition, even though the insinuations made her flush with a chaotic blend of pride and anger.

"He's the man I love," she finally said. She almost said she was carrying his baby, but didn't. She would wait for the final results. Maybe she wasn't really pregnant. "What did he say?"

"He only asked if you were here. I don't approve of you being with a farang. You know that farangs are no good, don't you?"

The way her mother said the word *farang* made her skin crawl. She started to say so, but held her silence. Instead, she called Mike. There was no answer. She would keep trying for as long as it took to connect with him.

~~~

Mike showered, shaved, and dressed in the sharpest clothes he had. If he was going to become the most hated man in Pattaya, he wanted to do it in style. At four o'clock he plugged the phone back in and went to the Suaee Dee Lady.

No one was there yet, so he let himself in and locked the door behind him. He went directly to the office, turned on the light, and sat at the desk. By habit he turned on the computer and connected to the internet. There were a few dozen emails. Most were spam peddling cheap software and male enhancement pills. The rest were from visitors to the website. He deleted the obvious spam in mass, and then read the other messages in turn. He hesitated when he saw the email from his sister Carol. He didn't remember ever giving her his email address.

"I haven't heard from you in a while," Carol's message said. "Please send me an email so I know you are okay." It was signed with love.

Mike's throat squeezed tight to the point of pain. It was all he could do to keep from crying. After a few hard swallows the cramp eased and he wrote a response. In it he told Carol everything. He deleted it before it was sent. In a while, he wrote another message. This time he said nothing about his illness. He tried to keep his tone light, but it didn't work. Finally, he asked her to forgive him for any hurt he might have ever caused. He decided to delete that one too, but hit the send button by mistake. It didn't matter; she would probably think he was just drunk and ignore it anyway.

He turned off the computer, rested his head on the desk, and waited for Itta. In a while he heard someone opening the bar for the evening. It could be Itta or Ohm or any of the girls Itta trusted. He thought he heard them outside the office door once or twice, but no one came inside and he never went out. He figured it wasn't Itta but he knew she would be coming soon. Silently he rehearsed what he would say.

Chapter 37

Itta arrived at the Suaee Dee Lady promptly at six o'clock. Ohm had already opened the door and a couple of the dancers had arrived. She turned on the music and washed the bar top one last time. Satisfied that they were ready to open, she headed toward the office to hide her purse and get the money she had stashed for the evening's cash drawer.

The first thing she noticed was the light coming from the office. She distinctly remembered turning the light off when she had left earlier. Jarapan was out of town and Mike had been sick for the last few days, so she knew neither of them had been here. She wondered if they had been robbed, and if the thieves were still here. Or what if it was Ian? Her heart raced. She tip-toed back to the bar area and took one girl by the arm, "Paw, please come with me."

"Arai na?" Paw asked.

"It's probably nothing," Itta smiled, hiding her doubts. "But I don't remember leaving the office light on and I'm afraid to go by myself. Will you come with me?"

Paw nodded.

They walked side by side. Their tension rose as they neared the door. It was slightly ajar and light shined from inside. Paw giggled, childlike, as her adrenaline surged. She cupped her hand across her mouth to muffle the sound. Itta gave her an annoyed glance but said nothing.

Itta put her face near the edge of the door and eased it open enough to see inside. There sat Mike, his head lay atop his crossed arms resting on the desk. Itta breathed a sigh of relief. "It's only Mike," she kept her voice low. "I think he's asleep. Maybe he went drinking this afternoon and stopped here instead of going home. Sorry if I scared you."

"Mai pen rai, never mind," Paw giggled again. "It was exciting."

Itta smiled and stepped inside the office.

"Sawasdee ka, Mike," she said. "I'm surprised to see you. Did you lose your way home?"

Mike raised his head. "Hello, Itta. No, I'm not lost." He didn't smile. "I came to talk to you."

His seriousness caught her off guard. She had seen Mike in his depressed moods before and this looked like grandfather of them all. He had once told her that he sometimes did unpredictable things when he was depressed. She wondered if he was about to do something unpredictable now. "Are you okay? You look upset."

He avoided eye contact as he fumbled with his cigarette pack. Finally he extracted one, raised it to his lips, and then laid it on the desk. "The doctor told me I should stop smoking." His thin smile looked forced. "Are you feeling well, Itta."

Itta's apprehensions gathered faster than a monsoon storm. She made a conscious effort to keep her smile in place. "Yes, Mike, I feel fine. I'm tired, but only because I didn't sleep well last night. Bad dreams all the time. You're the one who doesn't look well. Maybe you should be home in bed." She paused and then added, "I mean alone, no bar girls."

"You don't have to worry about that. There will never be a woman in my bed for the rest of my life. That much is sure one hundred percent."

Itta studied his face. It was emotionless except for his eyes and they oozed inner turmoil. "Did something happen between you and Jarapan?"

"You might say that."

She wondered if Jarapan had told him about the man with the scarred face. She was sure she hadn't, yet something wasn't right.

Maybe it had to do with Jarapan going home. Maybe they had argued. She decided that must be it. "Don't worry. She'll be back soon. Everything will be okay."

Mike's face twisted, as if someone had punched him. "You're wrong," his voice mirrored the emotions etching his face. "Everything won't be okay. Everything's all fucked up."

"Is Jarapan okay?"

He tried to answer but nothing came out.

"Mike, please tell me Jarapan is okay." She reached over to touch his arm.

He pulled away, "Don't come near me."

Itta jumped as if she had been shocked. "What's wrong with you? Are you on drugs or something? You're scaring me."

"I'm sick. Maybe you're sick, too. I want you to go to the hospital and be tested."

Itta's dread grew like bamboo on steroids. "What are you talking about? What do you mean *maybe I'm sick, too*? I'm not sick. Are you contagious? What disease do you have? What about Jarapan?"

Mike took a deep breath and told the only lie he had practiced. "I have pneumonia and I'm going to die."

Itta stared at him. She knew people didn't die from pneumonia unless they were very old or they didn't have proper medical care. "Your doctor told you that? Did he give you medicine? Why aren't you in the hospital if you're that sick." She held out her hand. "Come on, right now, I'm taking you to the hospital."

Mike leaned away. "I've been there already. They gave me antibiotics, but I'm going to die anyway." He paused for a second, gathering courage. Finally, he stood and said, "I have AIDS. I am so sorry." Without another word he ran from the room.

Itta felt like she might faint. A million emotions tore through her. Visions of death flooded her mind. She sat at the desk and took several deep breaths. Work was out of the question. Perhaps everything in her future was out of the question.

She made her way from the office to the bar. Already customers had come. She took a seat far from everyone and motioned Ohm to her side. "I need you to stay and close up for tonight. When Jon comes in, tell him I'll meet him at his condo later."

Ohm stared. "Are you okay?"

Despite her attempt to be calm, tears burned her eyes and hysteria distorted her face. "I'm fine. Please, just close down for me tonight." She picked up her purse and ran from the bar.

Outside she climbed on her motorcycle, sped away from the Suaee Dee Lady and turned north on Second Road. A few blocks later she turned left on Soi 5 and drove directly to the Pattaya International Hospital. She had to get tested now, tonight. Fuck waiting for tomorrow.

When she entered the lobby, the young receptionist motioned her to the counter. "Do you have an emergency?"

Itta wasn't sure how to answer. To her it was an emergency, but to anyone else it was probably something that could wait. "I think I have AIDS," she managed to whisper. "I want to be tested."

"Do you have money?"

"Yes, and a credit card, and insurance, too. I can pay for the test."

The girl nodded and stepped away. She made a short phone call, picked up some papers, and then returned to the counter. "Fill these out. Bring them to me when you're finished. The doctor has ordered a quick test and a long test."

Itta raised her eyebrows, "How accurate is the quick test?"

The girl shrugged, "It makes mistakes. So does the long test, but not very often. If you think you've been exposed, you'll want to be tested every few months for a while. The doctor will talk to you when the long test results are back."

Itta stepped aside to fill out the form. Her hand shook so hard she could barely write. After several minutes of effort, the forms were complete. The girl directed her down a hallway toward the lab. There a nurse slipped on rubber gloves, expertly extracted two vials of blood, then sent her back to the waiting room. Apparently, even the quick test would take a while.

As the minutes dragged on, Itta did an inventory of her health. She had felt tired lately, but she figured that was from working nights and trying to sleep through the daytime noises. She hadn't been sick except for a couple of headaches. She wondered if that was a symptom of HIV or AIDS. She had heard a lot about the disease but she couldn't remember what the symptoms were. Maybe there were none. Maybe the symptoms were only the inability to recover from other diseases. Maybe you didn't even know you were sick until you couldn't stop getting sick. The only thing she knew for certain was that AIDS killed people. The thought sent a hard chill through her.

Mike's face entered her mind. It had been a year since they first met. Back then they lived together as lovers and he had been as healthy as anyone she knew. As far as she could remember, she had only seen him sick once before now, just after he came back from Singapore. Except for a lingering cough he had healed. That didn't fit with what little she knew about AIDS.

In a while she was called to the counter that served as a combination pharmacy and cashier. She gave them her credit card and received her test results in return. She scanned the paper while she waited for them to process the card. One test was circled and it was checked negative. She almost exploded from the joy that single checkmark sent through her. Negative!!! Dear Buddha, she couldn't remember ever being so happy.

"Your official test results," the cashier said, "will be back from Bangkok in three days. The doctor has scheduled an appointment with you at two o'clock. Here's a reminder card. Please call if you can't come in."

Itta's elation disappeared faster than a Thailand sunset. Her real test results were coming! *The quick test makes mistakes!* That's what the receptionist had said. The quick test meant nothing. The real test didn't mean anything either. The nurse had told her she would have to be tested every few months for a while. What in

Buddha's name did that mean? How long was a while? A year? Two years? The rest of her life? She could be negative in three days but then test positive in six months or a year or even later.

She signed the credit card receipt and moved away from the counter. She knew she was walking because the exit door was getting closer, but she couldn't feel her legs moving. In fact, she didn't feel much of anything. Her entire body felt numb. Jon would be home in a few hours. She dreaded what the night would bring.

She steered her motorcycle left onto Second Road heading north. It was the opposite direction from Jon's condo. As she passed the bars of Soi 2, she caught a glimpse of Mike. He and the bar owner Lek were standing at the edge of the street, their expressions intense. She pulled to the side of the road and debated whether or not to tell Mike about her quick test. Surely he would be happy to know she was negative; or maybe not. She didn't know what he would think. She didn't even know what to think herself.

She turned the motorcycle around and drove against the grain of traffic until she was at the top of Soi 2. Before she could decide what to do, Mike boarded a baht-bus headed west toward Beach Road. She could catch him easily enough, but she didn't even try. Lek looked in her direction; a hard weariness lined her face. She knew Lek, but not very well. She and Mike had stopped at these bars before, and he had introduced her to Lek. Old friends, he had said. He had never mentioned that he and Lek had once been lovers, but she had heard rumors. From the scene she had just witnessed, she knew the rumors were true. Their eyes met as she approached.

"Good evening, Lek," she spoke quietly. "Are you okay?"

Lek glanced in the direction where Mike had gone, then back at Itta. "I should be asking you the same thing."

Itta blushed. "I've had a quick test. It was negative."

"It means nothing," Lek responded, her voice harsh. "But I'm sure you'll be okay. HIV isn't easy to catch." She paused briefly, as if deciding what to say, and then continued, "I've not slept with Mike in over two years. I have myself tested every three months.

The last time was five days ago." She held her arm out and pointed at the nearly invisible mark where her blood sample had been taken. "It wasn't a quick test; I'm okay. I'm worried about his friend, Jarapan. She and Mike have been recent lovers."

Itta was quiet as she digested Lek's words. She wasn't sure what to say in response. Finally she spoke her feelings, "If Jarapan is sick, it's my fault. I practically forced her to move in with Mike. I should have known better; bad luck seems to follow him around. He has made a disaster of my whole family. I wish we had never met him."

Lek stepped closer. "You listen to me. I have known Mike for a long time. He's not a bad man. I also knew your sister Math, and I know what happened to her. Her death was an accident. It wasn't his fault. I don't know how he caught AIDS, but it's possible it came from your own sister."

"My sister was not a whore," Itta hissed.

"I never said that," Lek retorted. "Mike told me that she had more than one medical operation. Who knows what diseases they put into her body? The only thing I know for sure is that Mike is the only one who is dying. Someone has killed him and he doesn't know who to blame, so he blames himself. How hard do you think it was for him to tell you and me that he has AIDS?"

Itta looked away. "I'm sorry. I haven't had time to think about how Mike feels. Lek, I'm scared. My long test will be back in three days. It could be positive."

"Or it could be negative."

"Yes, but it means nothing, anyway. I'm in love with a man, but after I tell him about Mike, I will lose him forever."

"Maybe you shouldn't say anything until your long test comes back."

"How could I live with a man knowing I might test positive next month, or the month after that? It's best if I tell him now."

"You mean Jonathan?"

"How do you know?"

"Nothing in Pattaya is top secret. I'm sorry for your situation."

Itta reached out, squeezed Lek's hand tight in hers, and then turned and walked away. Minutes later she was roaring north on Sukhumvit Road. She held the motorcycle's throttle wide open. In a while time worked its magic and she felt almost back to normal. The HIV/AIDS thing hung over her like a suffocating blanket, but the initial shock had faded. She turned back toward Pattaya. She was ready to talk to Jon.

Fifteen minutes later she parked her motorcycle in the garage area of Jon's condo. The boy at the front desk handed her the key without question and she went upstairs.

Jon wasn't home yet. She looked at her watch. He would be here soon. She went to his bedroom and packed her things. Then she sat at the kitchen table in total darkness and waited for him to arrive. As hard as she tried, she couldn't keep her fears and depression away. The threat of Ian coming was nothing compared to the other terrors creeping through her. Scenes from her life flowed like hot quicksilver. The things she had done and the decisions she had made, they all came down to this, and this came with the potential of destroying everything. She practiced what she would tell Jonathan.

Chapter 38

Mike had been in his condo for less than a minute when the phone rang. He knew it was Jarapan, no one else would be calling tonight—at least no one he cared about. His frayed nerves unraveled another strand.

"Hello."

"Sawasdee ka," Jarapan whispered through the receiver. "I miss you and love you teeluk. Are you okay?"

His throat cramped into a knot so tight that he couldn't speak.

"Are you still there?" Jarapan said when he didn't answer.

At that moment Mike knew he wouldn't be able to tell her. "Yes," he managed as the knot eased. He took a drink of beer and cleared his throat. "I mean, yes, I'm here." He changed the subject. "How is your family?"

"My family is well."

"I thought there was an emergency; I was worried." As hard as he tried to sound concerned, his words came out flat.

"Teeluk, I'm sorry I didn't call. Everything is fine here now. I will come back to you in quickly time."

"Don't worry Jarapan. Everything here is okay, too. Take your time. Have a nice visit with your family. We can talk by phone every day until you come home. Okay?"

"Okay teeluk. I'll talk to you tomorrow. I love you."

"I love you, too, Jarapan."

He hung up the phone and unplugged it from the wall. He hated himself for everything that was happening. Especially he hated himself for being such a coward that he hadn't told Jarapan the truth. He took three of the pills the doctor had given him, lay down in his bed, and prayed for sleep to come.

~~~

Jarapan had intended to tell Mike that she might be pregnant but there had been no clear opening. After a minute she decided he needed to know now. She called him back but he didn't answer. She tried again, dialing more carefully this time. Again there was no answer. Maybe he had gone out. She started to dial his cell phone but then remembered she didn't know the number. Her lips tightened in annoyance.

Her mother looked at her as if expecting her to say something. She knew her family's feelings about foreigners so she said nothing. She dropped her eyes from her mother's stare and walked away.

Her conversation with Mike played though her head. It had sounded like Mike and not like Mike at the same time. Not so much the words he had said but the way he had said them. His voice had been emotionless, almost cold. It messed with her mind.

She glanced at the clock, it wasn't yet nine. She would call again before she went to bed. She was irritated that she was so stupid that she had never memorized Mike's cell phone number.

Chapter 39

It was one 1:45 in the morning when Itta heard a key slip into the lock. As much as she had prepared herself, she nearly jumped from her skin at the sound. She stood as Jon entered the room. His face was a collage of worry and anger.

"I love you," she said before he had time to speak. "Now we must talk."

"What's going on? Ohm told me something was wrong. She thinks something happened between you and Mike. She said he came to the Suaee Dee Lady and that you were crying when he left. Did he hurt you? If he did, I'll kill the son-of-a-bitch. He's my friend, but I swear I'll kill him if he hurt you."

Itta had never seen Jon angry before and his threats unnerved her. She wasn't sure what to say. She steadied herself. "Mike would never hurt me on purpose. Please, come and sit down so we can talk." She pulled him to the kitchen, and then went to the refrigerator and took out a Carlsberg. "I bought you beer." The tone of her voice and the draw of her face spoke terror.

"What the hell is going on?"

Itta sat across from Jon, her arms resting on the tabletop. She tried to relax but couldn't. Her nerves were frazzled. "A long time ago, I had sex with Mike."

She looked for a reaction but there was none, not even a blink. "I thought I might love him but I couldn't," she continued. "I wanted you to know that."

Jon lowered his gaze. He already knew that Itta and Mike had once lived together. He'd even talked to Mike about it. It didn't bother him much because he wasn't exactly a virgin either.

Besides, at their ages it didn't mean anything. If Itta was worried about him finding out, she was worried for nothing.

He looked up and whispered, "I forgive you."

His response caught her off guard. She had been expecting jealousy, if not anger. She didn't deserve forgiveness. "You don't understand."

Jon sighed. "So you had sex with Mike. It doesn't bother me. I've had sex with other women too. That's life. Now, please tell me what I'm missing here."

"Mike is dying," her words rushed out. "He told me tonight. Mike has AIDS."

Jon opened his mouth to speak but no words came. He turned away from her, trying desperately to keep his composure. Conclusions formed with crystal clarity. She had had sex with Mike. He'd had sex with her. Mike had AIDS; she had said so. Did she have it, too? Could she have given it to him? "Are you sick?"

"My quick test was negative."

His mind ran wild. The quick test was shit and everyone knew it. How could she be so calm? For the first time since they had met, he wondered what sort of woman she was. He knew little about her except that she was half owner of a bar in Pattaya and that Mike was her partner. Now he knew beyond a doubt how she had convinced Mike to finance their business. Imagines of Mike and Itta having sex flickered through his head. He wondered how many other men she had slept with. He was sure it was more than a few. Suddenly he realized she was like every other woman he had ever met in Pattaya. Perhaps she was worse.

"I thought you were different," he hissed. "You are nothing but a whore. Just how many other men have you fucked?"

"I'm not a whore," Itta snapped back. Her worst nightmares were unfolding. The need to shed blame was acute. The pitch of her voice rose. "I've done nothing you haven't done. You are the one who had sex with me without a condom. If you remember, I was the one who was worried. As for how many men I have fucked, you are number forty-two. I was paid by thirty-six of them.

If that makes me a whore, then I guess I am."

A long silence followed. Finally she whispered, "I've packed my things. I'm leaving Pattaya tonight. I don't want to be here anymore. I'm going home." She retrieved her suitcase from the bedroom and went to the door. "I'm sorry for everything." Itta ran from the condo.

In the hallway, by the elevator, her legs buckled and she slumped to the floor. She laid her head against her knees and cried. When she finally looked up, Jon was there.

"I'm a whore, too," he said. "I want you to stay with me tonight. And when this is over, I want you to go with me to America and be my wife."

Itta's eyes filled with tears. How could he want her after everything she had just told him. No normal man would want her, but Jon did. "Are you sure teeluk? Are you really sure?"

He pulled her close and held tight. "I'm sure."

He took her luggage in one hand and guided her home with the other. Later that night they made love and they didn't use a condom. It was their personal confirmation to each other and to their future.

Chapter 40

Mike awoke at seven o'clock on Friday morning. The overcast sky and heavy grayness grated against his already black mood. He took a beer from the fridge, slid the balcony door open, and stepped outside. The few people astir on the streets below carried umbrellas in anticipation of certain rain. The buildings were drab in the subdued daylight. The dreariness matched his mood.

He couldn't believe he had ended up in Pattaya, a shit-hole of a town on the edge of nowhere. A modern day Sodom and Gomorrah that sucked love-weary men into its slick pools of lust like black widows to a web of deadly sex. If he had to do it all over again, he would never have come here.

A memory of Math slipped into his thoughts and he knew he was lying to himself. He wouldn't have missed loving her for anything, even if it meant his death. He stepped back inside the condo and tossed the empty bottle into the trash.

He started to get another beer but changed his mind. He had business to take care of and he needed to do it sober. He had to look clean and professional; it was the only way it would work. He headed toward the shower. Thirty minutes later he hired a baht-bus to take him across town.

The receptionist stood when he entered the law office. "Sawasdee ka, Mr. Mike. How are you this morning? "

"I must see Ms. Orapin. I don't have an appointment but it's an urgent matter. I would be most grateful if she could make time for me. It won't take long."

"Let me look." The girl scanned her planner. " I think it won't be a problem. Let me check with Ms. Orapin." She picked up the phone, pushed a button, and spoke in Thai. Then she smiled up and said, "She can see you now."

Mike entered the lawyer's office.

"I'm surprised to see you so early in the morning," the woman said. "And unannounced," she added, motioning him to have a seat. "It must be something important. Is business okay?"

"Yes, the Suaee Dee Lady is doing fine." he said, hoping his smile looked genuine. "I want to take care of some things I've have been thinking about for a while. I want to write a will and change beneficiaries on an insurance policy." He coughed once and then again. He covered his mouth with a handkerchief.

"Are you okay?" she stood from her seat.

His urge to cough was powerful. "The doctor says I smoke too much. Look, I've fallen in love with a wonderful young lady and want to make sure her future is taken care of... You know, in case anything ever happens to me."

The attorney eased back in her chair. "Are you sure? Some people in Pattaya are not what they seem."

"Don't worry, she's a good woman. She's not a bar-girl."

Thirty minutes later Mike had signed a will that split his ownership of the Suaee Dee Lady and his life insurance policy between Jarapan and his son Josh. There were strings attached.

Once Mike had left, Orapin reread the documents. Clearly something was going on, but she had no idea what. Mike had said it was something he wanted to do, but he had acted as if his death were imminent. And the restrictions he'd put on the disbursements of his assets were odd. His son would get half, but only if he did specific things. Same thing for a woman named Jarapan, except she would get her share regardless of what she did.

Orapin shook her head in confusion and filed the papers away. Mike's business partner had called earlier and set an appointment for ten. She was sure it wasn't a coincidence. She sat back to wait for Itta.

Chapter 41

First thing on Friday morning Itta called the Suaee Dee Lady's attorney and made an appointment for ten o'clock. Later she went to the law office and signed over her ownership of the Suaee Dee Lady to the attorney as a trustee. She didn't know what that meant other than she didn't have to make more decisions. The woman had a million questions and Itta had finally told her everything.

When Itta left the attorney's office, she went directly to her brother's house to collect anything she had left behind. During her search she found a photo album she had never seen before. It was filled with pictures of Mike and her sister Math. She would have Jon return it to Mike. She loaded everything into plastic bags, strapped them to her motorcycle, and drove back to the condo.

Later she went to the Suaee Dee Lady and told Ohm she wouldn't be in that night or any other night. She was finished with Pattaya. She instructed Ohm to take care of business from open to close until Jarapan came back. On impulse she took ten thousand baht from her purse. "A bonus for your extra work. I think you'll have to take care of the accounting and stocking, too."

Jon was home when she arrived. Packed suitcases sat near the door. He hadn't mentioned going anywhere, and his job here wouldn't be finished for another month, maybe longer. She gave him a questioning look.

"I'm going to Bangkok for a few days and then I'm going home to America."

Itta felt panic rushing through her. He hadn't mentioned her. *What about me?* she wanted to scream. If he was abandoning her, she didn't want to hear him say it. If he had changed his mind and was leaving her behind, she wished he would have gone before she came home. She lowered her eyes from his. "I understand. I will miss you Jon."

"You mean you're not going with me?"

She glanced at the absence of her suitcase in the row of luggage

He took her hand in his. "We'll both leave for America as soon as I can arrange a U.S. visa. I don't think it will be a problem. In the morning we'll go to Bangkok to start the paperwork. You can go to Phitsanulok to visit your family while we wait. I'd go with you but I may have to answer questions about your visa. Besides, I have reports to write for my company. With luck we'll leave for America in less than two weeks."

As Itta packed her suitcases, she thought about how her life was changing. She thought Jon was crazy for loving her. She hoped that never changed.

Later, she remembered the picture album and asked Jon if he would take it to Mike. Jon agreed saying he wanted to tell Mike goodbye anyway.

After Jon left, Itta called her mother. It was the first time they had talked in three months. "I'm coming home for a while, and then I'm going to America."

Nui made her usual biting comments, but Itta ignored them. There was nothing that could change her mother's mind about Jon, and she was ready to leave Thailand forever.

Chapter 42

When Mike arrived home from the attorney's office, he forced himself to sit down and write a letter explaining everything he was doing. He wrote it in longhand so there would be no questions whether it was from him or not. Finished he put it in an envelope and addressed it to his attorney. On the back he wrote, "Open only in the event of an emergency." He sealed it shut, applied stamps, and left the condo. He dropped the letter in the mail-drop at the edge of the street.

He walked to the nearest Seven-Eleven and bought several bottles of beer. Chang wasn't his favorite, but considering the circumstances anything better would be a waste of good money.

Back in his condo he opened a beer and headed toward the living room. The phone on the desk stood out like a beacon. His eyes flicked from the phone to the clock. It was nearly two. He knew he should call Jarapan and tell her the truth before someone else did, but he couldn't force himself to pick up the phone. He would do it later, after he had more time to think about what he would say.

Suddenly he felt hyper, as if he would jump from his skin. The strength of his panic attack set his feet in motion. He paced back and forth across the room pulling hard at the Beer Chang. He couldn't remember the last time he had felt hyper and depressed at the same time. Then on his fifth lap he did remember. It was the day Math had died. He hadn't killed himself then only because he still had people to live for. Now he had nothing. All he had left was Jarapan, and he had already sentenced her to death.

Halfway through his sixth lap his growing self-hatred

exploded. As if by magic, the empty beer bottle sailed from his hand and shattered against the wall scattering shards of glass across the countertop and onto to the floor.

"Shit fuck everything," he cursed into the empty condo. Images of him breaking furniture flashed through his head. The images were so real that his muscles jerked in response. He took a deep breath. In a moment his urge to destroy things passed. He headed for the refrigerator. A knock at the door stopped him short.

"Go away," he snarled at whoever was on the other side.

"Hey Mike. It's me, Jon, Greene County. I want to talk."

Mike grimaced as his blood pressure spiked. "I don't want to talk right now. I'm busy."

"You don't have to talk. All you have to do is listen. It would be easier if you open the door."

"I just want to be alone." Mike forced his voice quieter.

"I have something for you."

"I'm not in the mood for gifts."

"It's not a gift, Mike; it's memories. I promised Itta I would bring them to you."

"Whatever it is, I don't want it."

"Let me show you, and then I will leave."

Mike's shoulders slumped. It was obvious that Jon wasn't going to go away easily. For an instant he imagined that Jon had a gun and was here to kill him. That promising thought passed as quickly as it had come; Jonathan Yeager wasn't that kind of man. He sighed and opened the door.

"You look like shit," Jon said as he stepped inside.

"That makes us even," Mike replied over his shoulder as he walked to the refrigerator and extracted another Chang. "Who cares anyway?"

Jon's face reddened. "Your problem... I mean your condition... ah... it's not a death sentence."

"That's bullshit and you know it," Mike snapped. "What do you call it? A life sentence? Don't patronize me, Greene County. I'm not in the mood. Hate me if you want, kill me if you've got the guts, but don't patronize me." He put the bottle to his lips and pulled hard.

Jon dropped his eyes from the outburst. Hard silence permeated the room. Jon raised his hand and held the plastic bag toward Mike. "Itta wanted you to have this."

Mike closed his eyes and took a deep breath. Despite everything ripping his emotions to shreds, he knew was being an asshole. "Is she okay? I mean, has she talked to you?"

"We've both been tested. We'll have the lab results in a couple of days."

"I'm sorry for everything. I don't know what else to say."

"If I thought you had planned this, I would kill you." Jon pushed the bag closer. "Itta said this was yours."

Mike took the bag from Jon's outstretched hand. Inside was a photo album, his photo album. He hadn't seen it in almost two years, since before everything in his life had gone to complete shit. "Where did you get this?"

"Itta found it at her brother's house while she was packing for our trip to the US. She wanted you to have it. She said it was your memories."

Mike opened to a random page. A picture of himself in his army uniform stared back. So young, so healthy, so full of life. Even without looking, he knew he didn't want to see the other pages. He closed the album and tossed it into the trashcan like it was yesterday's newspaper. "Tell Itta I said thanks."

Jon stared at the album protruding from the top of the trash. In a second he looked up. "I have to go now. We're going to Bangkok early tomorrow. We'll leave for the US as soon as she has a visa, probably in a week or two. In case you are wondering, our quick tests were negative. I thought you would want to know. Take care of yourself Mike." He reached out to shake hands goodbye.

Mike pulled away, hiding his hands beneath his armpits. "I can't. Nothing personal, but touching people makes me uncomfortable."

"Yeah, me too," Jon replied and stepped backwards through

the doorway. Outside, lightning flashed and a sharp crack of thunder followed.

"Stay dry, Greene County."

"Yes, I will." Jon turned toward the elevator.

Once Jon was gone, Mike opened another beer and pulled the album from the trash. His life flashed before him as he flipped through the pages. His boyhood with his family in West Virginia, his tech-school days in Pittsburgh, his tour of duty in Vietnam, his wife and son in America, and finally his life in Thailand. Each memory evoked emotions so deep that they would live long after he ceased to exist. His book would make sure of that.

His book! He hadn't looked at it in weeks. Not since Jarapan had read it. Jarapan! He glanced at the clock. He would call her later. He walked to the computer and turned it on.

Chapter 43

Jarapan's Friday morning crept past even slower than her sleepless Thursday night. She had called Mike just before going to bed and several times since getting up. Her uneasiness grew each time he didn't answer.

Later she called what she hoped was Itta's cell phone. She couldn't remember the number exactly, but she called anyway. She got a recording saying the phone was turned off or out of range. Maybe it wasn't even Itta's number. At six o'clock she called the Suaee Dee Lady and Ohm answered.

"Hello, Ohm. This is Jarapan. May I talk to Itta?"

"Itta isn't here. She came by earlier and said I was in charge of the bar because she was leaving Pattaya."

"Arai nai?" Jarapan couldn't believe what she was hearing. "What do you mean Itta is leaving Pattaya? What about Mike?"

"I think Mike is the reason she's leaving. She left work crying last night after she and Mike talked. Mike didn't look happy either. He looked sick. Will you be here tomorrow?"

Jarapan's mind spun. Something was more than not right, something was totally wrong. Either Ohm was lying or Mike was lying. She glanced at her watch. "Yes, I'll be there tomorrow." She hung up the phone.

For a moment she couldn't catch her breath. When she did, it came in gasps. Her heart raced, thundering in her ears. Suddenly she became aware that her parents and her brother were staring at her. Questions lined their faces. "I have to leave," she blurted out.

"Your farang found another lady?" her brother asked, his tone snide.

She turned on him. "Don't ever say anything like that again."

"What farang?" her father interjected, his gaze shifting from Jarapan to his wife.

"An American," her brother answered. "Purachai told me about him. He also said that Jarapan has become a whore."

"Stop it!" Jarapan screamed. "I'm not a whore. I'm in love."

"With an old man's money," her brother taunted.

"A farang's money," her father added.

Jarapan's mother stood. "Leave her alone, both of you."

"She should never have gone to Pattaya," her father huffed. "No decent man will have her now."

"No man in Khon Kaen would have me before." Jarapan glared. "I wish I had never come home. I'm leaving and I'll never come back." She picked up her purse and ran to the door. "Ever!"

"Wait," her mother stopped her. "I'll give you a ride." Her stare focused on the two men. Neither of them moved nor spoke. "Jarapan, pack your things. We'll leave when you're ready."

Outside, her mother said, "There are no flights from Khon Kaen until tomorrow. I'll take you to the bus station."

"No, take me to the airport. I have a return ticket."

"Maybe you should just wait here until morning. It's still your home."

"It hasn't been my home since the day I was raped." At that moment she realized that she had used the word *rape* for the first time to describe *the incident*. "I'm ready to go now."

They rode to the airport in silence. It was deserted except for security and a few maintenance people. With nothing else to do, the two women sat outside and talked.

"Your friend," her mother finally broached the subject they had both been avoiding. "Does he have a good heart?"

Jarapan didn't know how to answer. She understood the question, but it was more complicated than that. "He loves me," she finally said.

There was a long pause before her mother responded, "Farangs are not the same as Thais."

Jarapan tensed, wanting to ask what she knew of farangs, but kept her nastiness in check. Still her words came out terse. "You mean because they don't look like us, or because they speak a different language?"

"Yes, that's part of it," her mother soothed. "But there's more. They grow up in a different culture, in a different world. When you think something is *never-mind*, they might believe it's a big disaster. They are not like Thais. They dream of big houses and fancy cars while we dream of perfect rain and a new motorcycle. They're not like us."

Jarapan stared for a moment before answering, "I know what you're saying, but Mike is different."

"Because you love him?"

"Because he loves me."

Her mother flushed. "It will never work. You know that."

"I'm pregnant."

"Oh dear Buddha," her mother brought her hand to her mouth. "Is it his?"

Jarapan bristled. "Despite what Purachai said, I am not a whore."

Her mother looked away, embarrassed. "That's not what I meant. It's just that I was worried about... well, you know... about what happened before."

This time Jarapan looked away. Memories of that day rushed through her. Memories of her recent encounter with the scar-faced man and his wife followed close behind. Suddenly she wished her mother would go away. "I'm trying to forget what happened before," she said harsher than she meant. "I wish everyone would just forget."

"Does the farang know?"

Jarapan stood. "His name is Mike and he's more than a farang. If it's any of your business, yes, he knows. I think you should leave now."

"Can I tell you a story?"

"Mother, please. I just want to be alone. I need time to think."

"When I was nineteen," her mother continued as if Jarapan hadn't spoken, "not long before I married your father, I knew a farang and I loved him. That's all. That's the story I wanted to tell you. I'll leave now. If you want to call me sometime, I'll be happy to hear from you. If you want to come home, you will be welcome. Your father and brother didn't mean what they said tonight. They love you and worry about you. Don't ever forget that."

When Jarapan didn't respond, her mother stood and walked away. She had started the motorcycle before Jarapan stopped her.

"Wait. I want to hear the rest of the story."

Her mother looked over, her eyes filled with a mix of worry, love, and embarrassment. In a second she turned off the ignition. "Then I'll tell you."

As they sat outside the deserted airport, her mother told a tale like Jarapan could never have imagined.

Her own mother had once loved a foreigner, a man from England. The man had been young, handsome, and rich. He had come to Thailand on business. Her mother had barely turned nineteen. She had been working at a small restaurant that the man and his friends frequented. She had fallen in love with him from the first day the men came. When he finally asked her out she hadn't refused. Nor had she protested when he took her home and stole her virginity. By the time the man returned to England, she was hopelessly in love. He had promised to come back for her, but he never did.

"That is how I know about farangs," her mother concluded. "And why I know it will never work. You should forget about him. Someday he will go home and never come back. That's what farangs do. When he leaves, the only things he'll take are your heart and your self-respect. You should have an abortion; I think that would be best."

Jarapan was shocked by her mother's confession of loving and sleeping with a foreigner. But she was angered by her mother's suggestion that Mike would abandon her, and that she should have an abortion. "Mike would never leave me," she said then paused, gathering her thoughts. "I'm not a little girl anymore. I'm old enough to know what's best for me. I love him and I would never kill his baby."

A tear slid down her mother's cheek. "You should come back home with me and stay for a while, a week or so. It will give you time to think. "

"I've thought already. I have to go to Pattaya. Something is wrong. I think Mike is sick and needs me. Besides, I can't stay here. You saw how my father and brother talked to me. I love you, but your house is no longer my home."

"Please don't say that. It's not true. I told you they didn't mean anything."

"I'm sorry mama, but it is true. I love you and papa, but I can't stay, I must find my own life and I won't find it here. I won't find anything in Khon Kaen but sadness."

Her mother pulled a tissue from her pocket and dabbed at her eyes. "I should be going home now. Your father will be worried."

"I'll call from Pattaya."

"We all love you."

"I know. Me too."

Her mother gave her a brief hug, boarded the motorcycle and drove away.

The evening had grown cold. Jarapan found a long-sleeved shirt in her suitcase and draped it across her shoulders. She passed the time thinking about everything that had happened in her past and praying for love and happiness in her future.

As the minutes became hours, the reality of her situation filled her head. She was pregnant, but she wasn't married. That alone stressed her to the edge of panic. But the things Purachai had told her brother, and her family's reaction, pushed her to depression. It was as if they were ready to believe the worst about her. And the phone call from Mike, and her conversation with Ohm—something was going on in Pattaya and it involved Mike and Itta, but she had no idea what.

Mike had been sick when she left Pattaya. She wondered if he had gotten worse and was running a fever like before. That would explain their bizarre conversation and maybe even the problem with Mike and Itta. She wondered if he had gone to the doctor. She suspected he hadn't since she wasn't there to make him go. She glanced at her watch: it was ten o'clock. Her flight wouldn't leave for hours. From the corner of her eye she saw a phone booth. She rummaged through her purse, found change, and then walked to the phone and dialed.

It rang a long time but Mike never answered. Finally she went back to the bench and waited for morning to come.

Chapter 44

After Jon had left, Mike reread the story of his life with Math. He cried for the misery he had caused and the pain he had suffered. By the end of the book he was drunk. It was almost eight o'clock. He picked up the phone. Three times his drunken fingers miss-dialed before he made a connection. The phone rang endlessly. He was about to give up when a woman answered. It wasn't Jarapan. It was the same woman who had answered before. He knew it was Jarapan's mother and he cringed. What does one say to the mother of a woman you have sentenced to death?

"Sawasdee krup," he said politely. "Khun Jarapan, please."

"Jarapan not here. Jarapan go Pattaya."

Mike's drunkenness dissolved into panic. "What do you mean, she go Pattaya?"

"Arai nah? Mai khow chai."

"When?"

"Mai phut Angrit. No speak English. Name you Mike?"

Obviously Jarapan had talked to her mother about him. "Yes, I am Mike."

"Jarapan have baby you."

Her words pounded his head like a jackhammer. His hand shook from the onslaught of emotions that tore at him like a pack of wild soi dogs. He hung up the phone when he realized he couldn't speak.

Jarapan have baby you! The woman's words tore through his head. Maybe he had misunderstood, yet he knew he hadn't. Jarapan was pregnant and he had AIDS. He was going to die. Most likely she was going to die, too. And the baby. What sort of life—or death—would the baby have? The answer was obvious.

A hard knot clamped at his throat like a pit-bull on crack. He took a deep breath. It triggered spasm of coughing that brought him to his knees. By the time he could breathe he was too weak to stand. He knew it was the pneumonia that was making him sick. The doctor had said it would go away in a few days if he got some rest and took the antibiotics. But he would get sick again and again until he died.

"Suicide!" The word pierced his thoughts like an ice-pick. Images of ways to commit kill himself flashed across his vision and a shiver of terror crept through him.

All his life he had put on a front of bravado about death. Everyone knew Mr. Michael Johnson wasn't afraid of death, he welcomed it. He had told that lie so many times that he had come to believe it himself. But now, staring straight into the eye of the grim reaper, he was scared shitless.

He forced himself from the floor, went to the bathroom, and splashed cold water across his eyes as if he could wash the away the visions. As he dried his face, he caught a glimpse of himself in the mirror. He looked more than sick; he looked terrible. He didn't remember ever seeing himself look this bad. He wondered if the pneumonia had suddenly aged him or if he had looked like this for weeks and never noticed. He couldn't imagine Jarapan ever loving something that looked like him.

Jarapan! He had sentenced her to death and he hadn't had the guts to tell her. She was coming to Pattaya; her mother had said that much. He wanted to see her and not see her at the same time. What would he say when she arrived? How are you? He already knew the answer to that question. Do you love me? He knew the answer to that one, too, once she learned the truth.

"Suicide," the thought came again. This time the mental images weren't so scary.

He put on a baseball cap to hide his mess of sweat-soaked hair, left the condo, and went directly to the Dockside Bar. His friend Meaw was busy with another customer and didn't see him. He ordered a beer and told the waitress to let Meaw know he was there. She nodded and hurried away.

In a moment Meaw arrived carrying his beer. Her smile reached from ear to ear. "Hello Mike. I'm happy to see you. A customer said you have been not well. I'm happy you better now."

"Yeah," he said. "I've not been well. I think I'll be okay tomorrow."

"You like play game?" she pointed at the connect-four board.

"I want you to do something for me."

"Sure! I would do anything for you." Her anticipation of getting bar-fined stood out like a Thai virgin.

"I want you to buy me some ganja, and yaba, too. Yeah, mostly yaba."

Meaw frowned. "What about me?"

"Sure, buy some for yourself." He knew she smoked ganja because she had told him so. He was guessing about the yaba.

"No. I mean about you and me. Do you want to take me home with you?"

His test results flashed though his head. Images of Jarapan on her way to Pattaya followed close behind. "I'll pay for your time.

"How much ganja and yaba do you want?"

He handed her ten thousand baht. "As much as that will buy. I'm having a big party." Then he threw another five thousand baht on the counter. "That's for you."

Meaw eyes grew wide. "I will love you all night for that much money."

"Tomorrow would be better. Tonight I want to be alone."

"Okay, tomorrow," Meaw didn't argue. "I know where you live. Can I come at eight o'clock, after your lady is at work?"

Mike rubbed his hands across his face to wipe away the sweat pouring from his forehead. At that moment he decided his fate. "Yes. Come to my place tomorrow night at eight. That's when the party begins."

Meaw was back in less than ten minutes and surreptitiously

slipped him the plastic bag filled with ganja and yaba.

"I'll see you tomorrow at eight." She smiled, and then went back to her customer.

Mike was glad to see her go. He finished his beer and left the bar. He walked to the nearest Seven-Eleven and bought more Chang beer. Five minutes later he was back inside his condo.

Out of habit he opened the Suaee Dee Lady website. The picture of Jarapan kissing him appeared on the screen. Immediately he closed the connection and went to his document folder. His book file stared out at him. Not only had he authored it, he had read it a thousand times. It was complete but still riddled with his West Virginia grammar. It would never be finished the way he had always dreamed. But that didn't matter anymore. Maybe it never had. He emailed the file to his sister without a subject or a message.

He took a yaba pill and chased it with a beer. When nothing happened, he took another pill and then smoked a joint to boot.

He spent the next hour chugging beer, smoking pot, and thinking. His son Josh came to mind, and then his sister Carol, and Itta. He had ruined their lives just by existing. Then came Math and Susan; he was responsible for their deaths, too, but no court would ever convict him. An image of Jarapan crept in and overwhelmed the others. Dear God, what had he done? He didn't know much about HIV and AIDS, but he figured that if he had gotten her pregnant, then he had probably infected her.

He stepped outside onto the balcony. The sky was clear and the moon had taken the place of the sun. Its brightness drowned out the stars. He stepped to the railing and looked at the parking area below. Most of the spaces were filled but no people moved about. He noticed that the monkey cage was gone. To his right he could see where the side-street intersected Beach Road. Motorcycles and baht-buses flicked across the narrow view. Pedestrians moved at a slower pace but they were too far away to be anything except faceless people.

He looked back at the parking lot. It was about thirty feet from the balcony to the blacktop. He remembered a story from the Pattaya Mail about a German man who had killed himself by leaping from this height. Images of himself falling thirty feet flashed crystal clear. His palms turned sweaty and he took a step back from the railing. Heights had never bothered him before, at least not like this. Of all the ways he could kill himself, jumping from the balcony wasn't one. He went back inside.

As far as he could tell, the two yaba pills had done nothing. He pulled another from the baggie and inspected it closely. He had never taken yaba and knew nothing about it. He didn't even know what it looked like. He put his nose to the bag of pills and sniffed. For all he knew Meaw had bought him aspirin. The pot was real though. He could feel it.

He finished the Chang, tossed the bottle into the trashcan, and opened another. He took ten yaba pills from the baggie and set them in a row on the table top. They stared up at him as if wondering what he was waiting for. He picked them up in one handful, tossed them into his mouth, and washed them down with the beer. He would kick Meaw's ass if she had bought him sugar pills or aspirin.

He opened his Yahoo account, clicked on compose, and entered his sister's email address. "Hi, Carol," he typed, "I'm not coming home."

He reread the sentence to himself; not sure if it made sense or not. He continued, "Ever!"

That seemed too final. He deleted it, and wrote instead, "Josh is now part owner of a bar in Thailand and potentially a rich man. Make him keep the bar open through the high season. If he does that, I'll be eternally grateful. My attorney has the paperwork and will contact you soon. Someday you will understand."

He pushed the send button before saying he loved her, but it didn't make any difference. After tonight, nothing would. He finished the Chang.

He wasn't sure if it was the alcohol or the pot or the pills, but he was suddenly engulfed in a confusing haze of elation and sadness. His heart thumped like a jackhammer. He didn't know whether to laugh or cry or destroy everything in sight. And then the dizziness started.

He weaved his way to the desk, found a pen and paper, and wrote a note to Jarapan. It was short, yet it said everything. The important things in his life had narrowed to a pinpoint. He taped the note to the computer screen. On a post-it note he wrote and even shorter message, taped it to his hospital report, and put in the desk drawer. He glanced at his watch; it was getting late. He picked up his cigarettes and left the condo.

The security guard and the boy working the front desk were engrossed in some Thai comedy show on TV and barely acknowledged Mike as he passed through the lobby. He walked the half block to Beach Road and turned south.

Meaw at the Dockside Bar called to him as he stumbled past but he ignored her. Two blocks farther he turned left and headed east toward Second Road. At the far end of the soi stood a half-dozen beer bars. He had seen them before, but he had never stopped at any of them. No one would recognize him there. He took a seat and ordered a bottle of Mekong whiskey, no ice, no cola. He drank it by the glassful. His skin felt like it was crawling across his arms.

At first the bar girls tried to talk to him but stopped when he ordered the second bottle of Mekong. This time he didn't even bother with the glass. When it was empty, he put two five-hundred baht bills in the wooden cup with his tab and staggered away. His head reeled in perfect sync with his wobbling gait.

Nausea pushed the acrid taste of Beer Chang and Mekong into the back of his throat but he managed to swallow it down. He picked up his pace. He had to get to the Alcazar show before the buses left. He puked on the sidewalk as he reached Second Road. It seemed to clear his head a little but his body wasn't impressed. He nearly fell as he boarded a baht-bus heading north.

He swayed like a drunken sailor as the vehicle made its way up Second Road. The other passengers edged away from his drunken reeling. His attempt to smile ended with a burst of vomiting that splattered at his feet. A Thai woman pushed the buzzer for the driver to stop. Everyone except Mike left the baht-bus. The driver came back and screamed something unintelligible but clearly threatening.

Mike could see The Alcazar Show not far up the street. He handed the driver a hundred baht and staggered away to the sound of Thai curses at his back. It took less than two minutes to reach his planned position at the south end of the Big C Shopping Center.

Before long the first of a half-dozen buses exited Alcazar's parking lot. The smaller vehicles on the street yielded as the buses bullied their way into the traffic. Once on Second Road they roared north, daring anything or anyone to get in their way.

Mike's heart raced as the lead bus passed by. He made note of the space and time separating the first bus from the second. His plan was good. It would look like an accident and the insurance policy would pay. He tensed his muscles, ready to run. When the third bus was in position, he dashed toward the street.

Suddenly his thoughts became clear, as if his drunkenness didn't exist. At that instant his eyes were drawn to the front-end of the third bus in line. It looked like the face of death. By reflex he tried to stop his forward motion. By accident he stumbled and continued his headlong plunge. He fell hard on the rough concrete sidewalk and slid to the edge of the street. Bus number three passed without incident; it didn't even slow down.

He stood and looked at his hands, they were bleeding; his shirt was torn and stained. Someone shouted his name. He turned to look; it was Sunee, from Toy's Bar. He wiped his bloody palms on his jeans as he backed away. "I'm okay."

"You don't look okay. Here, let me see your hands."

"Stay away from me," he warned. "If you come close, I'll hurt you. Now get out of here."

Sunee stopped. "I thought we were friends."

"I have no friends." Mike turned and staggered down the

street.

He had never imagined that suicide would be so hard. Or maybe he was simply a coward. Visions of his father's death slithered through his head. He wondered how his father had found the strength to pull the trigger. He shook the vision away.

Jarapan was coming tomorrow. If he didn't kill himself, he would have to see her face-to-face. He couldn't hide like some rat. Or could he? He already knew he was a coward. Maybe he could hide somewhere, but then what? Tomorrow would come, and the day after that, too. He had AIDS and that wouldn't change. Since he didn't have the guts to take his own life, he would die a miserable death unless he took medication. The doctor had said there were treatments. His thoughts raced. Maybe Jarapan wasn't infected. She was pregnant with his child but that didn't mean anything; it wasn't the kiss of death. He had learned that much from the internet. Maybe she was okay.

When he realized he was walking in the opposite direction of his condo, he turned and headed back. Jarapan would be here tomorrow. He would talk to her, make her get tested, and tell her he was going to America for treatment. She could go with him if she wanted, or he would give her everything he had before he left. It would be enough to take care of her and his child for years. His thoughts flew as he made new plans for his future. Maybe she would forgive him.

When Mike turned to cross Second Road, he made the most basic of expat mistakes: he looked in the wrong direction for oncoming traffic and stepped into the path of a dull-blue baht-bus. He saw it in time to dive toward the hood of the vehicle. His head and body shattered the plate-glass windshield.

Chapter 45

On Saturday morning, before her flight left Khon Kaen, Jarapan phoned Mike but he didn't answer. She called again when she arrived at the bus terminal in Bangkok. Again he didn't answer. She glanced at her watch. If her bus left on time, she could be in Pattaya by three. She went to the boarding area.

The afternoon sun blazed and there was no breeze. Exhaust fumes hung acrid in the humid air. It was suffocating. A bus arriving from Phitsanulok parked at the gate next to hers. Even from five meters away she felt the cold air sweep out when the bus opened its doors. She took a few steps closer and reveled in the coolness. Ten minutes later she boarded her bus to Pattaya.

Traffic was thin and they made good time. As they neared the outskirts of Bangkok, the landscape changed from shops and tall buildings to factories and warehouses sprawled on huge pieces of land. In a while she closed her eyes and slipped into the surrealistic world that separates sleep from consciousness, thoughts from dreams. The events of the past few days played through her head. Her meeting with the scar-faced man, her trip to Phitsanulok, Mike being sick, and her visit to the doctor—the images swirled like dust-devils on a windy day.

Her brother's face entered her thoughts. She wondered if Purachai had really talked with her brother, or if he had only made up his story. She knew there were rumors circulating through Khon Kaen. Anyone could have said something about her. Maybe it was Purachai or maybe not. Maybe no one had said anything at all. Regardless of who had put the thoughts into her brother's head, she couldn't believe he had said them aloud in front of their mother and father. He wasn't the brightest candle in the temple, but he was smart enough to understand what he was doing and saying.

Now that her mother had confessed her affair with a farang, Jarapan understood her father's reaction. She wondered how long he had known about her mother's past romance, or if he had always known. In a city like Khon Kaen it would be impossible for him not to know at all. But one thing she knew for certain, her father would never accept Mike as part of their family. She wondered how he would react when he learned she was pregnant by a foreigner. She was sure it wouldn't be good.

Images of Mike drifted through her twilight sleep. She remembered their last conversation clearly. The tone of his voice still bothered her. He had sounded depressed, cold, lifeless. She could tell he wasn't well, even though he had said everything was fine. She would be at the condo and taking care of him in less than two hours. She prayed he would be happy when she told him she was pregnant with his baby. In a while she fell into a fitful asleep.

Jarapan awoke as the bus entered the Pattaya station. She glanced at her watch: it was four o'clock. After collecting her suitcase, she hired a baht-bus to the condo.

The traffic was light and she arrived in less than ten minutes. She paid the driver and went inside. The girl at the front desk was turned away, talking on the phone.

"My key, please," Jarapan said.

The girl looked up, confusion lined her face. "You cannot. There are policemen upstairs."

Jarapan blinked rapidly, trying to make sense of the girl's terse announcement. "What are you talking about? Do you mean in Mike's condo?"

The girl nodded, her eyes wide.

"How did they get in? What do they want? Is Mike there?"

"Mike left last night and didn't come home. The policemen said they wanted to look around. They didn't say why. I gave them the key."

Jarapan's heart fluttered painfully. Something was wrong, terribly wrong. "I'm going upstairs."

"I don't think it's allowed."

"I don't think you can stop me." Jarapan turned to face the security guard moving in her direction. "And neither can he. If he so much as comes close to me, you'll need more policemen. Maybe an ambulance, too."

Neither the front-desk girl nor the day-guard moved. She raced to the elevator, stepped inside, and pushed the button for the third floor.

Her thoughts ran wild as she hurried from the elevator to Mike's condo. The door was slightly ajar. She pushed it open and stepped inside. Uniformed men turned and looked.

"Are you Ms. Jarapan?" one officer asked. His eyes glanced at her suitcase.

"I am," she replied. "Where is Mike?"

The policeman didn't answer. Instead he pulled a picture from his shirt pocket. "Do you know this person?"

Jarapan looked. It was the scar-faced man. His eyes were closed but he didn't look like he was asleep. Why did the policeman have a picture of that man in his pocket? She wondered if he had hurt someone else. Suddenly the room felt hotter than before. "We have met, but I don't know him. Where is Mike?"

"I have a mystery, Ms. Jarapan. I'm hoping you can help me solve it."

Sweat formed on her upper lip. "What are you talking about? Where is Mike? Is he in some sort of trouble?" Jarapan felt a powerful urge to run but her legs wouldn't move. "How do you know my name?"

The officer fished an envelope from his back pocket. "This was addressed to you here, at this condo. I've read it already."

Jarapan took the envelope from his outstretched hand. She wanted to read it and not read it at the same time. Her fingers slipped the paper from inside. Her eyes focused on the writing.

TEARS FOR THE THAI GIRL

"Dear Ms. Jarapan—You are the nicest person I have ever met. I truly appreciate what you have done for me. My wife called and we talked. I talked with my son and daughter, too. It was the first time since they went away. I'm eternally indebted to you. My wife said she loved me but wouldn't take me back. She has petitioned for divorce. I'm sorry for any pain or sorrow I have caused. Thank you for forgiving me."

Jarapan looked up. "I don't understand what's going on. Why are you here? Where did you get that letter?"

"Like I said, I have a mystery. When was the last time you saw Mr. Johnson?"

Jarapan caught her breath at the officer's question. The hair raised on her arms. It took a moment before she could answer. "What are you asking? I didn't understand your question."

"Please, I mean nothing. You don't have answer if you don't want to, but we'll find out anyway."

"Find out what? You're confusing me."

The policeman only stared.

After a long silence she said, "I saw Mike on Monday, five days ago, before I went to my home in Khon Kaen."

The officer made a note. "Why did you go home? Were you and Mr. Johnson having problems? You know, a lover's quarrel or something?"

His question kicked her tension up a notch. "Mike and I never quarreled." It was a lie; they had even separated for few days less than a month ago. "Sometimes we argued, but we never quarreled. I went home for personal reasons."

The Lieutenant raised his eyebrows. The look on his face said he was ready to wait as long as it took her to explain her *personal reasons.*

After an uncomfortable moment, Jarapan related her story of *the incident* , her coming to Pattaya, and her recent meeting with the scar-faced man. As she talked, things started falling in place. Something bad had happened and it clearly involved the scar-faced man. But why were they asking about Mike? It didn't make sense. There was no connection. She felt an urgent need too make that clear. "Mike knows about the incident, but I never told him about seeing the scar-faced man in Pattaya. Mike was sick and I didn't want to bother him with that."

The policemen exchanged glances. "When was the last time you saw him? The scar-faced man, I mean."

Jarapan couldn't help but notice the change in the Lieutenant's voice. "On Monday, the same day I went home. What's going on? I don't understand any of this."

"The man was found dead yesterday afternoon. He hanged himself; at least that is the official cause of death. But he would have died from a drug overdose anyway. He was determined to die."

"Oh dear Buddha," Jarapan whispered. "You don't think I had anything to do with that, do you? Or Mike? "

"I'm sorry if it sounded that way. At first we thought maybe you or Mr. Johnson might have had something to do with the man's death, but now I don't. He left a note addressed to the police telling the same story. I wanted to make sure it wasn't coerced. Unfortunately I now have a new mystery." He pulled another picture from his pocket. "Do you know this man?"

Jarapan took the picture and looked. The face was too bloodied to recognize, but the tee-shirt was unmistakable. It was identical to the shirt Mike had specially made for himself just last week. *I Love Jarapan*, read the caption across the front. Her mind refused to accept what her eyes were telling her. "Why is this man wearing Mike's tee-shirt? Please tell me Mike is okay."

"I have one more thing for you to look at before we talk." He held a piece of paper in her direction. "I found this on the desk."

Her hand shook as she took the paper from his outstretched hand. "Where is Mike?"

"Read the note first, and then we'll talk."

Jarapan glanced down at the paper. *"My Dearest Jarapan,"* it began. Mike never talked like that. She looked up at the policeman; his face was emotionless, but his eyes were softly compassionate. Suddenly she felt shaky all over. Her universe turned surrealistic. Her feet seemed detached from her legs as she walked to the desk and sat in Mike's chair.

"My Dearest Jarapan." The paper trembled in her fingers. *"I fell in love with you the night we met at Toy's bar. Since then, I have been happier than I can remember. I once promised to love you until the day I die. If you're reading this, I guess I've kept my promise."*

Jarapan bit hard at her lip hoping the pain would stop the rush of emotions overtaking her senses. She looked up at the policemen. Desperation etched her face.

"That sounds like a suicide note to me, but maybe I'm wrong. Mr. Johnson is at the Bangkok-Pattaya Hospital. His condition is not good. Do you know how to contact his relatives? If you don't, we'll contact the U.S. Embassy. We have to decide what to do with Mr. Johnson."

Jarapan couldn't respond to his question. Images of Mike's bloody face and his *I Love Jarapan* tee-shirt etched her brain. *His condition is not good!* She knew that meant Mike was dying, or already dead. Her shallow breathing became huge gasps. She tried to stop doing that but she couldn't. She wanted to get up and run away but her legs wouldn't move. Her throat cramped and her composure disintegrated. She slumped across the desk and broke into gut wrenching wails of grief.

One officer started in her direction, then stopped and waited. In a while her sobbing waned to numb whimpers.

"We can give you a ride to the hospital."

"I can get there by myself," she whispered. "Please, can you go now? I want to be alone. I want to pray in private."

The policemen exchanged glances. One nodded, and they left her alone.

After the men had gone, Jarapan sat at the desk trying to make sense of everything that was happening. There was no sense to be found. Finally she stood and left the condo. Outside she hired a baht-bus to the hospital.

The lady at the front desk politely informed Jarapan that Mr. Johnson was in ICU and that no visitors were allowed except immediate family.

"I'm his wife," Jarapan lied.

The girl stared. "May I see your identification?"

"I'm carrying his child."

The girl's face softened. "Let me ask my boss."

A moment later Jarapan was escorted to the intensive care section of the hospital. They made her put on a surgical mask, cap, and robe before allowing her inside the room.

Mike's head was heavily bandaged. A tube dangled from his right arm. An oxygen mask covered his nose and mouth. He wasn't moving.

"Is he asleep?" Jarapan asked.

"He has been like this since he arrived last night," the attendant answered. "I heard the doctors say he has a severe concussion and broken bones. They have done tests but I haven't seen the results. I'm sorry, but I must ask you to leave now. My supervisor said you could only stay for a minute."

"Will he live?" Her voice caught on her own words.

"I don't know."

Tears flooded Jarapan's eyes. "Can I hold him?"

The attendant shook her head sadly. "Maybe tomorrow."

Jarapan nodded and left the room. Her body felt disconnected from her head as she rode the baht-bus home. Everything around her faded to shades of black and gray as her world crumbled away.

Jarapan shuffled through the deserted condo in a numb depression. The little knickknacks she had bought to make Mike's condo feel like a home sat where they always had. Old copies of the Bangkok Post, Pattaya Mail, and Pattaya Trader lay stacked beside the sofa. The TV was silent. The air conditioner hummed in the background. She reread Mike's note. The policeman was right, it did sound like someone who knew they were going to die very soon.

As she walked back toward the kitchen, a photo album protruding from the trashcan caught her attention. She hadn't noticed it before. She sat down and opened it to the first page. A picture of a young baby stared out. White hair and blue eyes, slightly chubby, smiling. In the background stood a house. Not large and beautiful as she imagined all American houses to be but plain, not much better than her own in Khon Kaen. Below someone had written, "Mike, 2 years old." The careful form of the letters said the writer had been Thai.

Mike's life passed before her eyes as she flipped through the pages of his album. She recognized the farang lady and young man as his deceased wife and his troubled son. She stopped cold when she saw an entire page of photos of Mike and a Thai woman. Below each picture, someone had described when and where it had been taken. Each was titled Mike and Math. She stared closely. The girl was the same one whose picture Mike had once kept on the bookshelf. The last pages in the album were filled with faxes and emails from Mike and an occasional picture of the girl Math, alone, without Mike.

By the time she closed the album her depression had grown to painful depths. She wanted to cry but she couldn't. It was as if she wasn't capable of crying more today. Suddenly she didn't want to be in the condo. She had to be on the move, and anywhere but here. She picked up her purse and went to the lobby.

The girl and the guard both stared but said nothing. Jarapan left the building and walked toward Beach Road. She had to tell Itta what had happened, in case she didn't know already.

"Hey," a man shouted as she neared the main street. She turned to look. It was the same farang who had been rude to her so long ago. "Come sit with this fat old bastard," the man laughed loudly. His face was ruddy, as if he were drunk or had been in the sun too long.

Jarapan started to say an English insult she had learned from

Mike but then decided the man wasn't worth her breath. She turned away and waved down an approaching baht-bus. Three minutes later she paid the driver and walked toward the Suaee Dee Lady.

Everything looked normal. Two sleek dressed hostesses stood outside encouraging passing farangs to come inside. The girls' expressions changed when they saw her. One went inside but was back before Jarapan reached the entrance. The unusual activity set her on edge more than she already was. Neither of the girls spoke as she stepped inside the Suaee Dee Lady.

The bar was packed, the music was loud, and the dancers were naked. Nudity wasn't allowed. If the police happened to come, the bar would be fined or even shut down. Her eyes scanned the room looking for Itta but she was nowhere to be seen. Ohm was there, near the cashier, looking apprehensive. Jarapan walked to her. "Where is Itta?"

Ohm shrugged. "Ms. Itta said she was leaving Pattaya. She told me I was in charge until Mike comes back." She glanced around the bar. "Look. We have more customers than ever. Are you happy?" Her nervous smile said she knew better than to even ask.

Jarapan didn't answer. Apparently Ohm knew nothing about Mike's accident. Jarapan considered telling her, but then decided it was better to say nothing. "Mike will not be happy if the police come."

Ohm's smile disappeared completely. She turned to one of the hostesses, "Tell the girls to put their work clothes on."

"Thank you," Jarapan said. "Did Itta say how she can be contacted?"

"Yes, I almost forgot. Follow me." Ohm led her to the office where she picked up a sealed envelope and handed it to Jarapan.

Jarapan felt like she was still with the policemen as she took the letter. Everything handed to her today had been bad news; she expected this one to be the same. To her surprise her hands were steady as she took the envelope, opened it, and read.

"Jarapan. I'm sorry to leave without telling you or saying

goodbye. Jon is going to America and has asked me to go with him. I have signed my ownership in the Suaee Dee Lady to you. Mike won't mind. Please contact Ms. Orapin at the phone number and address at the bottom of this letter. She will explain everything. I love you like a sister."

There was no date on the note. "When did Itta give you this?"

Ohm's smile disappeared completely. "Yesterday, just after we opened."

"Do you know her cell number? I must talk to her but I can't remember her number."

Ohm wrote it on the back of the envelope.

Jarapan picked up the phone on the desk and dialed. It rang a long time before someone answered. It wasn't Itta. "Who is this?"

"My name is Chalamsee," the voice on the other end said.

"Sorry, I must have dialed the wrong number." She held the envelope toward Ohm. "This isn't Itta's number."

Ohm looked. "It is, for sure. You must have dialed it wrong." She dialed the number and handed the phone to Jarapan.

"Hello."

It was the same woman who had answered before. Jarapan disconnected the call without saying anything. She looked at Ohm. "It still wasn't Itta."

"Maybe someone has stolen her phone."

Jarapan sighed. "I think you forgot the number, too. Call me at Mike's condo if you remember it later." She wrote Mike's number on a piece of paper. "I have Mike's cell phone, too. Call that if you want. Look, I've been awake for a long time and I'm exhausted. For now, you're still in charge. Make sure the girls keep their clothes on."

Jarapan went home and fell into a sleep filled with nightmares of death.

Chapter 46

Itta had spent that same afternoon at her sister's house in Phitsanulok. Nuang's young daughter was walking now and pried into everything she could find. The two women spent as much time chasing after little Tippawan as they did talking.

In a while Itta broached the subject foremost in her mind. "Do you remember Mike Johnson? You know, the American who loved our sister Math."

Nuang glanced at her daughter and blushed. "Yes, I remember."

"I never told you, but he and I went into business together."

"I know that already. Our brother Anan told me. He also said you lived together for a while, but now you don't."

"Anan has a big mouth. What else did he tell you?"

"That you are now living with another farang, the one who is taking you to America. I hope he's a good man."

"He is a good man," Itta said, remembering the way Jon still wanted her after learning about Mike's illness. "I know that much for sure. Let me show you a picture."

At that moment Itta's phone rang. "It's probably Jon," she said. "Hello," she spoke into the phone.

"Itta, it's me. You'll not believe this but your visa has been approved already. The big boss at the refinery helped. We can leave as soon as you come back to Bangkok to sign the paperwork."

"Thank you, teeluk. I'll be there in quickly time. I love you."

Itta turned to her sister. "That was Jon; I'm leaving for America very soon, maybe tomorrow. The main reason I came home was to talk to you about Mike Johnson."

Nuang tilted her head as if she didn't understand. "What are you talking about?"

Itta glanced at little Tippawan for a brief second, and then back at Nuang. "I don't have time to be anything but blunt. Mike is dying from AIDS, and I know the truth about you and Mike. I know what happened after our sister Math died. I know the truth about your daughter. You need to be tested Nuang; so does little Tippawan. I've been tested already and I'm okay. I'm sure you will be, too."

Nuang opened her mouth as if to say something but nothing came out. Finally she said, "I'll do it tomorrow. Please don't tell mama or Surat."

"I'm leaving here tonight." Itta held her cell phone toward Nuang. "You keep my handy, I won't need it anymore. I'll call you when I get to America. You will have your test results by then. Tell mama I had to do something for my American visa and didn't have time to visit." Itta reached over and took her sister by the hand. "Everything will be okay. When this is all done, I want you to come and visit me in America. Promise me you will, okay?"

Nuang only nodded.

"If Jon calls, tell him I'm on my way." She repeated the words slowly in English, and then turned and walked away.

Thoughts tore through Nuang's mind in mass confusion. Itta's short announcement and rapid departure set her on a downward spiral that she couldn't stop. She hadn't felt like this since she was pregnant with little Tippawan. The thought of her daughter found its way to the forefront. She had to make sure little Tippawan was safe. She felt disconnected from reality as she walked toward her daughter. The cell phone rang. Itta had told her to answer and tell Jon something, but the exact instructions eluded her.

"Hello," she said.

"Who is this?" The voice was female.

"My name is Chalamsee," Nuang answered using her proper

Thai name. Suddenly she remembered the English words Itta had said and spoke without thinking. "I'm on my way."

"Sorry, I must have dialed the wrong number." The connection went dead.

Nuang stared at the phone. Maybe it was a wrong number or maybe it wasn't. Maybe it was the voices. Before she had time to think the phone rang again. She looked at it as if it were something evil. By the third ring she decided she was overreacting. "Hello."

This time the phone disconnected without so much as a word. Now she was sure—it *was* the demons from her past and they were taunting her. She turned the phone off. Terror and depression surged through her and left overwhelming exhaustion in its wake. She had to lie down.

She forced herself to pick up little Tippawan and carried her into the house. She put her daughter into the playpen and then lay on the nearby sofa. Within seconds she fell into a fitful sleep.

Chapter 47

Early the next morning, Jarapan rode her motorcycle to the hospital and checked on Mike. His condition was the same. Afterwards she drove to the temple on Buddha hill and said prayers for his health. She knew it was bad luck to cry, but she cried anyway. She couldn't stop herself. Later she prayed for inner strength and guidance, but divine inspiration eluded her.

After leaving the temple, she drove aimlessly through streets of Jomtien Beach and Pattaya hoping that God or Buddha would tell her what she should do. In a while she remembered Itta's note about a woman named Orapin who would explain everything. She stopped at the next public phone and called the number. It was Sunday and she didn't expect an answer. To her surprise, a woman answered on the third ring.

"Hello, this is Orapin."

"My name is Jarapan. Ms. Itta said I should call you."

After a short silence the woman said, "Yes, where are you?"

"I'm in Pattaya, near the Royal Garden Plaza."

"You're not far from my office. I don't work on Sunday, but we need to talk. I'll meet you there in ten minutes. Do you have my address?"

"Yes, I have it. But can't you just tell me on the phone. I'm not feeling well."

"I'll explain everything when we meet."

It took Jarapan fifteen minutes to find Ms. Orapin's office. The woman was waiting when she arrived. She smiled politely as she escorted Jarapan inside.

"Would you like something to drink?" Ms. Orapin asked. "Water, cola, or a cup of tea?"

"No, thank you," Jarapan answered. "Please excuse me but I'm upset and not feeling well."

"Then you know?"

"How can I not know?"

"I'm sorry. Are you okay? Is there anything I can do?"

"Itta said you can explain everything. I need to know why Mike tried to kill himself."

Orapin jerked at Jarapan's statement. ""What do you mean, *Mike tried to kill himself*? When?"

"Night before last."

"Dear Buddha!" Orapin covered her mouth. Suddenly Mike's reason for changing his will became clear. "Where is he now?"

"He's in the hospital and he won't wake up."

"Are you okay?"

"How can I be? The man I love is in the hospital. He may die."

"Then you don't know, do you?"

"Know what?"

"That Mike has been sick."

"Yes, I know that. He was sick when I left Pattaya last week. I think he had the flu or something. "

"Please sit down." Orapin pointed at the chair in front of her desk. "I want to tell you a story. Probably one you've never heard."

Jarapan sat.

"I met Mike not long after he first came to Thailand. I've lost track of the years, but it was a long time ago. I had taken my staff out to celebrate a contract we had landed with a large company coming to the Hemaraj Estates in Chonburi. A mutual friend introduced Mike and I. We talked and I flirted with him, but he didn't respond. Still, we became friends. When he opened the Suaee Dee Lady, he called me and I took care of everything for little cost. Then just two days ago he came to see me for the first time in weeks. He seemed upset but didn't say anything was wrong. Itta came to see me later that same morning. She said Mike was very sick but that it wasn't the flu."

"He has cancer, doesn't he?"

Orapin sighed, took a deep breath and said, "Mike has AIDS."

Jarapan's emotions whipped from dark depression to hot neon panic. "I don't believe you. Mike doesn't go with bar girls and he isn't gay. He doesn't even do drugs except for beer and ganja once in a while." She remembered the times he went out in the afternoon but never said where he went. Could he have been short-timing the bar girls on Soi 6? Tears welled. "I'm pregnant with Mike's baby."

"Oh dear Buddha." Orapin knelt beside Jarapan. " I'm sure you'll be okay. I've read that AIDS isn't easy to catch."

"And I've heard that I may test negative today and positive years from now. I'm not okay and I'll never be okay." Jarapan broke into hard sobs, this time from the fear of her own death.

"I will pray your tests are negative." Orapin held Jarapan's hand until she had calmed. "You need to know," she finally continued, "If Mike dies for whatever reason, you'll be a very rich lady. Over twenty million baht."

Jarapan stared, dumbfounded. "What are you talking about?"

"Three days ago Mike came to see me. It was early in the morning and he didn't have an appointment. He came to make a will and to make you a beneficiary on his insurance. I knew something was wrong, but he said he only wanted to make sure someone he loved was taken care of in case anything ever happened."

Jarapan's emotions rippled from love and gratitude to hate and self-pity. The sensation left her numb. She felt as though she had just taken a step further from reality. "I'm leaving now."

"Have yourself tested."

"I will."

"Don't do anything stupid."

Jarapan didn't answer. She felt cold and brittle like cheap crystal. She started the motorcycle and drove home. When she walked through the condo lobby, the front desk attendant caught her attention. "I have a message for Khun Mike. I don't know what to do with it. Can I give it to you?"

Jarapan sighed. "You can throw it away," she said and continued her way to the elevator.

"Wait," the girl stopped her. "The man said it was important."

"Was he Thai or farang?"

"The man who delivered the message was Thai. He said he had been trying to call Khun Mike but there was no answer. He gave me the letter and said it was important."

"What did you tell him?"

"I said nothing. Should I have?"

"Never mind." Jarapan figured some bill collector had heard the news and was trying to collect money from Mike while he was still alive. She took the envelope from the girl and shoved it in her purse. She would throw it away after she found what was so *important*. Inside the elevator she opened the envelope. The note was handwritten in English but with a Thai tilt to the printing.

"Dear Mr. Johnson," it read, *"I have tried to call, but there was no answer. You need to know there is a mistake on your test. Please contact me immediately."* It was signed Dr. Phansak.

Jarapan's heart did flip-flops. Mistake? What in Buddha's name did that mean? The implications overwhelmed her. When the elevator doors opened, she raced to Mike's condo, sat at his desk, and read the note a hundred times. A mistake. On his test. What test? His AIDS test was her first thought. But it could be any of tests that doctors did. But how many would be important enough for a doctor to deliver a personal note?

She glanced at the desk-drawers. Mike was a pack rat and never threw anything away unless it was growing mold. She slid the top drawer open and looked at the papers. Nothing recent. The second drawer contained an envelope with the Bangkok-Pattaya Hospital logo in the corner. Hesitantly she picked it up and slipped the document from inside. There was a yellow post-it note stuck to the front. It was Mike's handwriting.

"I knew you would eventually find this report," it read. "It tells you everything I was too much of a coward to tell you in person. If you haven't been to see my attorney Ms. Orapin, do it tomorrow. That's the last thing I'll ever ask of you. I'm sorry Jarapan. I love you. Please forgive me."

Even before she read the report she knew what it would say. Her eyes scanned for what she knew was there. The words stood out as if embossed. "HIV Positive. AIDS Confirmed."

She threw the paper on the desk as if it were tainted with death. It landed next to the note from the doctor. *There is a mistake on your test*, the words jumped out at her. *MISTAKE ON YOUR TEST*. The emotional wall that had appeared earlier evaporated like a speck of water on hot asphalt. *AIDS CONFIRMED—MISTAKE ON YOUR TEST*. Her mind snapped when the two thoughts collided. Mike had tried to kill himself for nothing. There was no other explanation for the doctor's note. She was carrying Mike's baby. Her world turned surreal. She managed to stand and walk to the bed. She curled herself into a fetal ball and cried herself to sleep.

Jarapan felt terrible when she awoke. Her mouth was dry and her head throbbed. She forced herself out of the bed, went to the bath, splashed water across her face, and brushed her teeth. Afterwards she felt better, but not much. She knew she should eat but the thought of food made her stomach churn.

She went to the desk and picked up the phone. No dial tone. She traced the phone cord; it was unplugged. That explained why Mike had never answered her calls. She plugged it in and called the number on the doctor's note. It was answered by the Bangkok-Pattaya hospital. She asked for Dr. Phansak. A moment later he came on the line.

"My name is Jarapan. I'm calling about the note you left for my husband, Mr. Michael Johnson. What mistake are you talking about?"

"Thank you for calling," the doctor responded. "Could you put Mr. Johnson on the phone please?"

"I can't. My husband is in intensive care at your hospital."

"What? That isn't possible. He had pneumonia and I gave him medicine for that. How long has he been here?"

"Since Friday night. I thought you would know already."

"I only treat walk-in patients. That's my job."

"Your report said he had AIDS."

"It was a mistake. Not mine, but the laboratory in Bangkok. Michael Johnson is a common name. They got two reports mixed up. I found out just yesterday. What happened?"

Suddenly she was sick. She made it to the bathroom just as her vomiting began. She heard the phone ringing in the background but she didn't care. She hoped she would vomit herself to death.

Five minutes later her retching ended but she was still alive. She called Orapin and told her about everything. "Mike doesn't have AIDS, but he might die anyway. I don't know what to do."

"I've already contacted Mike's family," Orapin answered. "Come to my office tomorrow; there are things you need to know."

Chapter 48

It was ten o'clock on Sunday night when the phone rang. Josh had spent the day and most of the evening watching football, drinking beer, and smoking pot. He wasn't in the mood to talk to anyone. He glanced at the caller I.D.; it was Aunt Carol. Definitely he was too stoned to talk to her. It stopped on the fourth ring. Seconds later it rang again. This time the ringing continued until the answering machine kicked on.

"Joshua, if you are there, pick up the phone. I need to talk to you."

Except for her tone he would have ignored her. She sounded over the edge, like she was going through instant menopause or something. He picked up the receiver. "You woke me up Aunt Carol. Can you call back tomorrow? I'm really tired."

"No, this can't wait. Don't go anywhere; I'll be there in ten minutes."

The desperation in her voice shook him. His marijuana buzz disappeared leaving alcohol numbness in its wake. He rolled up the dope baggie and shoved it into his pocket. Then he pulled it out again, filled his one-hitter, and took a quick toke. If he had to deal with some female hormonal thing, he wanted to do it completely stoned.

A few minutes later Aunt Carol knocked and he opened the door. Her face was twisted as if in horrible pain. The skin around her eyes was red and puffy. She had been crying. He stepped aside to let her in. "Are you okay? You look like crap."

He didn't mean to be insulting or anything but she did look pretty bad. When she walked her motions were quick and jerky.

Her breath came in short gasps. When she opened her mouth to speak, nothing came out. Something was totally fucked up. Anxiety ripped through him like a dose of bad meth.

"Is Dad okay?" It was the first thought in his head.

When she opened her mouth again, it spewed out a moronic moan.

Josh took her by the shoulders and made her look at him. "Please tell me Dad is okay."

She moaned again but this time her words were perfectly clear. "Your daddy has been in an accident. He's in the hospital. The doctors say he could die at any time."

Josh's eyelids blinked rapidly. He felt himself freaking out and he couldn't stop it. "You're lying. Why are you saying that?"

Carol tried to respond but couldn't. Instead, she held out several sheets of paper. Josh read them in turn. He didn't know what to expect, but it was anything except what he saw. The first was an email from Dad. It was short and confusing.

"Josh is now part owner of a bar in Thailand and potentially a rich man," it read. *"Make him keep the bar open through the high season. If he does that, I'll be eternally grateful. My attorney has the paperwork and will contact you soon."*

The second was a fax from a place called the Bangkok-Pattaya Hospital; it was brutally blunt. *"Mr. Michael Johnson was admitted Friday night with a history of pedestrian/vehicle collision. The patient suffered a severe concussion but tests indicate no intra-cranial hemorrhage. Multiple fractures and lacerations were noted and treated. The patient is currently in a coma. He is on life support until further notice."*

The third paper was from the Pattaya Police. Most of it was written in Thai but with a few comments in English. One readable side note said "possible suicide". The words etched an indelible image in his brain.

The last was an email from someone named Orapin. *"I am Michael Johnson's attorney. It is important that his son comes to Pattaya as soon as possible. There has been an accident and the prognosis is not good. I have asked the hospital and the police to send you their official reports. There is much at stake here. Contact me with your arrival date."*

Waves of raw emotions assaulted his senses. His body throbbed like the rush of smoked crack as his sanity deserted him. It was someone else, who called Aunt Carol a mother-fucker. It was someone else who pushed her out of the apartment. It was someone else who went into a rage and destroyed his TV and his stereo and all of the things he loved most. It was someone else who cried like a baby for the man he had tried so hard to hate.

Josh vaguely remembered calling one of his suppliers and making a deal for more coke and meth than any one person could possibly need. The man had the stuff and Josh had the cash. The rest of the night passed in a blur of drugs and alcohol. The world as he knew it had ended with Aunt Carol's weeping announcement and the hideous notes. His father, the man who would never die, was already dead and didn't even know it.

Chapter 49

The 747 was huge. Narrow rows of coach class seats stretched from the end of the business section at the front to the community toilets in the rear. Josh Johnson had requested, and been assigned, an aisle seat. His dad had always talked about the advantages of an aisle seat, and for the first time in his life he had followed his father's advice.

His seatmate was an older gentleman, probably in his mid fifties. The man was neither fat nor thin, nor ugly or handsome. He was just average for his age. He seemed to know the flight attendants' routines better than they knew it themselves. The man ordered rum with a glass of orange juice, polished it off, then immediately ordered another. This one he sipped at a slower but still rapid pace. He seemed anxious yet relaxed. Josh wondered if he was a businessman or one of the sex tourists he had read about.

"Where are you headed?" Josh asked when the man looked in his direction.

"Thailand," the man answered, giving Josh a short inspection. "What about you?"

"Me too," Josh answered, deciding the man probably wasn't going to Thailand on business. "Have you been there before?"

The man smiled, "More times than I care to remember."

"I apologize for asking, but could you tell me about Thailand? What's it like? Any advice on how I should behave? Can you teach me a few words?"

"Are you going there on business or pleasure?"

Josh wondered what that had to do with anything. This wasn't a pleasure trip, but it wasn't exactly a business trip either. He considered telling the man the truth, then decided against it. "It's a business trip," he finally said. "I'm meeting some people in a place called Pattaya. Ever been there?"

"What's your name?"

"I'm Josh. What about you?"

"You can call me Carl. If you're going there on business, I do have advice. Dress the best you can. Thais put a lot of stock in a man's appearance and personal presentation. Be confident but not smug. Smile a lot and tip well. If you take someone to dinner, make it a class restaurant. It may cost you more but it will gain you a lot of respect. Businessmen in Thailand have a fixation with class."

"So do a lot of people in Pittsburgh."

Carl laughed. "Same in Cincinnati. But there are things you shouldn't do, too. Never lose your cool, no matter how pissed off you get. If you do lose your temper for whatever reason, just walk away."

"You mean Thais never get pissed off?"

"I didn't say that. They get just as pissed as anyone; they just don't let it show as much as you and I might. It's a cultural thing or something. But if they're pushed too far, they explode, and it's usually when you least expect it. Don't put yourself into a position where you might become the focus of their outburst, if you understand what I mean."

"I've been around the block once or twice; I know when to be cool."

"That's good, but being cool in Pittsburgh isn't the same as being cool in Thailand."

"What does that mean?"

"Do you speak Thai?"

"Well, no. I speak some Spanish though."

"That won't help you much in Thailand."

"Is it important?"

"It depends on your perspective. Sometimes it's nice to know what they really think of you; sometimes it's not. But since you can't speak Thai, just remember this: they don't think the same way you think, and they're skilled liars. I think they must teach that in school or something."

Josh smiled, "I'm a pretty skilled liar, too."

"But the Thais are experts. Don't ever forget it." He didn't return the smile.

"Sounds serious."

"I don't mean to make it sound bad. I love Thailand and so will you; but only when you understand that you'll never understand a Thai."

Josh just stared. "Could you say that again?"

The man laughed, "Probably not."

A stewardess came by with earphones. Carl plugged his in and their conversation ended.

Josh mused over what the man had said. Skilled liars had nothing on him. He could bullshit with the best of them. And he could spot another bullshitter a mile away, at least he could in Pittsburgh. But how does one spot a bullshitter in Thailand, especially if they're all accomplished liars and they aren't even speaking English? The concept made him uncomfortable.

Josh read for a while, watched the in-flight movies for a while, and then slept for a while. Then he woke up and did it all over again. Outside stayed daylight, even when his watch said it was nighttime in Pittsburgh. He imagined they were chasing the sun across the Pacific. It was early evening when they arrived in Tokyo. Carl had slept through the entire trip.

Narita International Airport was modern to the point of making the Pittsburgh and Detroit terminals look antiquated. It was also security minded. The Japanese even made the deplaning passengers go through a security check. Considering recent world events, he wasn't surprised.

Inside the terminal was a mass of humanity like he had never seen. Languages he couldn't identify drifted through the air. People of every race wandered to-and-fro. There were more Asians than not. He moved through the crowd like an awestruck kid at his first circus. He nearly jumped from his skin when he felt a hand on his shoulder. He turned to see Carl.

"I can get us into the Executive Lounge. If you're old enough, I'll buy you a beer."

Josh blushed, "I'm twenty-two. You can buy me all the beer you want. Do you mind if I smoke?"

"I would mind if you didn't." Carl patted his shirt pocket. "Come on, there's a smoking room on the way."

The executive lounge was remarkably empty compared to the main terminal. Carl pointed him to a seat and then went to get them beers. In a minute he returned with drinks in hand, "Are you staying the night in Bangkok?"

Josh shook his head. "I have a hotel reservation in Pattaya."

"Never mind then. I just thought maybe we could share a taxi fare into downtown, that's all. I don't mean to pry, but what sort of business do you have in Pattaya?"

"Personal business."

Carl was quiet for a minute and then said, "Me too."

"How did you manage to sleep all the way to Tokyo?" Josh changed the subject.

"Just lucky, I guess. That plus the fact that I went on Thailand time a few days ago. It was past my bedtime before we boarded the flight in Detroit. I doubt I'll sleep much from here to Bangkok, though. What about you? Did you get any shut-eye?"

"I got something, but I don't think it can be classified as sleep."

Carl smiled. "You'll do better on the way to Bangkok." He pointed toward the restrooms, "I'm going to clean up. See you at the gate." He stood and walked away.

Josh waited a minute then followed Carl to the restroom. Carl must have been in one of the stalls because he was nowhere to be seen. Josh relieved himself, splashed some water on his face, and then left the Executive Lounge. He made an entire circuit of the terminal before finding his gate. The plane wouldn't board for another thirty minutes but the area was already jammed with passengers.

He passed the time guessing where the other travelers were from and where they were going. A couple of younger women caught his attention. They were Asian and they were very attractive. One of the girls noticed him staring and smiled. He wasn't sure how to react, so he turned away.

Carl arrived clean shaved and in fresh clothes. "I feel like a new man," he said.

Josh wished he had thought to bring shaving gear and a change of clothes. He hadn't even brought a carry-on bag. He sniffed casually at his armpits. "Do you suppose I could borrow your deodorant?"

Carl laughed, "Sure, why not? You may be sitting next to me on the flight to Bangkok." He pulled the deodorant from his bag and handed it to Josh. "By the way, what seat are you in."

Josh glanced at his boarding pass. "57-C. What about you?"

"I'm in 52-D, but I hope the deodorant works anyway." He pointed in the direction of the two women Josh had been ogling. "Maybe you'll have one of those girls for a seatmate this time."

"Fat chance of that happening. I'm not that lucky. No offense intended, but you see what I got for a seatmate the last time."

The terminal P.A. system came to life and a female voice made an announcement.

"That's us," Carl said.

Josh assumed the lady on the loudspeaker had spoken English, but he hadn't understood a word. He shuffled forward behind Carl, securing their place in line. As expected, he didn't sit next to either of the girls. The man who sat next to him was heavyset and overflowed his allotted space. Josh's narrow coach seat became even narrower. He hoped he would be able to sleep; otherwise it would be a very long flight.

Once they reached cruising altitude, the stewardesses handed out Thailand immigration and customs forms. Josh decided to fill them out right away in case he made a mistake and had to do them over again. It was a good decision because he managed to screw up the immigration form twice before he got it right.

Satisfied his papers were correct, Josh leaned his seat back, made himself comfortable, and was asleep in minutes. He remembered being awakened from time to time by stewardesses and passengers moving up and down the aisle, but mostly he slept.

When Josh awoke, the TV monitor was showing the general position of plane as it neared the Bangkok airport. Head winds, ground speed, and altitude were displayed in miles and kilometers, meters and feet. From his seat he couldn't see the ground except for an occasional short glimpse when the plane banked toward its assigned landing pattern. The expanse of sparkling lights spread for miles. He had read on the internet that more than ten million people lived in Bangkok. He saw no reason to doubt that statistic.

His ears refused to clear as they descended. He tried chewing gum, swallowing repeatedly, and everything else he could think of, but the pressure in his ears continued to build. He wasn't sure if his eardrums would implode or explode, but he was sure it would be one or the other—and that it would happen at any second. By some miracle his eardrums remained intact but the pain was excruciating. He could see people's lips moving but he couldn't hear a word they said. He wondered if his deafness would be permanent. His ears finally cleared with a series of squeals and pops just as the plane touched down in Bangkok. The relief was immediate.

When they arrived at their gate, passengers filled the aisles, anxious to be off the plane. Josh wanted to be off of the plane too, but there was no room to stand. Ahead he saw Carl pulling his carry-on from the overhead compartment. He hoped Carl would look in his direction, but he didn't. A few minutes later the crowd began shuffling single-file toward the exit. Josh stood and followed the others.

The first thing he noticed when he stepped into the terminal corridor was the smell of the air. It was neither bad nor good, but it was so distinctive that he knew he would never forget it. He wondered if all of Thailand smelled like that.

He trudged along with the other passengers as they followed the signs pointing toward Immigration Control. Five minutes later they entered an open area with long lines of travelers waiting to be processed by immigration officers. Josh picked a line at random and waited his turn. Twenty minutes he was taking the escalator down to baggage claim. Carl was waiting at the bottom.

"I'll be in Pattaya in a couple of days," he said. "Where are you staying? Maybe I'll look you up and you can buy me a beer."

"A hotel called the Amari or something like that. I have it written down in my suitcase."

"Must be the Amalee," Carl corrected his pronunciation. "Nice enough place. It's at the north end of Pattaya, near the Dolphin roundabout. I'll be staying there too. What's your last name? So I know who to ask for."

"Yeah, I guess that would help. It's Johnson, Josh Johnson. I'm not sure how long I'll be in Pattaya, but I'll buy you a beer if I see you."

"I never pass up a free beer," Carl winked. "Hey, there's my suitcase." He snatched it from the carrousel. "Look, I have to go. I want to get to downtown Bangkok before the bars close. A couple of beers will help me sleep."

Josh smiled, "I don't think I'll need anything to help me sleep."

"Don't forget what I told you about the Thais. Everything goes double for the bar girls." He turned and headed toward the customs checkpoint.

As Josh watched Carl disappear through the doorway, it dawned on him just how little he knew about surviving in this alien world. He wasn't even sure how to catch a taxi to Pattaya. In a minute his suitcase arrived and he passed through customs unsearched.

The official greeting area had barriers to separate incoming passengers from the people who had come to meet them. Some greeters held up signs with names printed in bold script. There were a couple of money changers and several places to hire a car with driver. Outside, through a glass wall, he could see a line-up of taxis waiting for a fare. He exchanged 200 US dollars for Thai baht. He wasn't sure how much he would need, but figured that would be enough.

He inspected the wad of Thai currency for a second, and then stuffed it into his wallet and walked outside. He didn't go directly to the taxis. Instead he stood on the concrete ramp just outside the doors. Below him two Thai men spoke loud enough for him to hear. To Josh it was melodic gibberish. What Carl had said came back to him. *"Sometimes it's nice to know what they really think of you; sometimes it's not. But since you can't speak Thai, just remember this: they don't think the same way you think, and they're skilled liars. I think they must teach that in school or something."*

Josh put on his most confident street smile and walked down the ramp to the sidewalk. Immediately a young woman approached him. She held an official-looking clipboard in hand. "You like taxi, sir?" she smiled wide.

Sir? No one ever called him *sir*. "You speak English?"

"Nit noy," was her reply.

"Huh?"

"I speak English nit noy, a little bit. You like taxi? Yes?"

This seemed almost too easy. "How much to Pattaya?"

"What name hotel, sir?"

He unzipped a pocket in his suitcase, pulled out a piece of paper and held it in her direction. "You can call me Josh."

"Okay, sir. Taxi to the Amalee is twelve hundred baht. Waiting line there."

Josh looked where she pointed; the line was long—probably thirty people or more ahead of him.

"Or," the girl continued, "You can ride Mercedes. Only four hundred baht more. Nit noy money."

He almost laughed at the way her statement sounded, but checked his urge to ask which girl was Mercedes. He did a quick calculation: Four hundred baht was about twelve dollars, chump change, nit noy money. "You sweet-talked me into it." A minute later he was on his way.

Josh was tired but sleep wasn't possible. They were on a freeway of sorts, but nothing like the ones in America. Speeding, tailgating, and sudden lane changes were the rules of the road. He had read about the notorious Bangkok traffic jams, but tonight they passed southward through the city unimpeded and at frightening speeds.

He wasn't sure what he had expected of Bangkok but he was surprised by what he saw. High-rise buildings and prominent hotels pierced the night sky. Oversized billboards advertised everything from electronics to automobiles. City lights sparkled as far as he could see. If he didn't know where he was, he would never have guessed Thailand.

Forty minutes after leaving the airport, the traffic thinned and the tall buildings were left behind. They were still on a freeway but on the far south side of the city. Here the highway was lined with a hodgepodge of roadside shops, restaurants, and light industrial complexes. Here, twixt neoteric Bangkok and rural Thailand, existed a society that was neither third-world nor first. Here, modern conveniences rubbed elbows with ancient customs. Josh was mesmerized by the world sliding past.

In a while the taxi driver stopped to refuel at a combination gas station and convenient store. A young girl came to the car, spoke briefly with his driver, then proceeded to pump gas. The driver exited the car and motioned for Josh to follow.

For the first time since landing in Thailand, Josh was about to step forth into this strange world of odd sights and even odder smells. He wasn't sure if it was from excitement or nervousness but he felt giddy. He opened the door and slid out of the taxi.

"Hong nam," the driver said pointing.

"What?" Josh asked.

"Him say toilet," the young gas attendant said. "Him say toilet over there."

Josh stared at the girl. He had understood her. "You speak English very good," he said.

The girl smiled, "Khop khun mak ka. Thank you. You speak English good too."

He didn't know what to say in response so he turned away and followed the taxi driver toward the *hong nam*. He smiled to himself. He had learned another Thai word and it was a useful one.

Josh had assumed the toilets would be western style with individual urinals and sit down commodes. He was wrong. The urinal was a tile-lined trough jutting from the back of the building. It was under cover, but still outside. His driver smiled as Josh rounded the corner of the building. At the end of the urinal was a doorway. He headed there figuring maybe he would do more than take a leak. To his distress there were no western conveniences. Instead there were squat toilets with footrests on both sides and a hole in the middle. Josh considered his urgency for a moment before deciding he could wait until Pattaya to do anything that required lowering his jeans. Surely the hotels in Pattaya would have western style bathrooms. He drained his bladder and headed back to the taxi.

The girl had finished pumping gas and was chatting with her co-worker. The two girls stared and whispered behind hands as he approached. "Khun cheur alai na?" the co-worker said.

Josh looked in their direction wishing he knew more Thai words than toilet. He shrugged and continued toward the taxi.

"She say what you name," the pump attendant smiled.

Josh allowed himself to smile back. He looked at her friend. "My name is Josh. What's your name?"

The girl didn't speak.

"She name Malee," the first girl answered. "She shy too much."

The co-worker stood up and hurried away, covering her face and giggling as she ran.

Josh wanted to laugh, but he wasn't sure if it would be impolite or not. He took the safe route. "I'm shy too." He slipped back into the safety of the taxi.

A moment later the driver returned and they continued their journey to Pattaya.

The shops and buildings grew sparser as they moved farther south of Bangkok. Long spans of countryside were interrupted with occasional towns and villages. All were asleep for the night. Road-signs, written in both Thai and English, noted their progress.

His heart raced when he saw a sign proclaiming Pattaya to be twenty kilometers away. He sat erect and paid attention as the first lights of civilization appeared. From everything he had read on the internet, Pattaya was going to blow him away. Party central, one man had posted. Disneyland for adults was another man's take. Whatever it turned out to be, Josh wanted to be ready.

Pattaya turned out to be a bust. The taxi moved through the northern part of the city without passing a single westerner. He saw a couple of places that could be outside bars, but they were mostly empty and the few customers were Thai. He didn't see anything but Asians until minutes before they steered into the Amari Orchid Hotel.

Josh settled his debt with the driver and then gave him a two hundred baht tip. The way the man bowed and scraped made Josh wonder if he had given him too much. He nodded at the man's gratitude and entered the hotel lobby.

His dad had stayed at the Amari; Aunt Carol had told him that much. Josh wondered if his father had known any of the employees, or if they knew him. The idea that he might meet some of his dad's friends unnerved him. What would he say if they asked how his father was? More than that, how would they react when he told them? Maybe they knew already. If they didn't say anything, neither would he.

To his left was the hotel lounge. Two men sat talking but no one was behind the bar. To his right was the reception desk. He headed in that direction.

"Sawasdee ka," the receptionist said.

Josh recognized the word from the magazine he had read on the airplane. She was telling him hello. "Hello. I'm Josh Johnson. I have reservations."

"May I see your passport, please?" The girl smiled.

"Oh, yeah, of course." Josh slipped it from his hip pocket.

She keyed his passport data into her computer then flipped to the form the immigration man had stapled to one of the pages. She entered that number as well. Big brother is watching you, he thought.

In a minute she looked up. Her smile stayed in place but her expression had changed. "We have expected you. We hope you have nice holiday." She motioned to someone behind him. "Boy show you room."

Carl's parting remark about having a beer to relax entered his mind. "Is the lounge still open?"

"Bar close already. You want something drink? Maybe can get from kitchen."

"A beer would be nice."

The receptionist's smile brightened. "Have cold beer in room already. We think everything for guests. "

Josh looked back at the bellboy and smiled. "Okay Jose, I'm ready whenever you are."

As he moved from the counter, the girl said, "I give you a special room. Have pleasant dreams."

The room was nice, but he was too tired to appreciate anything except a hot shower, a cold beer, and a soft bed. He was asleep as soon as his head hit the pillow.

~~~

In Bangkok, Carl mulled over his conversation with the young man named Josh Johnson as he rode in the taxi from the airport to his hotel. It crossed his mind that the kid could be a relative of his friend Mike, but he doubted it. More likely it was just a coincidence. For all he knew half of the plane passengers were named Johnson. He would be in Pattaya in couple of days and he would look up young Mr. Johnson. His curiosity could wait that long.

After checking into his room, he called the Amari and told the girl on duty that she had a special guest coming, Mike Johnson's son. He instructed her to give him the best room she had and to put a few extra beers in the mini bar. She knew Mike and was happy to comply. Maybe the kid wasn't Mike's son, but at least he would get treated like something special.

Carl went to the nearest beer bar and forgot about Mike and the kid.

Chapter 50

Jarapan lay in bed waiting for sleep that wouldn't come. Today she had gone through the motions of living the same as she had every day since returning to Pattaya. As always, her first stop had been to see Mike. Nothing had changed except that he was out of intensive care. He was still on life support for liquids and nourishment, but he breathed on his own and he wasn't brain dead. He was asleep. Afterwards she had gone to the temple and prayed he would wake up. Her praying had been useless so far, but it was the only hope she had left.

The rest of the day had been normal until five o'clock when Ms. Orapin called to inform her that Mike's son Josh was traveling to Thailand today. She didn't know if he was spending the night in Bangkok or coming directly to Pattaya. She didn't even know where he was staying. From what Mike had said, his son Josh had an attitude problem and drug problems as well.

Jarapan wondered what sort of person he was really like. Would he make sure his father had the best of treatment, or would he order the life support turned off out of spite for the past? And what would Josh think of her? Would he be able accept that his father had fallen in love with a woman young enough to be his daughter, and that she had fallen in love with him? She knew what some thought of Thai women with farangs, but it wasn't like that for her and Mike. They really did love each other.

At that moment a new thought entered her head; she was pregnant with Mike's child. She wondered how his son would react to that. A dozen scenes flashed through her head and none of them were happy. She feared what the coming days would bring.

Chapter 51

Josh awoke at six o'clock in the morning. His head was fuzzy with exhaustion but he couldn't force himself back to sleep. He finally got out of bed after twenty minutes of pretending he would eventually doze back off.

He stumbled his way to the bathroom and splashed cold water across his face and eyes. It helped some but not much. He felt like the shitty tail end of a three day binge. It was going to take more than a little cold water to shake this dog. He turned on the shower, adjusted the taps, and stepped inside. The water shifted from hot to cold several times before he managed to get himself clean.

After shaving he brushed his teeth using the bottled water provided by the hotel. He had read on the internet that the tap water wasn't fit to drink and he didn't want to take any chances that the article was only being cautious. He rinsed his mouth with Listerine just to be safe.

At seven-thirty he went to the free breakfast buffet included with his hotel package. The fruits looked delicious but he figured they weren't much safer than the tap water. There were lots of unidentifiable Asian dishes that didn't look much like breakfast and smelled like things he wouldn't eat even if they were. One short row of tables held pans of runny scrambled eggs, half cooked bacon, and sausages that looked more like miniature wieners than Jimmy Dean's finest. Eventually he settled on toast without butter or jam. He figured he would starve to death if he stayed in Thailand more than a few days. He intended to do neither. He would take care of business and then he would leave.

He nibbled at his dry toast and gazed about the restaurant at the others who had come for breakfast. There were a handful of Asians, but mostly they were westerners. The few voices he heard weren't speaking English—not American English anyway. The whole situation made him uncomfortable. Here he was, ten thousand miles from home, in a world that was nothing like he had just left, and he was a minority. For all he knew he was the only American for miles. Finished eating, he went back to his room and reviewed his plans.

His first stop would be the hospital. Images of Dad flashed across his mind. Not real memories but photos from the past, the last being a Thai woman kissing Dad on the cheek. But as hard as he tried, he couldn't picture his dad lying in a coma. He wanted to see his father, yet he dreaded what he would find.

His second stop would be the attorney who had contacted Aunt Carol after Dad's accident. Her name was Ms. Orapin. Her emails had been polite but terse. She was the executrix of his father's will in the event of death. Before leaving Pittsburgh he had sent an email telling her he was on his way to Thailand and that he would come to her office as soon as he arrived.

His last stop was to be the police headquarters. The reports he and Aunt Carol had received from the Thai police stated facts, but with an unsettling side note. In the end he and Aunt Carol had decided that the only way to learn the facts was to be there in person. He glanced at his watch. It was eight-thirty. He looked at his schedule: Hospital, attorney, police. There seemed no reason he had to go in that order. Josh left his room.

"I want to hire a taxi," he told the girl at the front desk.

She conferred briefly with another worker. "It will be here right away, sir. You can sit there and wait." She pointed to the wicker chairs and sofas between the front desk and the hotel exit. Paddle-fans whirled overhead.

Josh took a seat and waited. He picked up a worn Thai-English phrase book laying on the end table and scanned through the pages. He learned that the prayer-like bow people were making was called a wai, and that coon was really *khun* and was a polite form of address or the word *you*, depending on when or how it was used. He also learned that *mai pen rai* meant *never mind*, and that *mai khow chai* meant *I don't understand*. He filed the phrases away for future use.

His taxi arrived within ten minutes. The driver spoke little English but he carried a rate chart which he handed to Josh. It listed a lot of tourist's attractions and rates by the hour, the day, and half day. Josh pointed at the half day rate and the driver nodded his agreement. He handed the man a piece of paper listing the names and addresses of the three places he wanted to go to. He pointed at the hospital.

The man stared at the paper for a long second. Finally he looked up, "No read English."

Josh took the paper to the reception desk and handed it to one of the girls. In a minute she had written the words in Thai script. The driver smiled. "Okay, we go now."

As far as Josh could tell, the taxi was heading away from the main part of town, but since he had no idea where he was, he couldn't be sure. He saw a lot of Thais but only few Westerners. Smoke-spewing motorcycles and small blue pick-up trucks seemed to be the main forms of transportation. He saw motorcycles carrying entire families and small pick-ups loaded with more people than seemed safe, or even possible. He was glad he was inside the taxi and not on one of the motorcycles or overfilled trucks. As often as not, the locals would stare at him through the taxi's windows as he passed by. He wondered what they thought. Probably they had seen enough foreigners that he wasn't a novelty.

The drive to the hospital took less than ten minutes. Explaining who he was and why he was there took twice as long. After a lot of hand gestures he was escorted to his father's room.

Dad lay motionless. Wires were attached to his arms and chest. A tube snaked from his nose. A heart monitor beeped at regular intervals. The sheet rose and fell at each breath. Any casual observer would think he was only asleep.

"Dad?" Josh stared at the profusion of stitches and scabs that crisscrossed the right side of his dad's face. He reached out and touched his shoulder. "It's me, Josh."

His father didn't respond.

"You can wake up now. Your joke isn't funny anymore."

A zillion thoughts raced through his head. He couldn't count the number of times that Dad had asked him to grow up and start acting like a man instead of a punk teenager. *Give me just one year of peace before I die*, his father had begged a thousand times. Josh remembered telling his friends about that and laughing. He had always known that Dad would live to be an old man, and that he would give him one good year long before either of them died. His lifestyle had nothing to do with Dad. It had to do with fast highs and faster women. Any man could understand that. He struggled with his emotions for a few minutes and then left the hospital. The taxi drove to the police station.

The policemen were polite enough, but not in any great hurry. Eventually an officer handed him the same document that had been sent to his Aunt Carol. "Pedestrian/Vehicle Accident," was the official explanation. "Possible suicide attempt," the side note read. That side note was the main reason Josh had come to this third-world dump.

"What does *possible suicide attempt* mean?" Josh asked.

"The letter your father left for a woman named Jarapan. The investigating officers reported that it sounded like a suicide note."

"Can I read it? I want to see what he wrote. I want to make sure it's his handwriting."

The police officer stiffened; his polite smile hardened. "We don't have it on file."

Josh started to say something about their incompetence but bit his tongue. "Do you know where I can find this Jarapan person?"

"I'm sorry sir, but I do not. We have more important things to do than track every woman named Jarapan. We do know she had nothing to do with your father's accident. She wasn't in Pattaya when it happened. That has been confirmed. We have investigated this thoroughly, Mr. Johnson."

"Yes, of course," Josh responded. From what he had learned in his research, the death of a foreigner meant little in Thailand as long as it was anything except obvious murder. He crumpled the report and tossed it into a nearby trashcan.

The officer frowned. "Will you be staying long, Mr. Johnson?" His tone was curt and he didn't use the word *khun*.

Never lose your cool in Thailand, Carl's words echoed through his head. "No longer than I have to," he smiled.

"Please enjoy your stay in Pattaya," the policeman didn't smile back.

Josh nodded and walked away. The taxi was waiting outside.

The drive to the attorney's office took just over five minutes. He hadn't made an appointment for a specific time, but he figured it didn't matter. The lawyer knew he was arriving today. The driver waited in the taxi while Josh went inside.

The office was stark, but tastefully so. Beach scene paintings hung on two of the walls of the reception area, and a blown-up picture of Pattaya as seen from someplace high hung on the third. The fourth wall was taken up by the reception desk and a door to the inner offices. The woman at the desk looked up when he entered. "Sawasdee ka. May I help you?" she asked.

He unfolded a piece of paper and slid it toward her. "I'm here to see this person."

The girl scanned the paper. "You name what?"

"Josh Johnson."

"Oh, Mr. Johnson. Ms. Orapin not here. She leave letter for you." She pulled a paper from her in-basket.

He took the note and read, "Dear Mr. Johnson, I'm very sorry, but due to a personal situation I will be unavailable for a day or two. Please leave your phone number so I can call you when I return; we have important matters to discuss. Until I come back, take some time to learn about Thailand. That will make your father happy."

Her written English was perfectly clear, but in effect the note said nothing. He slipped a pen from his pocket and wrote at the bottom, *I'm staying at the Amari Orchid Hotel. I don't know the phone number*. He handed it back to the girl. "Tell your boss to call me as soon as possible."

He turned and walked away. This wasn't happening at all like he had planned. He had figured the attorney was his best chance of learning the truth about the side-comment on the police report, but she wasn't here and might not contact him for days. The schedule he had planned was going to shit.

Back outside he slipped into the rear seat of the taxi. The driver turned and said, "Bai nai?"

Josh had no idea what the man had said, but assumed he was asking *What now?* or something to that effect. "Amahlee," he mimicked the Thai pronunciation he had heard earlier. The driver pulled away from the curb and headed back from whence they had come.

At the hotel, Josh paid the driver the agreed rate. He had used the taxi for less than two hours but paid for half a day. He would have bargained with the man for the hourly rate but he didn't know how. It was easier to just pay and forget about it.

Josh stood inside the open air lobby of the hotel deciding what he would do with the rest of his day. Even in the shade and with fans twirling overhead, the heat and humidity were stifling. It took less than a second to decide to go to his room while he made up his mind. At least it would be cooler there.

When he'd left his room earlier that morning, it didn't occur to him that the oversized key-chain might also be the device that turned the air conditioner on and off. His room was almost as hot as the lobby. He slid the key handle into its slot and the air conditioning came to life. The maid, he noticed, had come and gone in his absence. The bed had been made, there were fresh towels in the bathroom, and the mini-bar's refrigerator had been restocked with beer and water.

He took a beer from the fridge and then propped himself on the bed. It wasn't yet noon and too early to be drinking, but his body felt like it was midnight regardless of what the clock said. He fell asleep before the beer was empty.

Chapter 52

Josh was awakened by a soft knock at the door and the sound of a lock being opened. He jerked upright, confused by his surroundings.

"Sawasdee ka," a female voice came from the doorway. "Excuse please. I have fresh fruit for you."

"Never mind," he said, remembering where he was. "I was only resting my eyes."

A slender young woman entered the room, sat a plate of fruit on the small table, and headed back toward the door. Before leaving she put her hands together in prayer-like fashion and brought them to her face. "Thank you sir. Goodbye sir."

He recognized the gesture, it was a *wai*. He smiled and nodded in return. The girl pulled the door closed behind her.

He tried to go back to sleep but couldn't. Finally he got up and inspected fruit. He didn't recognize any of it except one stubby banana and an undersized orange. He was hungry, but not hungry enough to eat anything that hadn't been cooked well-done.

He picked up his half-finished beer, pushed back the curtain, and looked outside. The midday sun beat down on the gray sidewalks and black asphalt streets. Shimmering waves of heat radiated upward engulfing everything less than three meters tall. Local Thais and foreign tourists passed back and forth in front of the hotel at lumbering paces. Cars, trucks, and motorcycles moved along the street in synchronized disorganization. Palm trees, bushes, and bright flowers formed intricate patterns across the hotel lawn. He dropped his hand and let the curtain fall back into place.

He looked around the room as if seeing it for the first time. It was actually very nice—Ritz luxury at Holiday Inn prices. If nothing else, the Thais did their hotels right. Free fruit plates, orchids on the pillows, and other little things that meant more than they cost. The little trick they did with the air conditioner wasn't too cool though. Yeah, definitely not cool. He smiled at his own inane pun.

He turned on the television but found nothing understandable except an English news channel. He wasn't in the mood to listen to talking heads bashing America so he switched to a Thai music station. He had no idea what the words meant, but the girl singers were cute and that he understood quite well.

Memories of his visit to the police station crept through his head. *Accident. Possible suicide attempt.* From what he had read on the internet, those seemed to be the standard police explanation for the death of any foreigner in Thailand, unless a heart attack or some such thing was more convenient.

A letter that no longer existed—unconfirmed suspicions. Josh supposed it was possible his dad had tried to kill himself, but it didn't seem likely. His dad wouldn't just wake up one day and decide to end his own life. At the same time, Dad wasn't a careless type of person who would accidentally walk into the path of something as large as a truck, either. If it had been on purpose, there had to be a reason, and a damned good one at that.

He glanced at his watch. It was after two. He figured he wouldn't be able to fall asleep with all of the noise seeping into his room from the hallway and from the street traffic outside his window. He considered going back to the hospital but decided against it. There was nothing he could do there except sink into miserable depression. On the other hand he would go crazy if he stayed cooped up in the hotel room. He decided to go outside and look around while it was daylight.

Suaee Dee Lady. The words bobbed to the surface of his thoughts. That was on his list of places to go, but he hadn't planned to go there until after he had talked with the attorney. He suspected the Suaee Dee Lady was probably all of his father's *substantial assets and important matters*. There was really no reason he couldn't go there before talking to the attorney. No one would know who he was. He could check out the place and see exactly what sort of business it was and no one would be the wiser. He might even see his dad's business partner or the woman named Jarapan, the woman his father had supposedly loved. He warmed to the idea. Those were two people he definitely wanted to meet. Whatever had happened to his dad, he figured their hands were in it all the way to their elbows.

He checked to make sure his passport, plane ticket, and Traveler's Cheques were still in the room-safe. Satisfied his few valuables were as secure as they could be, he left the room.

He stopped at the front desk and asked a receptionist for directions to the address he had printed on a piece of paper. He sensed she was answering in English, but he didn't understand a word she said. After a frustrating minute the girl wrote in Thai on the same paper and handed it back. She pointed outside at a small, dark-blue pick-up with an open-sided cap over the bed. "Baht-bus," she said and waved him in that direction.

He stepped outside into the muggy heat. As he approached the truck, he realized he wouldn't be riding in air conditioned comfort. He handed the piece of paper to the driver. "How much?"

The driver stared at the paper for a moment then looked up, his smile faded. "Fifty baht." His tone left no room for negotiation.

Josh nodded. Compared to the taxi it was a bargain. He stepped into the bed of the baht-bus and sat on one of the bench seats that lined both sides. As the driver pulled into the flow of traffic, he understood: Baht was the Thai currency and this truck was a bus; it made sense. The baht-bus turned south on the road that ran parallel to the beach.

To his left sat a jumble of shops, restaurants, open-air beer bars, and go-go nightclubs. To his right lay the Gulf of Siam. The sidewalks were busier now than they had been earlier in the day. The street-side shops were open and the foreign tourists outnumbered the locals. The bright contrasting colors that the Thais seemed to love couldn't hide the broken sidewalks or the overall dinginess of the city. Pattaya was nothing fancy, not even close. He couldn't imagine what magic had caused his dad to stay in this decorated slum.

The traffic was thick with motorcycles, cars, and other baht-buses. He guessed they had traveled a kilometer or so when his baht-bus braked to a halt. "Suaee Dee Lady," the driver said, pointing down the side-street.

Josh exited the vehicle, handed the driver a one hundred baht bill, and stepped away. It was double what had been agreed on, but a good deal compared to the morning's taxi. The baht-bus was gone before he reached the curb. He walked toward the Suaee Dee Lady.

The afternoon sun was brutal and the humidity merciless. Beads of sweat had formed on his forehead by the time he reached the bar. He pulled at the door but it didn't budge. His eyes focused on a sign that declared business hours from six until closing. Josh glanced at his watch, it was three o'clock. He never thought the bar might be open only at night. Suddenly he felt foolish standing in front of the locked door. He glanced around but no one was looking. He turned and walked back to the main street.

A steady stream of vehicles rolled down Beach Road, a one-way avenue heading south. His hotel was to the north. He didn't know how to get back except by the way he had come. It would be a long walk—much too long for this heat.

A flash, high and to the right caught his eye; a low thunder followed. A bank of dark clouds had already covered more than half of the afternoon sky. The breeze shifted and intensified, noticeably cooler. A large drop of rain splattered near his feet. Another put a cool spot on his shoulder. A downpour was coming. He decided to find shelter instead of walking anywhere.

He spotted a cluster of open-air bars not far from where he stood and headed there. A heavy sheet of rain arrived as he stepped inside the covered area. He took a quick survey: There were eight bars, each about fifteen feet by twenty-five feet in size; two were open. A few men, clearly tourists, sipped at drinks, mostly beer. He sat on a stool far inside where the rain wouldn't blow on him.

The girl tending bar came over. "You like some drink?" she asked, her English broken and heavily accented.

Josh hesitated. He wasn't used to being served without being asked for proof that he was over twenty-one. "Budweiser."

"Mai mee Budweise. No hab Budweise."

Josh noticed a Carlsberg beer sign on the side of a cooler. "I'll have a Carlsberg."

The girl looked at him, puzzled.

Josh pointed at the sign, "Carlsberg."

"Oh, Callsabuhg," she smiled nervously. "No hab Callsaberg. Hab Heineken."

He fought back an urge to laugh. "Okay, Heineken, then."

In a moment she delivered his beer in a styrofoam sleeve and his bill in a wooden cup. "You like play game?" she asked clear enough that he understood.

Josh shrugged. "Why not?"

He spent the afternoon drinking Heineken, playing Jinga, and getting his ass beat at Connect Four. The time passed quickly. When he finally looked at his watch, it was ten minutes past six. He paid his bill, gave the girl a generous tip, and left the bar.

The rain had stopped but it was still overcast. He was lightheaded from the several beers he had consumed but his steps were steady. He walked toward the Suaee Dee Lady. This time he noticed there were other bars on the same street. He hadn't noticed them earlier. Sexy young women sat outside the open bars luring passing tourists inside. Loud dance music spilt out each time the doors opened.

"Hello hansum man," a girl shouted as he neared the Suaee Dee Lady. "You come to this bar. Very nice, have air con, beautiful ladies. You like too much."

As bad as the girl's English was, it was better than most he had heard in Thailand. A badge pinned to her blouse said *Noi*. He pointed to the sign over the door. "Name mean what?" He kept his English basic.

"Suaee Dee Lady? Name mean beautiful lady."

Suaee Dee Lady, Josh repeated to himself. *Beautiful lady.* Suddenly it occurred to him that he could make an entire Thai sentence. "Khun suaee dee lady."

"Khun phut bpaak wan," she smiled. "Phut Thai chai mai?"

"What?"

"I say you talk with sweet mouth. Do you speak Thai?"

"Nit noy," he answered remembering the girl at the airport. "I know more but I can't remember it right now."

Noi laughed. "I think you speak Thai very nice. Come inside, hab suaee dee lady."

Josh intended to go inside whether she invited him or not. He wanted to see the establishment his father owned. Considering the way the girl was dressed, he was sure it wasn't a coffee shop. He stepped toward the door.

Noi took him by the hand. "You buy me drink?" The hopefulness in her voice reflected the anticipation on her face.

Josh figured that if she worked here she would know as much as anyone about his dad and what had happened. "Can we talk?"

"You buy me drink, okay?"

Josh nodded and followed her inside. The coolness was a welcome relief. An old song by the Bee Gees thumped from hidden speakers. Christmas tree lights dangled haphazardly from the ceiling. Four bikini clad girls danced on the raised stage. A few customers sat at the bar or at the high-top tables. Most stared at the dancers. Noi led him to a table in one corner of the room where they could talk.

"What you like drink?"

"Heineken," Josh answered, remembering his earlier experience.

Noi smiled and hurried away. She returned in a minute carrying drinks. His was a beer and hers was something in a small brown bottle.

"What's that?" he asked.

"Lipo. Give me power." She did a Charles Atlas stance to emphasize her words.

Josh laughed. "I think you have enough power already."

Suddenly she stood. "I go dance now. You wait me, okay?" She went to the far side of the raised dance floor and stripped off the skirt and blouse she had worn outside. She stepped on stage as one song ended and another began. Compared to the other dancers, Noi was stunner. Slender, sexy, and very attractive, maybe even beautiful. She smiled at all of the customers as she danced, but mostly she smiled at him.

His Heineken was gone before Noi had finished her dance set. He ordered another. It disappeared as quickly as the first. His third had arrived by the time Noi had dressed and come back to his table.

"You're a good dancer," Josh said as she sat next to him.

She lowered her eyes away from him in mock modesty. Suddenly she pulled him close and put a sniffing kiss on his cheek. "I like you too much. Where you from?"

"I'm from America."

"America? I like men America. What name you?"

"Josh. Josh Johnson. The man who owns this bar is my father."

Noi stiffened. She had thought him just another tourist. She hadn't expected to meet Mike's son. Her practiced come-on lines escaped her. "I never see you before."

"I have never been here before. I came to find out what happened to my father. Someone said maybe he tried to kill himself, but I don't believe them. It's not his style." He paused, wondering just how good her English was or how much she knew. "Do you understand what I'm saying?"

"I understand your words but I don't understand what you said. Khun Mike is your father, he is my friend. I think him go home America. What you mean, kill?"

The expression on her face said she wasn't aware of anything. "Never mind. I'm looking for a woman, my father's business partner. Can you point to her?"

"Ms. Itta not here. Two weeks ago she have married and go to America."

He hadn't expected that piece of news. "Are you sure?"

"Yes, sure, hundred percent."

"Who is managing the bar?"

"Ms. Itta said for Ohm to take care until Khun Mike come back, but she not here now. Ohm go home because mama her sick too much. Now Dao is boss." She pointed at the girl behind the bar. "That girl, she name Dao."

"Then you don't know where my father is?"

Noi shook her head. "Maybe you ask him wife."

Josh was caught off guard. Wife? Dad had once told Aunt Carol that he loved his accountant but he had never said he was married. "Is her name Jarapan?"

"Yes, you know she?"

"No, but I want to meet her. Can you help me find her?"

Noi hesitated; this was none of her business. Still, maybe there could be something in it for her. "I not sure. You pay bar fine, maybe I help."

Bar fine? What the hell was a bar fine? "How much?"

"Five hundred baht. Nit noy money."

Josh did quick calculations. It *was* nit noy money. "Okay." He handed her a 1,000 baht bill. "For the bar fine, the drinks, and your tip."

Noi smiled demurely and left the table. She returned a short while later dressed in tight jeans and a midriff length tank top. "Okay, let's go."

Josh chugged his beer and followed her toward the exit. At the door he lost his balance and staggered. Noi grabbed his hand and pulled him outside. "Ms. Jarapan go home to Khon Kaen, but my friend know family. Maybe have phone number."

Neither spoke as they walked. She seemed to know where she was going so he followed. She led him up and down streets and in and out of shops until he was hopelessly lost. Finally, she stopped at a small nondescript bar.

Noi spoke in rapid Thai to the working girls. A Heineken and a Lipo appeared on the table and Josh paid. One girl brought a cell phone, dialed a number, and handed it to Noi. A short wait was followed by a sing-song conversation.

Josh didn't understand Thai but he heard the politeness in Noi's tone. She said his name at least once. She disconnected the call and then dialed another. This time the conversation was longer.

In a while she turned off the phone and said in her clipped English, "Jarapan cannot meet you now. Maybe later." She shouted at a girl behind the bar and two more drinks appeared. "She said me buy you beer. Pay me later. Chok dee!" Noi raised her glass.

Josh raised his beer by reflex and they drank.

Noi turned away and talked with her friends while Josh eyed the bar girls and sipped at his beer. Before leaving Pittsburgh, he had read extensively about Thailand and the men who traveled here. Farangs, that's what the Thais called them. Supposedly it mean *foreigner*, but Josh figured it more likely meant *rich fools*. The stories of the unlucky ones were eerily repetitious. They would come to visit, decide they were in love, and then abandon their pasts to stay. For them the allure of cheap sex with svelte young women was overpowering. While their money lasted, they were Gods. When things got tight, their young Thai lovers would dump them and disappear—usually with another man. Sometimes the result was suicide.

Josh wondered if that was what had happened to Dad. Had he fallen in love with some Asian trollop who had fucked him over to the point that he wanted to die? He couldn't picture his dad flipping out over a hot piece of ass or a few bucks, but anything was possible.

He glanced at his watch. Five minutes had passed. He hurried to finish his beer and then ordered another. Thoughts of his father being shit on by some Thai whore paraded through his drunken mind. By the time the bottle was empty he was sure this Jarapan woman had somehow caused his father's death. No doubt she was a gold-digger. Why else would she be hanging around a man old enough to be her father? Or even her grandfather. Maybe she had taken his dad for everything he had and then dumped him, leaving him to react like the others. Or maybe she had been the cause of his accident but had somehow made it look like attempted suicide. He forced the thought from his head. He couldn't imagine anyone being so cold and calculating. *Remember where you are*, Carl's words echoed through his head. *Thailand ain't like America.*

His body jerked like he was falling asleep. He rubbed at his face. His lips felt numb and the world around him had dissolved into alcohol-induced surrealism. This was the first time since his overdose that he had consumed more than four beers in a single day. Worse, he hadn't eaten anything in the last twenty-four hours except dry toast and he had slept even less. He could feel the alcohol bypassing his liver and going straight to his head. He nudged Noi with his elbow, "I'm getting drunk. How long does it take someone to say no?"

"Slowly, slowly," Noi smiled. "We wait. If you drunk, I think no problem. I take care for you. We drink and have happy- happy."

Josh sighed. "I need to find a toilet. *Hong nam*," he added remembering another Thai word.

Noi pointed. "Over there. Three baht."

He stood and headed in the direction she pointed. It took his total concentration to keep from staggering.

Chapter 53

Jarapan arrived at the Happy Night Bar less than ten minutes after Noi called, but she didn't see was anyone who looked like the boy from Mike's pictures. She caught Noi's attention and mouthed in Thai. "Where is he?"

Noi nodded toward the three-baht toilets.

Jarapan was tempted to look but didn't. Instead she kept her face straight ahead and ordered a cola.

In a moment he appeared. He was older than in the picture and he looked more like a man than a boy, but she recognized him easy enough. He didn't look much like Mike, yet he was handsome in a bad-boy sort of way. It was obvious that he was concentrating on walking as he made his way back to his seat beside of Noi.

Noi was famous for having a man every night since she had been in Pattaya. There were even rumors that she sometimes had two men at a time and that she was a nymphomaniac. Jarapan had never seen the two-at-a-time thing, but she had seen Noi with enough different men to suspect the rumors might be true. The way she was fawning over Josh said that she had no intentions of spoiling her *hard*-earned reputation. Every few seconds Noi glanced around in the bar and smiled. She had laid claim to Josh for the night and was making it clear to everyone.

Jarapan was annoyed by what Noi was doing, but it was really none of her business. Josh was a grown man and he could do what he wanted, but she felt responsible for him because he was Mike's son and because she knew the reason he was here—and it wasn't to have sex with Noi. But Josh was drunk, and Noi was aggressive, so she figured Noi would have her way.

In a minute Noi and Josh began a game of connect four. She could only imagine what the bet was.

~~~

"You like play game?" Noi asked Josh and pointed at the Connect Four game on the bar.

Josh shook his head, "I played already. I lost every time."

Noi smiled, "Maybe you win now. I not play good, but I like. We make bet. More fun, nah? "

"What sort of bet?"

She thought for a minute, her face serious. "I win, you give me 700 baht. You win, I go your room for free. Okay?"

Josh considered her odd proposal for a moment. He had made more than a couple of bets in his life, but none had ever involved an ante like this. His money against her body. She was attractive and quite sexy, but he wasn't sure if having sex with a Thai bar-girl was such a good idea. He'd never had sex with a prostitute before. He'd had his share of loose women though, a couple of whom probably had more sex partners than all the whores in Pattaya. It didn't matter anyway, his chances of winning were slim and none. "If I lose, will you show me the way back to my hotel?"

"You stay Amahlee, yes?"

"Yeah, Amahlee," he parroted her pronunciation.

"I win, I take you. I lose, I take you. Never mind."

Her English, as stilted as it was, was perfectly clear. "Okay," he smiled.

The game of Connect-Four consists of a thin, stand-up, plastic panel with holes through the sides and slots in the top. Each player has a supply of poker-chip-like disks which are dropped into the slots to fill the holes. The goal is to put four of your disks in a row while blocking your opponent from doing the same. If both players are of equal skill, the game ends in a draw, a stalemate. Intelligence and forward thinking are important, but experience overshadows everything.

Josh was surprised at the way their game progressed. He didn't lose right away as he had earlier. In fact, most of the holes were already filled when he made a losing move. He looked up, certain she saw his mistake.

If Noi noticed, she didn't let it show. She studied the board closely. After a moment she picked up one of her few remaining disks and dropped it into a slot. Not the winning slot, but one at the opposite end of the board. Not only had she only passed on an easy win, but she had set him up for certain victory. She looked at him and smiled, "Okay, now your turn."

Josh couldn't tell if she had done it on purpose or if she really didn't know she had just lost the game.

A couple of the bar-girls who had been watching them play giggled and pointed at the Connect Four board. Noi shushed them quiet. She looked back at Josh and said, "What you do is up to you."

It was clear that she was losing on purpose. Josh hesitated a moment then dropped a game piece into the winning slot.

She looked up at him and smiled coyly, "I win."

Josh was drunk, but not incoherent. He pointed at the game, "I have four in a row. How can you win?"

Noi fingered a lever that cleared the plastic disks from the board. She gave him a quick but erotic inspection, "You win me. I like too much. I win too."

Josh wasn't sure how to respond. Here he was in the sex capital of the world, and a lady of the night was happy he had won her—and for no money. It cut against the grain of everything he believed about Pattaya. He glanced around the bar. He was by far the youngest customer, and the thinnest as well. One man who looked older than his father eyed him as if he were an intruder.

He turned back toward Nui, "I don't understand."

She took his arm and hugged it briefly, "Tonight you win. I win too. Big surprise for you, nah?" She pushed her leg against his. "Okay?"

"I don't think the woman is going to call back. I'm too drunk to talk to her anyway. I think I'm ready to go to my hotel. I've had all of the *happy-happy* I can stand."

Noi nodded. "Up to you. We finish our drinks first." She looked across the bar at Jarapan. "I think Ms. Jarapan call soon."

~~~

Jarapan had seen all she wanted to see for tonight. Noi had said that Josh was drunk and she had been correct. From what she could see he didn't seem to be an annoying drunk like many of the tourists who came to Thailand, but she was too far away to hear his words so she couldn't tell if he was obnoxious or not. She had already decided it was time to make her call when Noi made it clear that Josh would be leaving soon.

Jarapan asked one of the waitresses to total the check-bin for Noi and the farang. She was careful not to mention Josh by name. A minute later she handed the girl eight hundred baht, enough to pay for everything and more. She stepped from the bar. When she was far enough away not to be obvious, yet still close enough to see everyone, she dialed the last number on the caller ID. She watched as Noi answered the phone.

"It's me, Jarapan. Is he going home now?"

"He said he's tired and drunk. What should I tell him?"

"Tell him I'll meet him tomorrow night at seven. I'll call you by six to let you know where."

"I'm going to the hotel with him. Does that bother you?"

"It would bother me if he was so horrible that you wouldn't go with him."

"What do you mean?"

"I mean nothing," Jarapan answered. "Just make sure he uses a condom." She turned off her phone and walked off into the crowd.

Chapter 54

Josh and Noi finished their drinks and left the bar. Noi led him through a winding maze of beer bars and narrow alleyways until they came to a major street.

"Second Road," she said as if it meant something. She flagged down a baht-bus. "Amahlee, no stop," she said to the driver in both Thai and English.

"Fifty baht," the man responded.

"I'll give you thirty," she countered.

"Forty."

Noi nodded her agreement. She led Josh to the back of the baht-bus and the driver headed north. She took Josh's hand in hers and brought it to rest on her thigh. He tensed but didn't pull away. Noi smiled to herself. Within a minute they were stopped by the traffic light at Second Road and Pattaya Central.

"Do you like Pattaya?" she asked while they waited for the light to turn green.

Josh looked at her like she was from another planet. "It's too hot."

She snuggled close and smiled seductively. "Yes, Thailand is hot and my room no have air con. Only have fan. I sweat too much. I think I like sleep in you room tonight."

The baht-bus jerked forward before Josh could respond.

"I know papa you long time," Noi said as they crossed the intersection.

Josh remembered that she had mentioned that earlier when they first met. At the time he had wondered just how well she knew his father. Now a more disquieting thought entered his mind.

Was it possible that this woman, somehow, was also involved in Dad's *suspected suicide attempt*? After all, she had known him a *long time*. Josh pushed the thought from his head. He was just being paranoid. "How long have you known him?"

"Three years. When I first came to Pattaya."

He wanted to ask if she ever had sex with his dad but couldn't bring himself to do that. Instead he asked, "Did he ever pay your bar-fine?"

"Many times," she bragged then reconsidered her words. "But friends. Khun Mike same my uncle. I sleep in his air-con."

Noi reached up and pushed one of the buttons mounted along the edge of the truck-cap. A buzzer sounded and the driver pulled to the curb. She paid their fare from her own pocket, and then took Josh by his hand. "I show you something, okay?"

She lead him across Second Road through a frightening maze of speeding vehicles and into a beer-bar complex similar to the one they had just left, only this place was smaller and there were a lot fewer customers. She took a seat and he followed suit.

"What do you want to show me?"

"First we have some drink."

She ordered him a Heineken and a whiskey-coke for herself instead of her usual make-you-strong concoction in the little brown bottle.

There were eight bars here, nothing compared to the number he had seen earlier. The few customers got plenty of attention from the abundance of working girls. The ladies without customers looked mostly bored. "What did you want to show me?"

"Condo," she pointed to her left, away from Second Road.

Josh leaned back and craned his neck to get a good view. "You brought me here to see that?"

"Papa you sleep before."

Her English was screwed up but he understood her perfectly. He figured it must be the Pinewood Condos. That was where his father had stayed the first time he came to Thailand. Josh remembered it from the letters and pictures his dad had sent home.

He wondered if his father had ever come to these bars, and if any of the girls who worked here had known him, or slept with him. "Did you ever have sex with my father?" he asked.

Noi cocked her head to one side. Her smile faded noticeably. "What you say?"

Even in his drunkenness Josh felt like a jerk for asking such a stupid question. It was none of his business and it didn't matter anymore anyway. "Never mind. Just thinking out loud.

"Mai pen lai," she said. "Mai pen lai means *never mind*."

"Mai pen lai," he repeated. "Thanks. Now I know another Thai word."

"What words know already?" she asked.

"Mai pen lai, hong nam, suaee dee, and nit noy." Josh laughed at his limited vocabulary.

Noi laughed with him. "While in Thailand, I teach you many Thai words. Okay?"

"Yeah, sure. Why not?"

Suddenly everything caught up with Josh. The day, the night, the lack of sleep, and the beer—everything had worn him down. "I think we should go soon."

"Okay." She finished her drink. "I sleep in your room, yes? With air con. You never say me before."

"Only sleep?"

"Maybe you buy me food from the restaurant, too. I eat very quiet."

Josh laughed despite his exhaustion. "Okay, but no TV. It'll keep me awake."

Noi smiled wide and nodded her agreement. "Thank you Khun Josh. You nice man. Have good heart."

She took his hand and led him to the hotel.

~~~

Noi was gone when Josh awoke at ten-thirty the next morning. He checked his wallet and the safe. If anything was missing, it wasn't obvious. One set of towels in the bathroom had been used, but he couldn't tell if she had showered last night before going to sleep or this morning before leaving. His toothbrush and razor had been put handles-down into a glass. His shave cream, tooth paste, and mouthwash were neatly aligned on the vanity top. Wedged beneath the edge of the mirror was a piece of paper. The carefully formed letters said the handwriting was by a Thai.

"Meet you in hotel lobby at six o'clock," the note said. "Ms. Jarapan see you tonight. I take you. You snore too much. Love, Noi."

Josh didn't know he snored at all. He figured she was joking. But the rest of the message wasn't a joke. Since his dad's business partner had skipped town, Ms. Jarapan was probably the only person who would know what had really happened.

He glanced at his watch, not yet eleven. He called the hospital and, after struggling through the language barrier, learned his father's condition was the same. He took a quick shower and went to the restaurant downstairs. He wasn't surprised to find the breakfast buffet gone. He noticed a small restaurant at one end of the breakfast dining area. It was enclosed, it was air conditioned, and it was open for business. He went there.

After scanning the menu for food that he thought would be safe to eat, he settled on spaghetti marinara. Not many germs could survive the boiling involved in the preparation of that. After eating he went back to his room. Exhaustion accompanied his full stomach and he lay down and slept for the next three hours.

By five o'clock he was sitting on a stool in the open-air lounge of the lobby bar. Noi had said she would meet him there before six. He didn't want to risk missing her. The Heineken went down smoother than he expected considering all he had drunk last night. It fact, it tasted good. He settled back in his seat and stared at the activity around him. Every few minutes he looked toward the hotel entrance. Noi should be here any minute.

Chapter 55

Carl Rand stared at the Thailand countryside as his taxi made its way southeast from Bangkok to Pattaya. This was the first time he had been here in nearly three years, and he didn't recognize a thing. Either it had changed or his memory was failing. A few industrial complexes jogged vague recollection but the rest looked different from everything he remembered. The small shops, roadside restaurants, and gas stations looked familiar but so mundane that he could have been anywhere in Thailand. In a while he saw a sign proclaiming Pattaya to be 60 kilometers ahead so he knew they were on the right road.

As they entered the northern edges of Pattaya, the scenery finally meshed with his memories; not completely, but enough that he felt like he was coming home. By the time the taxi pulled into the Amari Hotel complex, his anticipation of spending a few days in Pattaya for old-times sake made him smile. His first stop would be Toy's Fun Bar on Soi 2. If he was going see anyone he knew from the old days, it would be at Toy's. After that he would go to a place called the Suaee Dee Lady, or something like that. It belonged to Mike Johnson, his friend and former co-worker at the refinery. He and Mike had worked together here a few years back and had shared more than one misadventure. He'd often wondered what happened to Mike after the project had ended. The day he had seen his friend's face on a Pattaya website he'd nearly laughed himself to death. It was a picture of Mike being kissed on the cheek by a very cute Thai girl. That was all it took to inspire this trip. Mike would be surprised and Carl figured he might even get a few free drinks and bar-fines at a discount.

Carl followed as the bell-boy wheeled his suitcase from the taxi to the front desk. The layout of the open-air lobby was the same as he remembered, but the décor had changed from Thai rustic to tropical modern. The only person he recognized at the check-in counter was Jintana. She had gained a few pounds but she was still very sexy. She smiled at him briefly and then returned to the customer she was registering. He was sure he had seen recognition on her face, but she hadn't waved or anything. Maybe she was just embarrassed she didn't remember his name. He would talk to her later when the front desk wasn't so busy. He filled out the forms, showed his passport, and let them scan his credit card. A minute later he followed the same bell-boy to his room.

The Amari wasn't the best hotel in Pattaya, but it had a breakfast buffet worth killing for. He had lived here once for a more than a year, so for him it was a no-surprises hotel. He unpacked his suitcase, put on a clean shirt, and headed out.

The front desk was less busy now but Jintana was nowhere to be seen. The lobby bar was completely empty too; even the waitresses were missing. He glanced at his watch: not yet five, too early to start drinking. He left the hotel and walked south.

Carl never thought it was possible to add more bars to the Pattaya scene but he was wrong. Every available shop-space and open piece of real estate that had once existed on the east side of Second Road was now occupied by small bars and open-air entertainment complexes. A few had customers but most were empty. Considering the heat and the time of the day, he was surprised there were any customers at all.

Ten minutes later he reached Soi 2 and Toy's Fun Bar. Except for one old woman sleeping it was as deserted as the other bars he had just passed. He flagged down a baht-bus headed toward Beach Road and hopped aboard. The TQ would be a better place to start the evening. It was air conditioned, offered a late afternoon happy-hour and, from what he remembered the go-go dancers were pretty hot, too. There were worse places to pass some time in Thailand.

Chapter 56

Josh saw Noi as soon as she entered the hotel lobby. He stood
and waved her toward him. "Where are we meeting Jarapan?" he
asked when she was within earshot.

"You buy me drink?"

"Do we have time?"

"Sure, have time." She motioned the bartender over, ordered a
Heineken for him and a Lipo on ice for herself. "No hurry. Ms.
Jarapan not call. Maybe she call soon."

He wondered what that meant, if it meant anything at all.
Before he could form a response, Noi's cell phone rang. He heard
the same politeness he had heard the night before. He wished he
knew Thai so he could understand the conversation. In a minute
she ended the call.

"Ms. Jarapan meet you at the Suaee Dee Lady in one hour."

Josh tensed. He had been expecting their meeting to be more
private. The bar would be anything but that. "Call her back and tell
her I'd prefer to meet someplace less noisy, and with fewer people
listening."

"Today no problem," Noi said. "Ms. Jarapan say bar not open
until eight thirty. Special night for you, nah?" She finished her
Lipo in a single gulp and then waved at the bartender. "Now have
time for more drinks." This time she ordered a glass of wine.

At six forty-five Josh paid their tab and they left the Amari
Hotel. Noi stopped when they reached the street. "Too far to walk.
We hire baht-bus taxi."

Josh nodded.

Noi flagged down a passing baht-bus and spoke with the

driver. After a short but intense exchange of words the driver nodded. She turned to Josh and held out her hand, palm up. "One hundred baht. He'll take us there and won't stop for anyone else. Okay?"

Josh knew it was too much but didn't say anything. He handed over the money and they climbed into the back of the truck. As the baht-bus made its way through the heavy traffic, twisted scenes of his father being pushed in front of a speeding vehicle flickered through his head. Images of the pusher flashed clear as glass. An unknown sense told him the pusher was a woman. Logic told him the woman's name was Jarapan. The thought burned itself into his brain and refused to let go. A chill crawled up his back in defiance of the sultry evening.

Within ten minutes they arrived at the narrow street leading to Suaee Dee Lady. Noi paid their fare and the baht-bus sped away.

"The driver didn't want to come here," she said as they walked toward the bar. "Today someone told him about Khun Mike's accident. Now he thinks the Suaee Dee Lady is bad luck."

When they reached the bar, she nodded toward the entrance. "The door isn't locked."

Josh looked. She was right; the door was slightly ajar. His tension wound tighter. "Will you come with me?"

Noi took a step back. "No, I cannot. This is your business. You go talk to the lady; I will go talk my friends." She eased further away and pointed to the bar next door. "See you later, okay?"

Josh watched as she walked away. After a moment's hesitation he turned back to the Suaee Dee Lady. His nerves had rubbed his emotions raw. He pulled the door open and stepped inside.

Chapter 57

A single amber spotlight shined down on the raised dance stage. A woman sat at a table in the shadows between dark and light. In front of her was a drink in a tall glass. To her right sat a beer. A cigarette burned in the ashtray. The beer and the cigarette were too far away to be hers.

"You are Ms. Jarapan?"

She nodded. "Please have a seat."

He walked forward tentatively, half expecting an unseen person to step from the shadows. He forced his eyes to focus on her face. She was the most beautiful woman he had ever seen. He understood how his father could have fallen in love with her. It would be easy for any man to have his head turned by her beauty. He glanced at the beer and smoldering cigarette. "Are you alone?"

She reached over and crushed out the cigarette. "It was a present for someone special, but I think he will not come here tonight." She slid the beer bottle across the table toward him.

Josh wasn't sure what to make of her comment. He doubted she was talking about him. He wondered if she was referring to his father. Considering that his father was in a coma in the hospital, it didn't seem reasonable that she would be expecting him here tonight. Maybe it was some weird Thai custom or maybe the woman was plain crazy. He took a seat and stared across the table at her. "My father said he loved you."

"And I him."

For some reason he expected her to say more. He picked up the beer, brought it to his lips, and then quickly put it back down. It didn't seem like a good idea drinking from an open bottle offered by a person he didn't know. If his instincts were correct, this woman couldn't be trusted. If Carl were here, he would be telling him not to drink the beer. "Can you tell me what happened to my father?"

"Khun Mike was hurt in an accident." Jarapan dropped her eyes from his stare.

Josh knew the official cause already. It was the side-notes to the official cause that he wanted to know about. He considered carefully before saying, "That's what I've been told. The police said he wrote a note, but they don't have it anymore. They thought maybe it was a suicide note." He raised his eyebrows but didn't ask the question foremost in his mind.

"I have the note. Your father was upset. He believed something that wasn't true. I don't want to talk about it. It disturbs me to think about what happened." She closed her eyes and took a deep breath.

Josh paid intense attention to her words and her body language as she spoke. Her agitation was obvious, or perhaps it was distress. What could his father have believed that wasn't true? Something so bad that he wanted to die. It didn't make sense. The posts on the web boards and the headlines from the Pattaya Mail newspaper whipped through his head. While their money lasted, the foreigners were Gods. That was the take of most web-board posters. When things got tight, their Thai lovers would dump them and disappear, usually with another man. That was the general opinion. According to the newspapers the results were often suicide. His mind buzzed from the four Heinekens he had drunk at the Amari. Suddenly everything became clear. Maybe she hadn't pushed his father like he had imagined before; maybe she had only done something to trigger one of his dark depressions. If that were the case, it would have to be something really bad. "How did you make my father so crazy he wanted to die?"

She looked up. "I did nothing. I loved him."

Her face twisted but Josh couldn't tell if it was from emotional pain or panic. She sounded sincere, but in his heart he knew she was lying. Carl had already told him all Thais were expert liars. The closer he looked the more he knew Carl was right. He decided on an aggressive approach; one that had served him well in Pittsburgh. "Come on," he said, his tone haughty. "Let's be honest with each other. I've read all about you Thai women. What did you do? Screw around on him? Did he catch you with another man?"

His insinuation stung like hot poison from a cobra's bite. Her anger flared. "You are a stupid man." she lashed back, her words more caustic than his. "You're nothing like your father. I'm leaving now."

Her sharp reaction surprised him. He had expected lies and denials, not a direct rejection. Carl's warning about angry Thais flicked through his head. "Please wait. I'm sorry; I'm upset. I only want to know what happened. I came here hoping someone could tell me what is going on."

Jarapan was quiet for the longest time. In a while she calmed enough to answer. "I will tell you a story. Five months ago I met your father. He is a good man, very polite. He filled an empty part of my life. We dated, we laughed, and we loved. I tried to make him as happy as he made me. We made plans for our future, but now it is ended. That is all I know."

He considered her words for a long second and then said, "I don't believe you."

Silence echoed above the droning of the air conditioner. They stared at each other in the dim amber glow. "I don't care what you believe," she finally responded with measured calmness.

He didn't move. "I came to find what happened to my father. You know the truth and I won't leave until I know the truth, too."

She turned her face from him. In a moment she looked back and said, "If you think I had anything to do with his accident, then our conversation is finished."

"I suspect everyone in Thailand."

Jarapan shook her head ever so slightly. "There are things you don't want to know. You should go now. Go home with your memories, nothing else is important."

"Listen to me. Mike Johnson was more than just my father. He was the man who taught me to swim. He was the man who taught me to drive a car. He was the man who loved me when I didn't deserve to be loved. I want to know everything."

Jarapan let his English words become Thai and she understood his need to know. She touched lightly at her stomach, "I have Mike's baby inside of me."

Her pronouncement hit him like a sledgehammer. Of all the things he thought he might hear, he hadn't expected to hear that. He fought to keep himself under control. His response came as a reflex without thought. "My father wouldn't kill himself because you are pregnant. He loves kids. No, that's not it at all. You did something to hurt him. You hurt him so much he didn't want to live." When she didn't respond he added, "It's not his baby, is it? I know because I can see it in your eyes."

Jarapan bristled, "Then you're as blind as you are stupid. You are nothing like your father. I love Mike and would never hurt him. I love him more than life itself. He's the only man who ever shared both my heart and my body." Her expression turned resolute. "If you want to know the truth, then I'll tell you, but I think you should just go away and forget we talked."

Josh's confidence shrank a few degrees. He wondered if he could be wrong. He lowered his voice to a whisper, "I have to know why my father wants to die."

Jarapan looked away briefly as tears formed then subsided. She reached into her purse and withdrew an envelope. She handed it to Josh. "Please, read this."

A coldness crept down his arms and hair stood on the back of his neck. He took the envelope. Hesitantly he slid the piece of paper from its jacket and tilted it forward to put more light on the print. It was an official document from the Bangkok-Pattaya Hospital. His eyes scanned through a combination of Thai and English. They froze on one entry. *HIV Positive - AIDS Confirmed.* The words etched a gruesome image in his mind. "Is this your fucked up idea of a joke?"

"It's not a joke—it's a nightmare. A nightmare that may kill your father."

Suddenly he realized the consequences of what she had told him. If she was telling the truth, she was pregnant with his father's baby. If his father had AIDS, was it possible he had infected her? Or maybe she was the one who had infected him. Without thinking he picked up the beer and finished it in one long swallow. "What about you?"

She ignored his question. "There is one more thing you need to know."

Josh felt his world unraveling. He struggled to keep his emotions under control. "How can there be more?"

She pulled another piece of paper from her purse and pushed it toward him. It was typed in Thai on hospital stationery.

"What does it say?"

"It says there was a mistake, a mix up of names. Your father doesn't have AIDS; he has pneumonia." She stood, her face poised. "I'm leaving now. You can stay as long as you want. This was your father's business, but now it's yours. I have no use for it." She laid a key on the table and then hurried toward the door.

"Please, wait." Josh stood quickly, knocking his chair backwards to the floor. "We're not finished talking."

Jarapan stopped at the noise. Tears swelled and flowed down her cheeks. "I'm finished and I'm leaving." She ran from the bar.

Josh tried to follow but his legs felt awkward. His first thought was that the beer had been spiked. His second thought was that he'd had too many to drink. He burst through the door and ran directly into the man he had met on his flight to Thailand. He remembered the man's name was Carl.

Chapter 58

Carl had left the TQ at seven o'clock and meandered his way through the tourist jammed sidewalks. There was a slight breeze, but the heat radiating from the concrete and blacktop rendered it impotent. Beads of sweat slid through his hair and down his face. He mopped at his neck and forehead with a handkerchief.

If he remembered this area of Pattta correctly, the side-street to the Suaee Dee Lady was only a few blocks away. The thought of surprising his old friend Mike brought a smile to his lips, the heat and humidity were forgotten.

When he reached his intersection, he stopped and stared. This street had changed almost as much as the rest of Pattaya. Small bars and go-go's had sprouted like wild bamboo. He scanned the neon signs looking for one that identified the Suaee Dee Lady. In a minute he saw it, but the light was off and there were no greeters outside. He wondered if Mike had already gone out of business or if he had been busted by the police for some violation. Both occurred often for foreign owned bars; especially the go-go's. His excitement at seeing his old friend faded.

He headed toward the bar next to the Suaee Dee Lady. The way the bar-girls liked to gossip he was sure someone would fill him in on the facts. He was less than five meters away when the door to the Suaee Dee Lady swung open and a Thai woman appeared. There was no smile and she was in a hurry. She bumped into him as she raced toward Beach Road. He watched as she disappeared around the corner. When he turned back, another person emerged from the bar. He recognized the young man immediately. It was his seatmate from the flight. The boy looked as desperate as the girl who'd nearly run him over.

"Hey, Josh," Carl shouted, smiling. "The open bars are more fun." He pointed at the go-go next door." And the ladies don't run away from you either."

"Did you see a girl leave here?" Josh didn't acknowledge that Carl was more than another tourist.

"She went that way." Carl hitched his thumb over his shoulder but kept his eyes on Josh. "She seemed to be in quite a hurry."

"I have to catch her." Josh headed in the direction Carl had pointed.

Carl grabbed him by the arm. "Son, it's not a good idea to be chasing women in Pattaya. The only thing you'll catch is something you don't want."

Josh stiffened. "Don't call me son. You're not my dad. Now let go of my arm or you'll be catching something you don't want."

Carl noted the balled fist at the end of Josh's free arm. He let go. "Don't say I didn't warn you. You'll never catch her anyway."

The nearby tourists and bar-girls had turned their attention to the two farangs confronting each other. "You can take him, boy," one man egged them on. "Show him what you got," another laughed drunkenly.

Josh glared at the inciters and then ran to the end of the street. He looked up and down Beach Road before sprinting in the direction opposite of where the girl had gone. Seconds later he was back, panting from his fruitless chase. A sheen of oily sweat glistened his face. He pulled himself erect and walked back to where Carl stood waiting.

"Sorry for acting like an asshole," Josh said when he was within speaking distance. "I need to talk to that girl. That's all."

"Never mind. Come on, you can tell me about it over a beer."

"Yeah, sure. Thanks. I need to lock up first." He headed toward the Suaee Dee Lady.

Carl's eyes grew wide as Josh slipped a key the door. "You own this place?"

"Maybe, maybe not. That's what I wanted to ask the girl."

"I thought a man named Mike Johnson owed this joint."

Josh's expression switched from irritation to intense interest. "You know him?"

"I used to. We worked together a few years back. Did you buy him out or something?"

"Mike Johnson is my father."

Carl's face beamed. "Then call him up and get his ass over here. I'll buy us all beers for the night."

"You don't know, do you?"

A cold fist gripped Carl's chest. The worst thought possible exploded in his head. "Know what?"

"I think we need to talk. Come on, I'll buy you a beer."

"Let's go someplace quiet. Follow me."

As they headed out a woman shouted. "Khun Josh, where you go?"

Carl turned, searching out the voice.

"Oh dear Buddha," the same voice said. "Randy, is that you?" The woman ran over and threw her arms around him. "Not see you long time. Miss you too much."

"I thought your name was Carl." Josh said.

"Carl Rand," he replied. "Everyone here calls me Randy. Would you mind if Noi goes with us? She's an old friend."

Josh shrugged and Noi joined them.

They went to a cubbyhole bar near Beach Road where Josh told what he knew and repeated everything Jarapan had said.

When he finished, Carl said. "This woman named Jarapan, is she the girl you chased down the street?"

"Yes."

"Is her nickname Math?"

"Is it important?"

"I don't know. Next time you see her, ask what her nickname is. I'd be interested to know."

They sat in silence for a while, each contemplating everything in their own way. Josh was the first to speak. "I'm going to the hospital."

Carl glanced at his watch. "I think it might be past visiting hours. If it is, they won't let you see your dad. They have security guards and everything."

"I'll take my chances. Now, if one of you would help me with a baht-bus, I'll be on my way."

Carl pushed his leg against Noi's. "Maybe we could hire a baht-bus to hospital and then back to the Amari. What do you think?"

Noi only smiled.

Josh watched Carl and Noi as the baht-bus made its way to the Bangkok-Pattaya Hospital. Noi cuddled next to Carl while slipping sly smiles at Josh. Clearly this wasn't the first time Carl and Noi had been together.

At the hospital, Josh exited the baht-bus and Carl and Noi continued on to the Amari.

Chapter 59

The hospital lobby was deserted except for one receptionist and a lone security guard. If Carl was right, they wouldn't be too anxious to let him near the patients' rooms. He put on his best I'm-better-than-you face and strode confidently toward the elevators.

"Kaw tort ka," the girl at the counter said. "Khun bai nai."

He had no idea what she had said, but it didn't matter. "I'm a doctor," he said back, barely giving her a glance as he continued his way.

Ahead the security guard stood from his seat. Josh slipped his wallet from his pocket, and flashed it open briefly toward the guard. "Doctor," he repeated and was inside the elevator before the guard could react.

On the third floor he was greeted by a grim-looking nurse. He figured the receptionist and the security guard had alerted each floor to be on the lookout. Clearly his doctor routine was out of the question. He showed his passport to the woman and pointed at his name. "Johnson." He pointed toward his father's room. "Papa me."

The woman's expression softened as she stepped aside.

The light inside the room was soft enough to see but not enough to disturb sleeping patients. Monitors recorded vital signs with digital displays and regular beeps. His father's breathing was raspy and labored, each breath was a struggle. Josh wondered if the feeding tube was blocking his dad's airway. The tube wasn't very big, but it filled most of his father's right nostril. He remembered that the left side of dad's nose was narrowed by a deviated septum or something.

He stepped into the hallway, found a nurse, and tried to explain the problem. She either didn't understand or didn't care. Finally he gave up and went back to the room. Probably the tube wouldn't fit down the narrowed nostril anyway.

Dad's gasps for air now sounded more like moaning than a struggle for breath. The bitter reality of what was happening pounded at his senses. His father, the man who would live forever, was dying before his eyes and he couldn't stop it. Emotions he had never felt burned through his soul like hot acid on cheap cloth. A knot hard as steel gripped his throat. Tears filled his eyes. "I'm sorry Dad," he managed to whisper. "I never gave you that one good year you wanted."

Memories of his life flashed through his head. His childish manipulations that everyone hated, and the drugs and his tough-guy image that came later. Looking back he knew his dad hadn't been the cause of the tension in their home, it had been himself. He reached out and took his father by the hand. "I love you Dad."

His dad moaned in response.

The knot returned to Josh's throat like a battle-crazed pit bull. A tear overflowed and slid down his cheek. He knew he had to get away before he broke down and cried like a baby. He turned and hurried from his father's side.

When he entered the hallway he was confronted by the security guard and an older, professionally dressed man. "Can we help you?" the older man asked in clear English.

"I was just leaving," Josh answered.

"The nurse said Mr. Johnson is your father. Is that correct?"

An image of feeding tube entered his head. "Are you a doctor?"

The man nodded.

"My father can't breathe. I want you to take that tube out of his nose."

"That's how we feed him. If we take the tube out, he will starve to death."

Josh heaved a heavy sigh. "If you leave it in, he might suffocate. I don't think he'll starve to death in one or two days."

"Reinserting the tube isn't comfortable for the patient."

"He's in a coma for Christ's sake," Josh snapped. "I don't think he'll know the difference."

The doctor only stared. "If you will sign a paper saying you are his relative and that you want the tube removed, then I will do it. The choice is up to you."

The realization of what he was about to do struck hard. The hard knot returned to his throat and he couldn't speak. He nodded his decision.

Outside, a baht-bus was dropping people at the emergency entrance. Josh walked to the driver. "Amalee. How much?"

The driver scanned Josh from head to foot. "One hundred baht."

Josh didn't argue.

Twenty minutes later he was in bed, but not asleep. Every time he closed his eyes, an image of his father appeared. The accompanying moans sounded as real as when he had heard them at the hospital. Eventually he slept, but the images didn't stop. They haunted his dreams through the night.

Chapter 60

Jarapan jerked awake at seven o'clock the next morning. It took her a moment to realize the phone was ringing. She lifted the handset from its cradle. "Hello."

"This is Orapin. We met a couple of weeks ago. I'm Mike's attorney.

"Yes, I remember."

"Josh Johnson, Mike's son, is in Pattaya."

"Yes, I know already," Jarapan answered. "We talked last night. I gave him the Suaee Dee Lady. I don't want it anymore. Without Mike it means nothing."

For a moment only empty airwaves filled the phone connection. "It's not that easy," the attorney finally said. "I want you to come to my office at ten o'clock. There are things we need to discuss. I want young Mr. Johnson here too."

"I don't want to see him again. He's a rude and arrogant farang, nothing like his father."

"I can't help that. Be here at ten o'clock. It's important. I'll meet you outside my office so you won't have to be alone with him."

Before Jarapan could object, Ms. Orapin terminated the call. The last thing she needed was to see Mike's son again. Until last night she had hoped he would be someone to help share her pain and sadness. Instead he had accused her of somehow being involved with the accident. The whole situation depressed her.

By the time she had showered and dressed, she decided she would go to the meeting. Then she would find a willing doctor and have an abortion. That idea depressed her even more. Maybe she would just go home and let her family decide what to do. That's what a proper Thai girl should do.

For the last two weeks her morning routine had been to visit Mike and then go to the temple to pray. That wouldn't be possible today if she was going to make the ten o'clock meeting. She decided to go to the temple first and then visit Mike when the meeting was finished. At eight forty-five she started her motorcycle and headed out.

She stopped at a Seven-Eleven to buy a package of sweet snacks for the monks before joining the traffic up Buddha Hill. A whirlwind of thoughts filled her head as she drove. Mike was going to die. No one had told her that, but she sensed it in the way the doctors and nurses talked. She wondered what his son would do. Would he keep the Suaee Dee Lady open or would he just go home? And the feeding tube, what would he do about that? Before leaving the temple she prayed extra hard for Mike.

The feeling started before she reached the bottom of Buddha Hill. It felt like a vacuum growing in the pit of her stomach. By the time she reached Sukhumvit Road it had filled her entire body and she recognized it as despair. By the time she reached the attorney's office she was ready to explode. She prayed that Mike's son wouldn't be there.

Chapter 61

Josh awoke at seven o'clock. The dreams of his dad lingered like the smell of death. He wondered if he had done the right thing by having the doctor remove the feeding tube. He knew he wasn't thinking rationally and may have made a mistake. Images of his dad dying of starvation flickered through his head. He would go back to the hospital later and talk with the doctors again. This time he would do whatever they advised.

At eight he went to the restaurant for his free breakfast. Carl wasn't there. Josh figured he probably busy getting his money's worth from Noi. The scrambled eggs looked less runny today and he knew he couldn't exist on bread and beer alone. He put a spoonful on his plate and then selected some bacon that looked almost done; he would take an Imodium later.

As he passed the front desk on his way back to his room, he was stopped by one of the girls working reception. "Excuse please, Mr. Johnson. I have message for you."

Josh suspected it was from Aunt Carol wanting to know if he had made it there safe or not. He was supposed to call when he arrived but he hadn't. He looked at the note. It was written in Thai. He handed it back to the girl. "What does it say?"

The receptionist blushed. "I'm sorry, I forgot to write it in English. It says that you must come to meet with Ms. Orapin today at ten o'clock, and that you know her address already. She said it's very urgent that you be there."

He glanced at his watch: it was almost nine. "I have the address in my room. Can you call a taxi for me? I'll be back in a minute."

The girl nodded.

Ten minutes later he was back at the front desk and a taxi was waiting. It was the same driver he had hired before.

He arrived at the attorney's office at nine forty-five. The receptionist asked him to have a seat and wait. Either the attorney wasn't there or she was going strictly by her schedule.

At precisely ten o'clock the front door opened and a middle-aged lady entered with Jarapan at her side. Josh jumped to his feet. "What's she doing here?"

"Please come with me, Mr. Johnson. We have important business to discuss." She stepped past him and into her office.

Jarapan glanced in his direction, but didn't say anything. Whatever was going on, he didn't like it. He followed the two women inside.

Ms. Orapin motioned them to chairs. Once they were seated she moved away from the door. She walked to her desk and stood straight as a bamboo rod. Her face neither smiled nor frowned. Except for the dull hum of the air conditioner the room was quiet.

After a considerable pause she pulled an envelope from a file folder and held it out for view. "This was written by Mr. Michael Johnson. I received it nearly two weeks ago." She looked at Jarapan. "It was after I talked to you." She turned her focus to Josh. "And after I contacted your family." Her solemn expression shifted to a frown. "This letter is very short but says a lot. As odd as it may seem Mr. Josh Johnson, you may be the reason your father is in a coma at the hospital."

Josh stood, angry at her insinuation. "That's bullshit. I came to find out what happened to him, not to be accused of his causing his accident. I wasn't even in Thailand until two days ago and I have papers to prove it. That's more than I can say for her." He glanced at Jarapan, waiting for a response that didn't come.

Their silence kicked his paranoia into a higher gear. He remembered the papers Jarapan had shown him last night. He had no way to know if they were real, or forgeries to steer him away from the truth. He didn't know what was going on but something didn't feel right. He slipped into his toughest street-punk stance. "I don't know what your scam is lady, but it's not going to work." He shot another glance at Jarapan. "Or your scam either. Pregnant? I don't think so. I'm leaving now. I think the police will be interested in hearing about this."

"Stop," Orapin ordered. "It's not in your best interest to walk out that door."

"Is that a threat?" His smile was as sarcastic as his words.

"I don't make threats, Mr. Johnson. This letter contains your father's last wishes."

"You expect me to believe that letter is from my dad?" Josh grunted. "I believe that about as much as I believe the bullshit papers I saw last night. I don't know what's going on or how I'll be shaken down, but I can assure you the Thai police and the U.S. Embassy will hear about it." He started toward the exit.

"Joshua, I have often said I'm not afraid of death. That was a lie."

Josh stopped and turned, "What did you call me?"

"Those are words from your father's letter. I have a copy for you and for Ms. Jarapan. It was written by your father's own hand. If you have any love and respect for your own father, you should honor his wishes."

Joshua. No one had called him that since he was a kid. No one that is except his dad when they argued or when he was about to dish out unwanted advice. Josh figured his dad called him *Joshua* just to piss him off. Nobody else dared call him by that name. "You have five minutes, and then I'm going to the police."

Josh walked back to the chair, but he didn't sit. Orapin extracted papers from the envelope and handed him a copy. She was right—it was his father's handwriting. *Joshua*, the word stood out like a crooked cop. His heart raced as a spurt of adrenaline shot into his veins. He forced himself to sit.

Orapin nodded her curt approval and then proceeded to read in slow, carefully-pronounced English.

"Joshua, I have often said I'm not afraid of death. That was a lie. Tonight, as I write this letter, death is holding my hand and it terrifies me. The only thing that scares me more than dying is the thought of living.

"I don't have much time so I will get straight to the point: I have been diagnosed with AIDS. I don't know how or when or who. I only know it's not important anymore. The doctor said there are medications to keep me alive, but there seems no reason to live. The people I love will hate me. Whoever doesn't hate me will pity me, or be afraid of me.

"I considered coming home but I can't burden my sister Carol with all of this. You know how she is. She would have a breakdown. And you, Josh, I couldn't face coming home to watch you destroy your own life.

"I worked hard to make sure you and your mom had everything you needed. All I ever wanted in return was your respect and to see you grow to be a son I could brag on. I guess I don't have to worry about that anymore. Probably I never should have.

"In spite of all that has happened between us, I want you to know I still love you. If you are reading this, it means you have come to Thailand. Maybe you have come out of greed, but I will pretend you have come from love and respect. I feel better just believing you still love me.

"Before you leave Thailand, please clean up the mess I've made of my life here. Especially I want you to meet a wonderful young woman named Jarapan. Make sure she has everything she needs—everything! When you go home, take good care of my sister. - Love, Dad."

Orapin paused and looked up. Josh's face was expressionless. His head turned briefly toward Jarapan and then back to Orapin. He motioned as if he wanted to say something but nothing came from his mouth. His eyes glistened.

TEARS FOR THE THAI GIRL

"The rest of this letter is for Jarapan," Orapin said. "But you'll want to pay attention Mr. Johnson. Really, it has to do with you, too. She continued reading;

"Jarapan, I don't know what to say except I'm sorry. I love you more than anyone I have ever known; I love you more than life itself. I know you cannot feel the same for me after what I have done to you—and to our baby. Yes, I know about the baby. Your mother told me. Jarapan, please forgive me. You must believe I would never hurt you on purpose.

"Today I read about AIDS on the internet and maybe you aren't sick. Everything I read says that AIDS isn't that easy to catch and making love with someone doesn't mean anything. I hope and pray with all my heart that you will be okay. Still, Teeluk, I cannot wait for you to come back because I don't want to hear you say that you hate me. Maybe someday you be able to forgive me. I pray that you will live to be an old woman and our child will grow up to be someone special.

"I have included you in the disbursement of my estate. You and our baby will never want for anything. If my son Josh comes to Thailand, please be kind to him. He's young and still trying to decide who he is. Maybe before he goes home he will become a man. I will always love you, Jarapan. If we meet again in another life, I will make amends for what I have done in this one. Thank you for making me a happy man. I love you."

Orapin choked on the last words and she stopped reading.

Jarapan's emotions gave way. "Why, why, why?" she wailed. "Why couldn't he have waited another day? Why doesn't he know I could never hate him? Please, dear Buddha, I want to die, too."

Josh slid from his chair and knelt beside her. "If you love my father, you cannot die. You must live to be an old woman and raise his child to be someone special." He stood and glanced over at Orapin, "Everyone is talking like he's dead already. I saw him last night and he's only sleeping. Tomorrow he'll wake up and everything will be fine."

Jarapan looked up at Josh and said through her tears "The doctors think he will never wake up but that he might not die soon. It's all my fault. If I hadn't gone home, none of this would have happened."

Josh's face tightened. "Listen to me. I'm the reason that Dad didn't come to the US for treatment. Do you know how that makes me feel? It makes me feel like a piece of shit. Except for me, Dad wouldn't be in the hospital and we wouldn't be sitting here. Dad always wanted a child he could brag on, and that's what I intend to do for him. You're carrying his baby. He asked me to make sure you are taken care of, and I will do that."

"If only I hadn't gone home," Jarapan continued pouring out her self-blame. "Or if we had never met."

"Maybe it would have happened anyway. Maybe it was his fate. All I know is that we can't change the past, but we can change the future. I will honor my father's wishes and make sure that one of his children grows up to be someone special and I'll make sure you are taken care of."

Jarapan was quiet for a moment before she responded. "Thailand can be very cruel to fatherless children of foreigners. My baby will never be anything special except a farang-looking kid who speaks Thai."

"Then I'll take you to America."

"Visas to America are not easy for Thai women. Especially a woman with no reason to come home. The American Embassy thinks all Thai women are whores."

Josh's face blushed at her words. Until this very moment, he had thought the same thing. "Then I'll live in Thailand. I will be the father of your baby."

"Mike said you have a business in America. I think you will go back to that."

Josh blushed harder. "I'm tired of that business. I think it's time for me to do something else with my life."

No one spoke for a long moment.

"There is more," Orapin voice was steady again.

Jarapan and Josh turned.

"The rest of this is for both of you." Orapin turned the sheet of paper over and read the rest of Mike Johnson's letter.

"With luck, I'll be dead soon. With bad luck I will not. If you are reading this letter I'm either dead or wishing I was. It's possible that I'll screw this up like I have everything else in my life. If I somehow survive my attempt at suicide, please bring me a gun. If I can't function on my own, don't let me linger someplace between life and death. I have left exact instructions in my will.

"My insurance policy has an accidental death clause—it pays double—which beings me to this point: When I opened the Suaee Dee Lady, my only goal was to get back what I had spent. The spirit house that Itta put in the bar must have worked because our business has been very good since we opened. To recover my investment in one high season would make me a successful businessman. That is something that would make me happy.

"Josh, I want you to take charge of the bar and keep it open through the coming high season. You don't have to, but I would be proud of you if you did. I think Jarapan may not want to help you, and Itta may not be there, but Noi, Ba, and some of the other girls at the Suaee Dee Lady will take care of you if you take care of them. The decision is yours. My will contains instructions for that, too.

"That is all I have time to write. I have things to do tonight. There's an accident or something waiting my appearance. Tonight I will be center stage on Second Road. I love you Jarapan. And I love you Josh. Burn this letter after you have read it. People have always said that accidents don't just happen. Now I know it's true. It's best if the insurance company never finds out. Please forgive me for everything."

Orapin folded the paper and slid it back into the envelope. Silence permeated the room. Not even the air conditioner hummed.

Josh's numb expression deepened. Tears slid down Jarapan's pain-pinched face.

At that moment the phone rang and Orapin answered. Her expression faded quickly from serious to deathly grim as she listened to the caller. After a moment she hung up the phone. "My secretary has a friend who works at the hospital. She called and said something has happened. She doesn't know what. She thinks you should go there right away."

Jarapan put her hand to her mouth and began crying uncontrollably. Josh felt as if someone had just punched him in the stomach.

"Come," Orapin said softly. "I'll drive you."

Chapter 62

At 9:00 that same morning Carl Rand gave Noi two thousand baht and sent her on her way. It was more than the going rate but she had done more than most bar girls would. He had been with dozens of women in his life, but none who enjoyed sex as much as Noi. Multi-orgasmic and always ready. Considering she had insisted on making love more times than was prudent for a man his age, he reckoned she should have been the one who paid. He smiled at his memories of last night as he stepped into the shower.

By the time he arrived in the lobby the breakfast buffet was all but gone. He passed on the leftovers and ate a couple pieces of toast instead. He promised himself to come earlier tomorrow to make up for what he had missed today. It was 9:30 when he hired a baht-bus to the Bangkok-Pattaya Hospital.

Carl dreaded seeing his old friend. Josh had said Mike was in a coma and no one seemed sure if he would live or die. He wondered if things would be different if he had come to Pattaya sooner. He and Mike had been through a lot together. He was sure he could have stopped Mike from doing anything stupid, like trying to kill himself. He sighed and shook his head at the situation.

The girl who had bumped into him last night entered his thoughts. Josh had said her name was Jarapan but he didn't know her nickname, or if she even had one. Carl knew it could be the girl Mike had once loved, or maybe she wasn't. He would track her down later; or maybe not. Maybe he would just go home.

He wondered what Josh would do. If his father never woke up, would Josh keep him on life support forever? Or would he one day decide that enough was enough? Carl hoped that Josh would have the guts to make the right decision. He knew his friend Mike wouldn't want to live in the shadow of death. He remembered all the times that Mike had said he welcomed death as a relief from life. Back then it was nothing but beer talk, but now it had new meaning. He would talk to Josh about it later.

The hospital lobby was abuzz with patients and visitors. Carl went to the front desk and asked for information on Mike. The girl on duty directed him to room 306. Outside of Mike's room Carl paused, took a deep breath, and then went inside.

The scene was exactly like Josh had described except there was no feeding tube in Mike's nose. He walked to the bedside and took Mike's hand in his. "Hey buddy, I'm not sure what to think about this. You look like shit."

There was no response and he didn't expect one. After a minute Carl decided there was nothing for him here except massive despair. "Hey, I've gotta go, but if you ever need anything, I'll be here for you."

Mike's grip tightened as Carl started to remove his hand.

"Oh shit," Carl said, horror filled his voice. "Don't do this to me. I don't want to be the one to see you die."

At that moment Mike's eyelids fluttered open and shut like a movie projector on yaba. His eyes rolled in their sockets like a scene from The Exorcist. Carl struggled to pull his hand from Mike's death grip.

"I didn't know you were dead." The words hissed from Mike's throat like the devil himself. "I must be in hell."

Carl's horror shifted to panic. "I need help here," he shouted high pitched toward the doorway.

Suddenly Mike's eyes stopped rolling and focused on Carl. "Do they have beer in hell? I'm really fucking thirsty."

Every monitor in the room began beeping erratically. A nurse entered the room. "Oh dear Buddha," she screamed in English. "I'll get a doctor."

"They have doctors in hell?" Mike moaned.

Carl laughed and cried at the same time. "No, Mikey, but they do in paradise. And angels too."

Three doctors entered the room and swarmed over Mike. The nurse ushered Carl outside.

"What does this mean?" Carl asked, tears rolled down his face.

"It means he will live," the nurse cried with him.

At that moment the doctors pulled Mike's bed from the room and sped toward the elevator. "Don't forget my beer Randy," Mike whispered as he was wheeled past.

"All you can drink," Carl shouted in sheer joy.

"I have to tell his son and his wife," Carl said to the nurse. "When can I see my friend again?"

"I don't know," she answered. "Come back in an hour. I think that will give the doctors time."

Carl bypassed the elevators and raced down the stairs. Adrenaline coursed through his body by the gallon. He felt like he was twenty again. Outside he hurried toward Sukhumvit Road. He didn't know where the nearest sidewalk store was but he would find one. He had to buy beer. A bright smile shined from his face.

A silver Toyota entered the hospital area as he hurried toward the street. It stopped beside him. A window rolled down and Josh's face appeared. "Have you seen my dad? Where are you going?"

"I'm going to buy beer."

"What?"

"Your dad is alive. He asked me for beer." Carl slid into the front seat beside of Orapin. "Drive woman; I'm on a mission for my friend." He looked into the back seat, "Tonight we will celebrate the life of your father." The girl was not Math. "I don't know you, but if you are a friend of Mike's then you are my friend too." He looked back at the driver. "What are you waiting for? We have to be back here in an hour."

Orapin raised her eyebrows at his obstinacy but followed his orders.

Chapter 63

Mike Johnson stared at the image on his computer. *"Happy Birthday!"* the caption read. The picture of a baby filled most of the screen. His baby! In the background were Jarapan, Josh, and a crowd of tourists at the Suaee Dee Lady. Everyone was smiling.

Josh had taken control of the Suaee Dee Lady and the high season had been very good. Last month they had leased another place and the Suaee Dee Lady II would be open within the month. Josh had found a new niche in life and it didn't involve drugs.

Except for some problems with his balance, Mike had recovered completely. He still went to the Suaee Dee Lady every night, but he didn't drink and he never stayed long. He had more important things to do.

His sister had cleaned up his story about Math and submitted it to every agent and publisher she could find. No one had been more surprised than he when an agent called to inform him that she was negotiating a two book deal with an option for the third. Now all he had to do was write two more books.

He looked over at Jarapan and his daughter asleep on the bed. Nothing could be more perfect. His heart swelled with a love few people can understand.

He flicked a cigarette from the almost full pack, lit it, and then snubbed it out. He tossed the pack into the trash.

Mike shut down the computer, turned off the light, and went to bed. He fell asleep with a smile on his face.

Other Books Available
By J. F. Gump

From Bangkok Book House
www.bangkokbooks.com

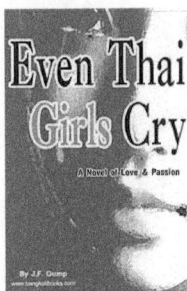

Even Thai Girls Cry
ISBN: 974-93100-4-7

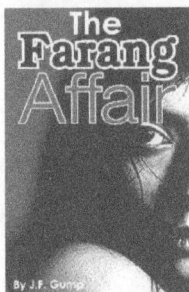

The Farang Affair
ISBN: 974-85123-6-3

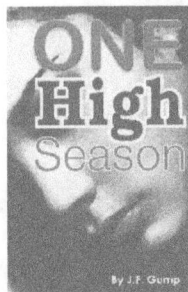

One High Season
ISBN: 974-85129-3-2

From Sabai Books U.S.
www.JFGumpNovels.com

Siam Nights
ISBN:978-0-9714855-2-5

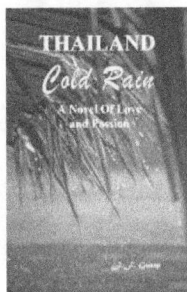

Thailand – Cold Rain
ISBN: 978-0-9714855-4-9

Blame It On Bangkok
ISBN: 1440473803

For Details Go To:

www.JFGumpNovels.com